Rereading the New Criticism

Rereading
the New Criticism

Edited by

Miranda B. Hickman *and*
John D. McIntyre

 The Ohio State University Press • *Columbus*

Copyright © 2012 by The Ohio State University.
All rights reserved.
Library of Congress Cataloging-in-Publication Data

Rereading the New Criticism / Edited by Miranda B. Hickman and John D. McIntyre.
   p. cm.
Includes bibliographical references and index.
ISBN-13: 978-0-8142-1180-9 (cloth : alk. paper)
ISBN-10: 0-8142-1180-1 (cloth : alk. paper)
ISBN-13: 978-0-8142-9279-2 (cd)
1. New Criticism. I. Hickman, Miranda B., 1969 II. McIntyre, John D., 1966
PN98.N4R47 2012
801'.95—dc23

2011040340

Cover design by Laurence J. Nozik
Type set in Adobe Sabon
Printed by Thomson-Shore, Inc.

∞ The paper used in this publication meets the minimum requirements of the American
National Standard for Information Sciences—Permanence of Paper for Printed Library Materials. ANSI Z39.48–1992.

9 8 7 6 5 4 3 2 1

CONTENTS

ACKNOWLEDGMENTS

T HE PROJECT of this volume began with a panel, "Rereading the New Criticism," that we co-organized for the Modernist Studies Association conference of 2006. The responses to our call for papers were so numerous, varied, and interesting that, over the next two years, we followed with a second panel for the MSA in 2008 and then a more general call for papers for a collection, which yielded an even larger, more diverse set of strong essays.

There was clearly keen interest in reevaluating the significance and legacy of the New Criticism, which has since the 1980s been regarded as superseded in literary studies—and has generally been read as emblematic of the apolitical, ahistorical practices of the discipline that had to be overcome through the revolutions in theory, historical scholarship, and politically engaged criticism of the last four decades. But over e-mail and at conferences, people in conversation with us underscored the value of revisiting a movement that was crucial to the foundation of the discipline as we know it now, especially to the development of "close reading" central to its development; and that merited reassessment toward reconsideration of the criticism, classroom practices, and commitments of our field. Ultimately, we had difficulty choosing the essays included in this volume from among the bounty that came our way.

We greatly appreciate the assistance of the Social Sciences and Humanities Research Council of Canada, whose support facilitated the production of this collection. Our thanks go to the many colleagues who offered supportive commentary on this project as it evolved, including Tim Newcomb, Leonard Diepeveen, Jessica Pressman, John Tiedemann, Elizabeth Loizeaux, Stephen Adams, and Ted Bishop. Above all, we are grateful to the contributors to this volume, the excellence of whose essays far exceeded our initial hopes.

Miranda B. Hickman, McGill University
John D. McIntyre, University of Prince Edward Island

Rereading the New Criticism

MIRANDA HICKMAN

I N 2008, Garrick Davis published an edited volume entitled *Praising it New: The Best of the New Criticism,* which gathers in one paperback a collection of landmark essays by leading figures of the New Criticism, the mid-twentieth century American movement in literary criticism fabled for its formalist approach to literature, and especially for its techniques of "close reading" that would become integral to academic literary studies in North America. The collection includes work by such major New Critics as John Crowe Ransom, Cleanth Brooks, and Robert Penn Warren. Noting the publication in the *Chronicle of Higher Education*, Mark Bauerlein recognized the cultural currents against which Davis was swimming to bring out such a volume: the project turns back to critics central to the foundations of literary studies as we now know it in North America, before the rise of poststructuralist theory in the literary academy of the late 1960s displaced their work from prominence. By the 1970s, New Critical influence had waned; the next decades of the literary academy would belong to theorists associated with poststructuralism and postmodernism, such as Barthes, Derrida, Foucault, Kristeva, Lacan and Lyotard. As of the 1980s, New Critical work, relegated to the status of superseded paradigm, was generally mentioned only in brief excerpts and caricatured shorthand terms. Davis's book thus makes widely available many essays that have been difficult to come by for decades, especially as an ensemble: its back cover frames the project as the "first anthology of New Criticism to be printed in fifty years." Our volume of critical essays, *Rereading the New Criticism*, participates in the recent wave of renewed attention to the New Criticism that Davis's project reflects. Contributors to this collection seek to reexamine in an interrogative spirit the development of the New Criticism, its significance, and its chief lines of thought, as well as to consider dimensions of its work relevant for contemporary literary and cultural studies.

The tale of the New Critics' ascent and decline is a familiar one: during the 1930s and 1940s, the New Criticism rose to preeminence in North American academic contexts during a time of rapid expansion and professionalization for academic departments of English. As the essays in this volume address, for more than two decades, New Critical methods would exert enormous influence in both criticism and classrooms across North America. The events of an international symposium on structuralism held at Johns Hopkins University in 1966 are often used to exemplify the poststructuralist turn in Anglo-American literary studies that would inaugurate the era, in Frank Lentricchia's phrase, "after the New Criticism." The widespread theorization of Anglo-American literary studies would follow—inspired by theoretical models from continental Europe and political developments of 1968 in France; informed by work in fields such as linguistics, psychoanalysis, philosophy, Marxism, and feminism; and fueling the rise of interest in deconstructionist and other forms of poststructuralist thought. As a wealth of new theoretical approaches in the literary academy sought to move, as Geoffrey Hartman's put it 1970, "beyond formalism," the New Criticism fell from authority; and as newer schools of thought often involved critique and even censure of New Critical techniques and assumptions, the New Criticism assumed a controversial status. In subsequent years, for many, the New Criticism came to emblematize irresponsibly formalist approaches to literature that showed critical practice at its narrowest. Focused on "the work itself," and "literature qua literature," New Critical methods were understood as unfortunately insensitive to authorial intentions and readerly response; to the historical conditions of literary production and reception; and to the cultural relevance and political significance of literary work.

More recently, however, a diverse body of critics have issued calls for a reassessment of the New Criticism and its legacy. Historicist scholarship from commentators such as Gerald Graff (1979, 1987) and Mark Jancovich (1993) has enlisted rereadings of New Critical work in its original cultural contexts to contest widely circulated misrepresentations of its assumptions, politics, and projects. Newer work from commentators such as Camille Paglia in *Break, Blow, Burn* (2006), Terry Eagleton in *How to Read a Poem*

(2007), and Jane Gallop in "The Historicization of Literary Studies and the Fate of Close Reading" (2007) likewise urges such reevaluation, emphasizing how New Critical methods of close reading inform contemporary practice in literary studies—often without acknowledgment—and considering how these might be adapted for today's climate. Other groups associated with an effort called the "New Formalism" seek to redirect attention to literary form, which they read as neglected in literary study of recent decades, and often point to the work of the New Criticism as important to this endeavor (see Marjorie Levinson's 2007 review essay "What Is New Formalism?"). The essay collection *Reading for Form* (2006), edited by Susan Wolfson and Marshall Brown, considers what a commitment to "reading" literature "for form" in these times might involve, at a point when not only the New Criticism, but also critical formalism more generally, is often construed as having "'outlived its usefulness'" (as the editors quote W. J. T. Mitchell as observing). Frank Lentricchia and Andrew Dubois's collection *Close Reading* (2003), meanwhile, recognizing the centrality of close reading to literary and cultural studies (despite its sometime relegation to the dustbin with the New Criticism), traces discussions and demonstrations of close reading from the New Critical heyday to the present, noting a continuity of interest in formalism where others have seen diminishment and rupture. Observing how responses to the specter of New Critical formalism have guided literary–critical evolution since the mid-twentieth century, DuBois maintains that "perhaps the central . . . debate in twentieth-century literary criticism is a debate between formalist and non-formalist modes of response" (1).

Inspired by this range of commentary reconsidering the New Criticism, the essays of this volume aim to reevaluate the New Critical corpus, trace its legacy, and explore resources it might offer for the future. More specifically, these essays shed new light on the genesis of the New Criticism; revisit its chief arguments for little-noticed dimensions and subtexts; illuminate its internal heterogeneity; interrogate received ideas about it; and consider how its theories and techniques might be drawn upon toward the reinvigoration of contemporary literary and cultural studies. Our collection follows a path highlighted by William J. Spurlin's and Michael Fischer's *The New Criticism and Contemporary Literary Theory* (1995), whose articles reflected on the implications of New Critical theory and practice and considered new ways of engaging New Critical methods in view of contemporary theory of that moment. A decade and a half later, in a different literary–theoretical climate, it is time for another such reexamination.

Through this project, we seek to facilitate reassessment of the New Criticism's significant contributions to the development of academic literary studies in North America; foster subtler understanding of the complex development of the work of the New Critics from their early Southern Agrarian commitments to their later association with supposedly apolitical and ahistorical critical formalism; clarify the central theories and methods associated with the New Criticism—which will often require reading past and against commonplaces about New Critical thought; and consider what New Critical theories and critical methods might offer for both literary and cultural studies in the twenty-first century.

Recovering the New Criticism

Accordingly, this collection aims to resist reductive understandings of what the New Critics did and stood for that have often pervaded accounts of them since their fall from disciplinary dominance. Although they are frequently invoked in today's climate, the abbreviated ways in which they are usually mentioned contribute to an occlusion of important dimensions of their work. And as Davis's project implies, such misunderstandings are frequently perpetuated by the limited repertoire of New Critical texts represented in prominent textbooks: generally, examples from New Criticism included in current anthologies feature only a small portion of their wide and diverse corpus. In the *Norton Anthology of Theory and Criticism* (2001), for instance, articles by John Crowe Ransom and Cleanth Brooks appear, along with W. K. Wimsatt and Monroe Beardsley's classic "The Intentional Fallacy" and "The Affective Fallacy." Julie Rivkin and Michael Ryan's *Literary Theory: An Introduction* (1998) includes two selections by Brooks, one an excerpt from his famous *The Well Wrought Urn,* the second an essay by Wimsatt on the "concrete universal." Thus while these two volumes do highlight widely known New Critical commentary, the selections included suggest much more homogeneity of thought within the New Criticism than actually obtained, indicating only a few of the many issues—philosophical, aesthetic, and cultural—with which the New Critics engaged. Also contributing to an atmosphere of misprision and cultural forgetting is the attitude with which the New Critics are generally noted in academic discourse: at best, they are presented as quaint and superseded, at worst derided as what Frank Lentricchia calls "repressive father figures" (*After the New Criticism,* xiii) and the discipline's favorite "whipping boy" (Suleiman, 5). And despite the historicization of scholars such as Graff and Jancovich that seeks to counter caricatures of the New Critics, New Critical work is still widely misrepresented as ahistorical, apolitical, and acontextual. The essays of this collection investigate these still tenacious assumptions about the nature and implications of New Critical approaches—to clarify their origins, redress distortions, and deepen understanding of their range and complexity.

In many contexts, the very gesture of returning to the New Criticism after the watersheds of theory and cultural studies can be construed as suggesting literary conservatism, even rearguard entrenchment. In part, this stems from a reflexive association between the New Criticism and "dead white male" cultural conservatism, and the way in which, as Jane Gallop notes, the "ahistoricism" widely connected with New Critical methods, along with the canon of literary work they tended to promote, have come to be "persuasively linked to sexism, racism, and elitism" (181). This volume contends, however, that the convictions and political perspectives associated with the New Criticism were multiple, diverse, and complex; that they were not always as we now often understand them to have been, nor as they later became as they evolved; and that, accordingly, they stand in need of reevaluation. Moreover, the project of rereading the New Criticism to which this volume is committed carries no one set of literary–political valences. In an article for *PMLA* (2007), Marjorie Levinson takes census of the trend known as the "New Formalism," composed of a diverse body of critics and scholars interested in revitalizing formalist approaches to literary analysis and interpretation, some of whom revisit the New Criticism for techniques and models. Her article emphasizes the coalitionary nature of this endeavor: New Formalists hail from widely varying schools of thought and political perspectives; what unites them is a conviction about the importance of formalist methods to literary study. A comparable range of viewpoints and political positions characterizes the contributors to this volume.

At this point, forty years after the fall of the New Criticism, it is important to revisit the papers in the disciplinary attic—to return, first, to both the letter and the spirit of what the New Critics actually said. They have often been misconstrued as presenting a monolithic school of thought, and accordingly, read as what Frank Lentricchia calls an "inconsistent and sometimes confused movement" (xii–xiii). The essays in this volume suggest instead that the New Criticism comprised a diverse collection of allied critics addressing shared questions and often contending with and contesting one another's claims. Through a widely circulated repertoire of myths, the diversity and subtlety of their arguments have often been elided, their debates and points of principled difference effaced. Many of the essays in this collection thus aim through historical analysis to recover the internal complexity of the New Critical effort, restoring to view important episodes and conversations in the history of the academic discipline of English in North America. Moreover, taking advantage of our retrospective position on the New Critics, these essays bring to the surface implicit or subtextual aspects of their arguments and cultural politics that the New Critics themselves did not emphasize and in some cases may not even have recognized—ones which chronicles of their work have overlooked.

Out of this work of reconsideration, several of these essays reflect upon what might now be derived from the examples, conversations, and debates of the New Critics toward the future of both literary studies, which finds itself at an early-twenty-first-century moment of reassessment and reorientation, and its sibling field of cultural studies. What we might now draw upon toward today's work are not only the techniques of "close reading" and "reading for form" widely associated with New Criticism (which can as easily be directed toward semiotic play in cultural texts in diverse media as toward forms of irony and ambiguity in texts marked as "literary"): also emphasized in the following articles are the New Critical commitment to pursuing ethical projects through approaches to aesthetics (Archambeau); the cultural politics animating their work and methods (Morrison, Shaheen, Hammond); and their pedagogical assumptions and approaches (Lockhart).

The Genesis of the New Criticism

What later became known as the New Criticism first emerged in the late 1930s, as a group of American Southerners—John Crowe Ransom, a professor at Vanderbilt University in Tennessee, along with a cluster of his former students (Robert Penn Warren, Allen Tate, and Cleanth Brooks)—gathered forces toward invigorating the practice of literary criticism and legitimating it within academic contexts. As of the early 1920s, Ransom, Tate, and Warren were all affiliated with a group of poets at Vanderbilt called the "Fugitives," devoted to discussion and critique of poetry, often new modernist verse and often their own, in the name of renewing the literature of the American South. Between 1922 and 1925, they published their verse and criticism in a journal entitled *The Fugitive*. Ransom was one of the earliest members of the group in the late 1910s; Tate and Warren would later join as undergraduates in the 1920s. Later that decade, all three came to be associated with Southern Agrarianism, a cultural movement catalyzed most immediately by the "Scopes Monkey Trial" of 1925 in Dayton, Tennessee, and the denigration of the American South which it fueled in many quarters. Spurred to organize by such attacks, the Southern Agrarians sought to defend distinctively Southern values and customs against what they perceived as the increasing hegemony of the industrialized North. Ransom, Tate, and Warren would all contribute to the symposium of articles that, in aggregate, became the Agrarians' major manifesto: *I'll Take My Stand* (1930).[1]

By the late 1930s, the nucleus around Ransom—with the addition of the slightly younger Brooks, then collaborating with Robert Penn Warren at Louisiana State University—had evolved into a group of allies making common cause. At that point, they turned energies to an effort to reform the discipline of English in the direction of greater rigor, prominence within the academy, and cultural authority—an endeavor that would eventually coalesce in the New Criticism. Specifically, they saw themselves as champions of rigorous literary criticism focused on aesthetics, which they opposed to approaches to literary study that emphasized historically-focused scholarly research, morally-oriented readings like those of New Humanists such as Irving Babbitt, and Marxist sociological analysis.[2] As distinct from such approaches, their criticism concerned itself with the literary "work itself" rather than with the author or historical conditions of its inception or reception; and with the aesthetic form of a literary work rather than just its thematic content: in their view, form and content were inextricably intertwined.

As of 1937, Ransom was drawn by an attractive offer to Kenyon College in Ohio, a congenial setting for his teaching and criticism, but one remote from the American South, signaling a removal from his former interests and allegiances. As of 1940, Allen Tate was at Princeton, his position suggesting and fostering a comparable distance on the American South. Alexander MacLeod's essay in this collection notes the pattern this indicates among the New Critics of turning away from their Southern Agrarianism as their commitments to literary criticism intensified. Rather than an abandonment of the Agrarian project, however, cultural historian Mark Jancovich reads this move from Agrarianism to New Criticism on the part of many nascent New Critics as a transposition into a different key of the group's ongoing refusal of the utilitarian, capitalist values they associated with the American North—a change of strategy rather than objectives (Jancovich, 208). In their articles for this collection, Aaron Shaheen and James Matthew Wilson likewise address this question of the relationship between the New Critics' Southern Agrarian and later literary–critical work.

As they sought to endow the academic study of English literature with greater precision and legitimacy, again, the proto–New Critics saw themselves as counterposed against the "historians," or "scholars"—i.e. those in literary studies devoted primarily to historical scholarly research. As Gerald Graff notes, historically-minded, research-oriented approaches to literary study had gained prominence in the American academy as "English" had emerged as a distinct discipline in the late nineteenth century, at a moment when academe was undergoing professionalization and accordingly increasingly favored a German research-specialist model of practice. In literary studies, this preference often resulted in the rejection of liberal-humanist, Arnoldian approaches to the study and teaching of literature in favor of data-oriented philological methods. In *Defining Literary Criticism*, Carol Atherton notes parallel developments in England at this time at Oxford and Cambridge.

In both the United States and England, however, from the time of the emergence of English as an academic discipline, the importance of philological study of literature had also been contested by many who were trying to establish the new field—sometimes for methodological and sometimes anti-German nationalist reasons. As Atherton observes of Oxford and Cambridge, "The evolution of English at both universities can be seen in terms of a gradual movement away from these philological beginnings" (37). In the context of the 1930s, the rising New Critics thus reprised in a new context and new moment this resistance to an approach to English literature focused primarily on philological and other forms of historical research.

As Graff observes, as they formed their sense of mission, the New Critics were also reacting against a number of other forces of the cultural climate, sometimes pressed by various adversaries in "conflicting directions" (146). They sought to define their program, for instance, against "generalist" approaches to literature prevalent in early-twentieth-century undergraduate classrooms, which often featured surveys of biographical and historical background rather than close engagement with the specifics of literary texts; as well as against what they read as merely impressionistic commentary on literature. They also sought to dissociate themselves from Marxist and Humanist readings that, in their view, focused on moral themes at the expense of attention to the implications of literary form.

And in the spirit of their work as Southern Agrarians, they were also reckoning with work in the sciences that enjoyed significant influence in the academy of this moment—which, as Steven Schryer suggests, they rejected as fostering "technocratic rationalism" associated in their view with the cultural power of the American North (670). But out of awareness of the pressures in their academic and cultural climate to gain legitimacy through scientific rigor, even as they resisted scientific values and perspectives, they also pursued their work with scientific precision. Specifically, Ransom and his compatriots sought precision in the theory and practice of literary criticism, at the time widely regarded as a merely subjective and lax endeavor unworthy of serious academic attention (Graff, *Professing Literature*, 124; Green, 62–63). In one of his essays designed to legitimate the work of literary criticism, "Criticism,

Inc.," included in *The World's Body* (1938), Ransom noted that he had heard "the head of English studies in a graduate school" observe, "'Well, we don't allow criticism here, because this is something which anybody can do'" (335). Ransom's ringing rejoinder in this essay—"It is not anybody who can do criticism" (336)—represented a shared line of thought, and a pivotal assumption, among the incipient New Critics.[3] In this essay, Ransom defined criticism as "the attempt to define and enjoy the aesthetic or characteristic values of literature" (332): to treat literary texts as art, rather than texts documenting history, social developments, ethics, or philosophy. In his vision, what was needed to make of criticism a newly rigorous, aesthetically focused endeavor was a new cadre of trained professionals, drawn from the university professoriate ("it must be developed by the collective and sustained effort of learned persons—which means that its proper seat is in the universities" [329]), as well as a scientifically inflected approach: "Criticism must become more scientific, or precise and systematic" (329).

As Gerald Graff points out, in view of such statements as the latter, the New Critics often came to be associated with, and "denounced for," "arid scientific empiricism" (*Literature against Itself*, 133). But given the cultural convictions informing their literary criticism, he maintains, in many respects the New Critics could not have been more distant from an allegiance to "science": science was "in fact one of the chief cultural ills that the New Critics themselves sought to combat. The New Criticism stands squarely in the romantic tradition of the defense of the humanities as an antidote to science and positivism" (133). As Southern Agrarians, the New Critics were committed to asserting in the face of the powerful North—which they read as industrial, capitalistic, technocratic and hyper-rational—the distinctive cultural practices of the South, whose way of life, in their reading, had been badly eroded during postbellum years by the Northern juggernaut. As their "Statement of Principles" in *I'll Take My Stand* observed,

> The capitalization of the applied sciences has now become extravagant and uncritical; it has enslaved our human energies. . . . [T]he act of labor as one of the happy functions of human life has been in effect abandoned, and is practiced solely for its rewards. (xxxix)

Thus although these critics' involvement in the rising New Criticism entailed a turn away from their earlier, more overtly Southern commitments, their critique of the "extravagant" "capitalization" of the "sciences" would continue to inform their literary–critical work. Ransom's claims in essays such as "Poetry: A Note on Ontology" certainly attest to an ongoing quarrel with the cultural practice of what he calls "sciencing and devouring" (52), which Ransom associated with the North, and which the approach to literature he advocated was intended to resist. The methods, epistemological claims, and values of the New Critics were often constructed in their work as a shoe thrown in the machine of industrial capitalism, Northern or otherwise, and the rational, scientific discourses it involved. When Ransom asserts that "Criticism must become more scientific, or precise and systematic" (*World's Body,* 329), then, the "precise and systematic" should be read as a qualification: Ransom means here that the rigor to which literary criticism aspires in the process of "sett[ing] up its own house" (345) should match that displayed by science, widely respected in the cultural climate of 1938, in order to gain legitimacy—but ultimately in order to achieve objectives that would countervail those of science.

Predecessors at Cambridge

In the mid-twentieth-century American context, as the New Critics-in-formation sought to legitimate literary criticism as an integral part of academic study of English literature, they were renewing an effort associated with the late nineteenth and early twentieth century in England.[4] As of the 1920s, criticism had been especially championed at Cambridge University, whose climate shaped the work of several critics from whom many New Critics would draw inspiration, such as I. A. Richards, William Empson, and F. R. Leavis.

When the emergent field of "English Studies" was reinvigorated at Cambridge after the Great War with the establishment of the English Tripos in 1917, I. A. Richards, like the New Critics who later followed his lead, sought to develop stringent techniques for analysis of literary work that would distinguish such analysis from and carry it beyond philological study, impressionistic belletristic commentary, and the "survey" style study of literature common in university programs. In the next generation of Cambridge English, F. R. Leavis would pursue a similar path.

Richards, trained in the mental and moral sciences, was concerned with the cultural health of an England struggling with the aftermath of war; accordingly, he argued that close, careful, trained engagement with literature could help readers to attain mental "balance," "poise," and "equilibrium" and promote forms of cultural healing. In an Arnoldian spirit, Richards maintained that work with literature could guard against a slide into "chaos" to which he read England as vulnerable during the postwar years. As he noted in *Science and Poetry* (1926): "Tradition is weakening. Moral authorities are not as well backed by belief as they were. . . . We are in need of something else to take the place of the old order." Concerned that the cultural center would not hold, Richards feared the upsurge of "a mental chaos such as man has never experienced." If this came to pass, he observed, "We shall be thrown back, as Matthew Arnold foresaw, upon poetry. It is capable of saving us; it is a perfectly possible means of overcoming chaos" (82–83).

While Richards focused chiefly on the psychological and neurological responses of skilled, trained readers, his students, such as William Empson and F. R. Leavis at Cambridge, as well as the American critics who admired his work such as Ransom and Brooks, were more concerned with what was increasingly conceived of as "literature itself": the formal features and practices read as distinctive to literature. What they drew from Richards were his exhortations about "how to read a page"—and his insistence on attending to words on the page as the primary site of consideration. As F. R. Leavis would put it, "literature is made of words, and . . . everything worth saying in criticism of verse and prose can be related to judgements concerning particular arrangements of words on the page" (Leavis, 25). As Brooks would note in a 1981 retrospective about the impact of Richards on the generation of American critics who succeeded him, Richards offered "a pioneering effort that broke with the literary training of the time—with the traditional British training as well as the American" (587). Brooks recalls becoming aware of Richards's books during his first academic year as a Rhodes scholar at Oxford in 1929–30:

> As I remember, it was Robert Penn Warren, then at Oxford also, who called my attention to *Principles of Literary Criticism* and *Practical Criticism*. I read both books eagerly. In *Practical Criticism* I was especially interested in the students' comments on thirteen selected poems. Richards had omitted the titles of the poems and the names of their authors to see what the students could make of the naked texts. (587)

The critics who would become the New Critics were thus primarily concerned with "the naked texts," rather than, as was Richards, in what occurred in students' minds as they engaged with them. Brooks admits that he and compatriots were suspicious of Richards's psychologizing ("It was Richards's psychological machinery that got in the way for me and many other theorists" [587])—which, when Richards's books first appeared, was considered courageous by some and by others inappropriately "scientific" for literary study. As Brooks notes of John Crowe Ransom's skeptical distinction between his own New Critical emphases and those of Richards: "what the reader had before him as positive evidence was the text itself, not certain presumed goings-on in the reader's head" (591).

Accordingly, what the New Critics would focus on and invest in was the construct of "the text itself" as the appropriate object of literary study. They also aimed for greater precision about that object of study: they sought to identify what literature offered that no other form of verbal communication provided and to promote systematic engagement with its distinctive qualities and techniques. This is why the received wisdom about the New Critics links them so easily, often too readily, to T. S. Eliot, who famously declared in 'Tradition and the Individual Talent" (among the essays of the *Sacred Wood* by which Richards was deeply influenced when first teaching at Cambridge) that criticism should be directed "not upon the poet but upon the poetry" (40). In the preface to the second edition of *The Sacred Wood,* Eliot would reinforce this point by advocating reading poetry "as poetry and not another thing" (viii). Eliot's statement entailed assumptions that would become axiomatic for the New Critics: that poetry (here used as a metonym for literature) should be read as ontologically separate from other forms of expression and accordingly, merited a criticism equipped to do justice to its distinctness and autonomy. Eliot was not actually as intimately involved with the New Critics per se as many accounts suggest, but his essays and complex poetry provided a crucial impetus—one might say "catalyst"—for New Critical work, both literary and cultural.[5]

The Era of Consolidation

The New Critics began their project at a moment of intense debate about where the discipline of English would direct itself next: as Ransom noted to Tate in 1938, the same year that saw publication of his major study, *The World's Body,* "I've just come back from the Modern Language Association at Chicago. The Professors are in an awful dither, trying to reform themselves, and there's a big stroke possible for a small group that knows what it wants in giving them ideas and definitions and showing them the way" (*Selected Letters,* 236). Ransom and his "small group" would attempt this "big stroke" with their effort to render literary studies a more stringent academic discipline with a focus on critical practice. The movement's name would emerge through the title of Ransom's book of 1941, *The New Criticism,* which in turn permuted the title of a 1910 essay by Joel Spingarn of Columbia University (Graff, *Professing Literature,* 153).

During the 1940s and 1950s, representatives of the New Criticism, both the former Southern Agrarians and others who became part of the movement's momentum, would gain prominent posts at a range of American universities—Ransom at Kenyon College in Ohio; Tate at Princeton, later the University of Minnesota; Warren at Louisiana State, the University of Minnesota, and Yale; Brooks at Louisiana State and then also at Yale, where René Wellek and W. K. Wimsatt would teach as well. As Vincent Leitch notes, as compared to critical schools contemporaneous with the New Criticism such as the Chicago Neo-Aristotelians and the New York Intellectuals, by the mid-twentieth century, the New Critics "influenced more colleagues and students, controlled more journals, had wider access to presses, and produced immensely more publications" (80). They disseminated their work and consolidated their program through periodicals such as *The Southern Review,* which Warren and Brooks founded in 1935; *The Kenyon Review,* which Ransom founded in 1939; and the *Sewanee Review,* of which Tate served as editor beginning in 1944. A cluster of landmark New Critical texts appeared in the late 1930s and 1940s: Ransom's *The World's Body* (1938) and *The New Criticism* (1941), along with Brooks's *Modern Poetry and the Tradition* (1939) and *The Well Wrought Urn* (1947). Also appearing at this time was the group of textbooks that Tara Lockhart's essay in this collection addresses—textbooks that would carry the New Criticism to high-school and university classrooms throughout North America and make of it a widely influential movement, such as Brooks and Warren's *An Approach to Literature* (1936), *Understanding Poetry* (1938), *Understanding Fiction* (1943), and Brooks and Robert Heilman's *Understanding Drama* (1945).

In part, the New Critical effort at consolidation, toughening, systemization, and legitimation of academic English took hold in American universities because the methods advanced by the New Critics allowed for a kind of democratization of literary study;[6] since, unlike philological study, which required years of groundwork, training in the close analysis of textual particulars was available to undergraduate students of all backgrounds. This was especially attractive during a time when, thanks to the G.I. Bill, many soldiers were returning from wartime committed to completing their educations. Moreover, as Veysey notes, "The war veterans made up only one segment" of the "dramatic increase in the number of students from 1940 to 1964, which more broadly reflected an awareness within a greatly enlarged sector of the middle and skilled working classes that some version of college was necessary in order to keep economically afloat" (15). While the precise, thoroughgoing criticism that the New Critics offered suggested a vision of literary study as accessible only to an elite of highly trained specialists,[7] the techniques of New Criticism nonetheless came to be widely used by a large and diverse student population. By the early 1960s, New Critical methods of analysis and interpretation had achieved dominance in English departments at many North American universities, and, through the major New Critical textbooks, also exerted significant impact on North American secondary-school pedagogy.

The rise of the New Criticism was also importantly bound up in, and facilitated by, the ascent of literary modernism, emergent at the same time that figures who would become New Critics were beginning their careers. Modernist literature featured complex texts for which New Critical methods of close reading were particularly apt, often even developed to address. In a climate of what would be widely referred to as modernist literary "difficulty," readers sought expert guides to help them to navigate the modernist labyrinth. It was the work of poet-critic modernists such as Eliot and Pound that first inspired many of the New Critics. New Criticism and modernism thus quickly became involved in a cultural symbiosis, with New Critics such as Brooks building their reputations on readings of modernist texts such as Eliot's *The Waste Land* and modernism enjoying wide cultural play in critical fora and classrooms thanks to New Critical attention. But as Adam Hammond's essay suggests, New Critical conceptions of modernism captured only a subset of the diversity of work associated with the modernist experiment of 1914–45, leaving much of the work of modernism in shadow, shaping limited received ideas about what modernism entailed. By the same token, assuming too close an alignment between the New Criticism and modernism can attenuate critical understanding of the many facets of New Critical work, some of whose animating objectives and values differed markedly from those suggested by modernist poetry and fiction.

Critiques of the New Criticism

Over the years, New Critics have frequently been disparaged as head-in-the sand formalists: even before the poststructuralist revolution, they were charged in such terms by contemporaries such as Northrop Frye and Lionel Trilling—as unconcerned with, even oblivious to, anything outside the text. But as several essays in this collection demonstrate, their methods were in fact often intended to register and encourage certain attitudes toward art and culture, as well as certain ethical and epistemological stances; and often, in the tradition of Matthew Arnold, they assigned powerful cultural roles to both poetry and the reading thereof. To whatever degree we are willing today to countenance their views on how literature and literary criticism can affect the world beyond the text, the New Critics did hold such views. Their famous devotion to the "autonomy" of both literature and literary criticism (for them, the "autonomy" of both placed them as independent disciplines operating by principles and rules distinct from those of other fields such as history or sociology) did not so much preclude as enable their impact on the world outside the literary sphere.

But from the beginning, critiques of the New Criticism were thick and varied, and such critiques often misrepresented what the New Critics had actually asserted. Their contemporaries the Chicago neo-Aristotelians, whom Ransom credited with undertaking a kindred project of differentiating literary criticism from other practices, often jousted with them: Chicago critic R. S. Crane accused them of generating critical "monism" with their methods, failing to take sensitive account of differences among texts, especially those having to do with genre. Frye suggested that they had not done enough to make of criticism a rigorous autonomous discipline. In 1949 in *PMLA*, Douglas Bush critiqued the New Criticism for cliquishness and elitism. And many castigated them for generating what Eliot once wryly termed in the late 1950s the "lemon squeezer school of criticism" ("Frontiers of Criticism," 537), involving mechanically reiterated readings about irony, ambiguity, and paradox.

Sometimes these attacks struck home, especially when they addressed what the New Criticism had become once it had achieved prominence in the North American academy. One of this volume's objectives is to reassess the aspects of the New Criticism that came under fire; another is to return attention to the New Criticism's analyses of literature and culture before their methods became, in the hands of some, mere mechanical routine.

Contributors

The collection's first four essays reread the genesis of the New Criticism to reveal dimensions of New Critical thought generally underemphasized or misrecognized in critical accounts. Robert Archambeau's "Aesthetics as Ethics" features the ethical emphases of the New Criticism's supposedly purely "formalist" work that allegedly distanced them from ethical concerns: his essay points up the little-noted indebtedness of several figures important to the New Criticism to German Romantic idealism, especially to Schiller's philosophy of artistic contemplation as a means of achieving ethical balance.

Reassessing political diagnoses of the New Criticism, Alastair Morrison's essay, "Eliot, the Agrarians, and the Political Subtext of New Critical Formalism" attributes to the New Critics a subversive illiberalism. Although the hegemony of the New Criticism in the mid-twentieth-century academy has sometimes led to its being regarded as exemplifying the dominant values of its liberal democratic Anglo-American culture, Morrison argues that through their formalism and the Southern Agrarian values underwriting it, the New Critics sought actively to undo a group of key liberal humanist assumptions.

The third and fourth essays in the collection, bringing to light neglected aspects of New Critical thought, enlist these to account for turns within the New Criticism's development from its Southern Agrarian beginnings to academic authority. Aaron Shaheen calls attention to John Crowe Ransom's concern with two distinct forms of "androgyny"—for Ransom, one a sign of cultural deterioration, the other indicative of an ideal culture—for fuller understanding of the conservative gender politics informing Ransom's critical work. Ransom's struggle with these two models of androgyny, Shaheen argues, informed his move from Southern Agrarianism to literary criticism marked as apolitical. James Matthew Wilson's "The Fugitive and the Exile" likewise focuses on the New Critical shift away from Agrarianism, highlighting a little-considered impact of the Frankfurt School on the thought of John Crowe Ransom. Wilson suggests that two of Theodor Adorno's 1940s critiques of American culture, published in Ransom's *Kenyon Review,* contributed significantly to Ransom's turn away from his Southern allegiances.

The next three essays in the collection engage with work by the New Critics and their predecessors that significantly shaped understandings of literary modernism. Bradley Clissold's "No Two Ways about It" reconsiders the work of William Empson, the Cambridge-based critic crucially influential on the New Critics. Clissold maintains that although Empson theorized "ambiguity" in response to the complexities of modernist literature, and despite the close association between modernist literature and New Critical work indebted to Empson's, Empson himself devoted almost no critical attention to modernist literature. Clissold considers the implications of Empson's surprising silence on modernist literature for how we should understand Empson's impact on the New Criticism, ultimately suggesting that Empson still nonetheless might be considered an "enabler" of both New Critical and modernist preoccupations with ambiguity.

Connor Byrne's "In Pursuit of Understanding" questions the pervasive misconception that the New Criticism remained divorced from popular criticism of its day. Byrne considers how apparent antagonisms between New Critics and their contemporaries occluded commonalities between their approaches to modernist poetry and those of other critics in their milieu who reached wider audiences. For instance, although New Critical techniques were roundly critiqued by Louis Untermeyer, a self-styled popular critic, Untermeyer's reading methods in fact shared much with those of the New Critics. Byrne's case study focuses on commonalities between readings of William Carlos Williams's "The Red Wheelbarrow" from, on the one hand, Untermeyer, and on the other, Brooks and Warren.

Tracing the evolution of James Baldwin's uneasy relationship to the New Critical vision of modernism, Adam Hammond reconsiders the New Critics' anti-urban bias and the racist elements of Agrarian thought informing New Critical cultural commitments. Behind the anti-modernism of Baldwin's *Another Country,* which for Hammond indicates both Baldwin's self-parody and a rejection of the New Critical conceptions of modernism, lies a surprising history of Baldwin's conflicted support for the New Critics' anti-capitalist, anti-industrial cultural program.

The collection's last three essays reread New Critical thought with attention to aspects of New Critical theory and practice that might be used today toward revitalization of theory, criticism, and pedagogy. The first two highlight overlooked facets of New Critical thought with a particular emphasis on how these might be set in dialogue with contemporary developments. Alexander MacLeod's "Disagreeable Intellectual Distance: Rethinking the New Critics and Their Old Regionalism" focuses on the little-acknowledged complex theory of regionalism forged by the New Critics during the early Agrarian years, which MacLeod argues could benefit contemporary theoretical work on regionalism and cultural geography.

Tara Lockhart's "Teaching with Style" addresses New Critical pedagogy and its theoretical ramifications through a little-known area of New Critical work—on the genre of the essay. She features Cleanth Brooks and Robert Penn Warren's *An Approach to Literature* (1936), the earliest and least-known of their highly influential textbooks, which, anomalously in their series, addresses pedagogical approaches to the essay. Generally, their textbooks featured poetry and short fiction, genres to which they most readily turned their methods and with which they showed greatest comfort; in contrast, their treatment of the essay registers a struggle, made evident through successive editions of *An Approach to Literature,* which Lockhart reads as especially revelatory of their commitment to teaching literature "as literature." Calling for finer understanding of the evolution of New Critical pedagogical convictions, her article also suggests that contemporary literary pedagogy, particularly that concerned with the enigmatic category of "style" on which *An Approach to Literature* focuses in its discussion of the essay, has much to gain from Brooks and Warren's example.

The volume's closing essay, Cecily Devereux's "'A Kind of Dual Attentiveness': Close Reading after the New Criticism," points back to the New Criticism in an article that, aligned with contemporary work from Jane Gallop and Terry Eagleton, seeks a renewal of "close reading." While Devereux remains wary of rehabilitating the kind of "close reading" advocated by the New Critics, "as the New Criticism represents . . . a problematic, exclusionary, and deeply biased notion of the literary and of the discipline," she nonetheless suggests that the emphasis the New Critics placed on close reading is one we should reconsider today. As she explains what's at stake: "The call for a return to close reading is a call for English studies to define itself again" and clarify what constitutes the discipline's distinctive object of study—what differentiates it from neighboring fields such as history, sociology, and philosophy. The problem facing contemporary critics, however, is how to do so, and how thereby to reaffirm "the literary," without "undermining the crucial late-twentieth-century expansion of the literary . . . beyond a limited, male-dominated, Anglocentric, white canon of particular genres" associated with the New Criticism.

Together, these articles seek to illuminate aspects of New Critical work that offer resources for rethinking contemporary approaches in literary and cultural studies, as well as the direction of the profession more generally. In 1970, retrospecting more than two decades after the heyday of the New Criticism, just as its academic sun was setting, Richard Ohmann reflected upon the "relevance" of literary culture as significantly shaped by the New Criticism in academic contexts of the mid- to late twentieth century. Looking back on the previous two decades, cknowledging the wide impact of the New Criticism on the generations of readers that it had trained and inspired, he noted that, "[T]he New Criticism was the central intellectual force in our subculture during those years." Accordingly, the educational culture in departments of English, he maintained, was far more robust during the New Critical heyday than it had been in previous generations. In 1970, however, acute awareness of an increasingly politicized counterculture in America and controversies about Vietnam was exposing the painful limits of a vision of the "study of literature" built from New Critical ideals. At that point Ohmann meditated on the changing profession for a new wave of academics in English who would not be able so easily to avert attention from uncomfortable political realities as had academics of the 1950s and 1960s. In Ohmann's view, the New Critical vision had left professors of English—along with those who followed their ideas of a richly moral life derived from the study of literature—unfortunately insulated from the forces of the surrounding culture.

Forty years after this time of transition, this collection seeks to reopen the question of what the New Critics' literary and cultural theory, approaches to close reading, vision of literary study, ethical directions, and pedagogical approaches, might offer us today. As the articles in this collection make clear, the New Criticism provided much of the foundation for what we still do now in literary studies; and if we are to reassess our situation at the outset of the second decade of the twenty-first century, if we are to avoid the kind of insulation that Ohmann laments, we need to understand more richly the New Critical matrixes of conviction, professional drives, and intellectual and artistic commitments from which so many of our contemporary practices derive.

Notes

1. For useful information accounts of the Fugitives and the Southern Agrarians, see entries on the Fugitives and *I'll Take My Stand* in *The Companion to Southern Literature*, ed. Joseph M. Flora, Lucinda Hardwick MacKethan, and Todd W. Taylor (Baton Rouge: Louisiana State University Press, 2002).

2. For fuller discussion of the various schools of thought within the discipline of English against which the New Critics defined themselves, see Graff, *Professing Literature*, especially Chapters 8 and 9, and Graff, *Literature against Itself*, Chapter 5, "What Was New Criticism?"

3. See also Allen Tate's representation of this view in "Miss Emily and the Bibliographer" (141).

4. See Atherton, Chapter 2.

5. Eliot, in fact, would wryly distinguish himself from the New Critics in "The Frontiers of Criticism" (1956), deflecting the widely held belief that New Critical work "derived" from him: "I fail to see any critical movement which can be said to derive from myself" (529).

6. On this point, see Graff, *Professing Literature*, 173.

7. See Guillory, Chapter 3, "Ideology and Canonical Form: The New Critical Canon."

Bibliography

Atherton, Carol. *Defining Literary Criticism: Scholarship, Authority, and the Possession of Literary Knowledge, 1880–2002*. Basingstoke: Palgrave Macmillan, 2005.

Baldick, Chris. *The Social Mission of English Criticism, 1848–1932*. New York: Oxford University Press, 1987.

Bauerlein, Mark. "What We Owe the New Critics." *Chronicle of Higher Education*, 21 December 2007.

Brooks, Cleanth. "The Critics Who Made Us." *Sewanee Review* 89.4 (1981): 586–95.

Bush, Douglas. "The New Criticism: Some Old-Fashioned Queries." *PMLA* 64.1 (March 1949): 13–21.

Davis, Garrick, ed. *Praising It New: The Best of the New Criticism*. Athens: Ohio University Press, 2008.

Eagleton, Terry. *How to Read a Poem*. Malden, MA: Blackwell, 2007.

———. *Literary Theory: An Introduction*. Malden, MA: Blackwell, 2008.

Eliot, T. S. "The Frontiers of Criticism." *The Sewanee* Review 64.4 (October–December 1956): 525–43.

———. *The Sacred Wood: Essays on Poetry and Criticism*. 2nd ed. London: Methuen, 1928.

———. *Selected Prose of T. S. Eliot*. Ed. Frank Kermode. New York: Harcourt Brace Jovanovich, 1975.

Gallop, Jane. "The Historicization of Literary Studies and the Fate of Close Reading." In *Profession 2007*, ed. R. G. Feal, 181–86. New York: MLA, 2007.

Graff, Gerald. *Literature against Itself: Literary Ideas in Modern Society*. Chicago: University of Chicago Press, 1979.

———. *Professing Literature: An Institutional History*. Chicago: University of Chicago Press, 1987.

Green, Daniel. "Literature Itself: The New Criticism and Aesthetic Experience." *Philosophy and Literature* 27.1 (2003): 62–79.

Guillory, John. *Cultural Capital: The Problem of Literary Canon Formation*. Chicago: University of Chicago Press, 1993.

Jancovich, Mark. *The Cultural Politics of the New Criticism*. Cambridge: Cambridge University Press, 1993.

Leavis, F. R. *How to Teach Reading: A Primer for Ezra Pound*. Cambridge: The Minority Press, 1932.

Leitch, Vincent B. *American Literary Criticism from the Thirties to the Eighties*. New York: Columbia University Press, 1984.

Lentricchia, Frank. *After the New Criticism*. New York: Routledge, 1983.

———, and Andrew DuBois, eds. *Close Reading*. Durham, NC: Duke University Press, 2003.

Levinson, Marjorie. "What Is New Formalism?" *PMLA* 122.2 (March 2007): 558–69.

Ohmann, Richard. *English in America: A Radical View of the Profession*. New York: Oxford University Press, 1976.

Paglia, Camille. *Break, Blow, Burn*. New York: Pantheon Books, 2005.

Ransom, John Crowe. *The World's Body*. Baton Rouge: Louisiana State University Press, 1938.

———. *Selected Letters of John Crowe Ransom*. Ed. Thomas Daniel Young and George Core. Baton Rouge: Louisiana State University Press, 1984.

Richards, I. A. *Complementarities: Uncollected Essays*. Ed. John Paul Russo. Cambridge, MA: Harvard University Press, 1978.

———. *Science and Poetry*. London: Kegan Paul, 1925.

Richter, David. *Falling Into Theory: Conflicting Views on Reading Literature*. 2nd ed. Boston: Bedford/St. Martin's, 2000.

Schryer, Stephen. "Fantasies of the New Class: The New Criticism, Harvard University, and the Idea of the University." *PMLA* 122.3 (2007): 663–78.

Spurlin, William J., and Michael Fischer, eds. *The New Criticism and Contemporary Literary Theory*. New York: Garland Publishers, 1995.

Suleiman, Susan. "Introduction: Varieties of Audience-Oriented Criticism." In *The Reader in the Text: Essays on Audience and Interpretation*, ed. Susan Suleiman and Inge Crosman, 3–9. Princeton: Princeton University Press, 1980.

Tate, Allen. "Miss Emily and the Bibliographer." 1940. In *Essays of Four Decades,* 141–54. Chicago: Swallow Press, 1968.

Twelve Southerners. *I'll Take My Stand: The South and the Agrarian Tradition.* New York: Harper Brothers, 1930.

Wolfson, Susan J., and Marshall Brown, eds. *Reading for Form.* Seattle: University of Washington Press, 2006.

Veysey, Laurence. *The Emergence of the American University.* Chicago: University of Chicago Press, 1965.

PART I

Rereading the New Criticism

O NE OF the chief objectives of this volume is to revisit and interrogate the many myths that the concept of the New Criticism has accrued over the years—in order to shed new light on their origins, complicate them, and sometimes to overturn them. The essays featured in the volume's first section pay particular attention to addressing such received ideas, and other essays throughout the volume engage them as well. Connor Byrne's essay opens by noting that this effort is certainly not new: as early as 1951, in "The Formalist Critics," Cleanth Brooks famously sought to encapsulate and refute some of the "misunderstandings" about the New Criticism which had already accumulated by only a little more than a decade after its emergence. Many such misconceptions--what Robert Archambeau calls the "straw-man versions" of the New Criticism--stem from the assumption that the New Critics, qua formalist critics, were concerned solely with the "work itself" and what F. R. Leavis called "particular arrangements of words on the page" (by which, it is usually maintained, they meant matters of aesthetic technique only) at the expense of attention to all matters outside the realm of aesthetics that literature might address. After all, in "Criticism, Inc.," the essay-cum-manifesto that culminated John Crowe Ransom's *The World's Body* (1938), Ransom sharply differentiates the "proper business of criticism" from that of "historical studies," "moral studies," "linguistic studies," and "personal registrations." This was a book in which Ransom, later regarded as prime mover behind the professional consolidation of the New Criticism, launched many of the ideas that would become fundamental to the New Criticism. The result of the New Critics' accordance of prime attention to the "work itself" has been a raft of assumptions about what they ruled out of their critical ambit and thus are understood to have dismissed as unimportant. They have widely been seen as unconcerned with either authors' intentions or readerly responses and as unengaged with politics, history, ethics, and societal conditions relevant to a work of literature.

The strategic disciplinary move that the New Critics made in order to establish the distinctness of the literary–critical endeavor also contributed to this widespread understanding of their criticism as dismissing what was beyond the text: they turned decisively away from approaches in the field of English that focused on literary history, read literature for philosophical insights, or appraised literature through overtly moral criteria. The polemical way in which they did so—in order to define and legitimize criticism during an era when criticism was widely regarded as a slight endeavor that "anyone could do"—often suggested that the work of these other approaches was less worthwhile than that of literary criticism. But according to New Critics such as Ransom and Brooks, New Critical distinctions between the "work itself" and what lay beyond it, and between criticism and other kinds of work with respect to literature, never implied that commentary that engaged extratextual matters was without value, nor that they themselves ignored such matters altogether.

Robert Archambeau's opening essay focuses specifically on the myth that the New Critics remained aloof from ethical issues. Even when Ransom ruled out "moral studies" from the kind of literary criticism he supported, he was not banishing moral considerations from New Critical attention. Instead, he suggested that in order for the critic to discern the moral dimension of a literary text, rather than search for a moral "message" detachable from its aesthetic form, he had to assess what it implied morally as an organic whole, aesthetic dimensions and all. And as Archambeau notes, tracing the New Critics' debt to German Romantic idealism—specifically to the ideas of Schiller as transmitted through Coleridge, Arnold, and I. A. Richards—the New Critics in fact take an ethical position by way of their concern with aesthetics: one that reads the disinterested stance enabled by aesthetic contemplation as conducive to a balanced subjectivity, which in turn provides the foundation for ethical conduct. Other essays in this module, such as Alastair Morrison's, similarly bring out the implicit ethics of the New Critics' devotion to an anti-instrumentalist perspective on the world, which they viewed as demonstrated and fostered both by the literature they admired and the critical methods they espoused. During the late 1920s and early 1930s, when several figures who would later dominate the New Criticism were allied with the cause of Agrarianism in the American South, this anti-instrumentalist outlook was also associated by some of them with the Southern "way of life"—focused on art, beauty, gallantry, respect for tradition and custom, and stewardship of the land—which they opposed to a Northern ethos they understood as aridly rationalist, technophilic, pro-scientific, and capitalist.

Morrison's essay presses most on a second myth, related to the first, that the New Critics advocated a literary criticism that was "apolitical," "politically quiescent," or politically "neuter." He homes in on a politics implicit in the New Critical formalist method—the "covert social and political agenda of formalism." Even aside from the politics implied by the Southern Agrarian position; apart from the commitment of Cambridge critics such as I. A. Richards and the Leavises to improving society through criticism (which Morrison reads as much more unabashedly political than the allegiances of their American counterparts); and besides the conservative politics suggested by the statements of T. S. Eliot, whose ideas often stand behind those of the New Critics, the political connotations of New Critical theory and formalism were, in Morrison's reading, profoundly illiberal. In suggesting this, Morrison also addresses another prevalent misreading of the New Criticism: that it was the handmaiden of a hegemonic liberal democratic order. Morrison ultimately maintains that we need to differentiate between, on the one hand, what New Critical theory, manifestic statements, and practice implied as the movement coalesced, and on the other, what the New Criticism later became in the hands of those who made use of it.

Aaron Shaheen, meanwhile, addresses the misconception that the New Critics were unconcerned with history and culture. Starting from Mark Jancovich's contention in *The Cultural Politics of the New Criticism* that "the New Criticism never intended to divorce itself from history and culture," he stresses that John Crowe Ransom, for one, should be read as grappling with cultural problems not only in his overtly Agrarian phase but also afterward, when he turned to a literary criticism only ostensibly separate from his Agrarian commitments. Shaheen traces a specific way in which Ransom carried out engagement with cultural developments of his historical moment through two distinct conceptions of androgyny that played out in both his cultural and literary criticism. Likewise focusing on Ransom, James Matthew Wilson debunks the related widespread belief that, because the New Critics were supposedly not concerned with culture, their commitments were starkly different from, even opposed to, those of Frankfurt School philosophers such as Theodor Adorno, and that certainly there was no commerce between them. On the contrary, Wilson notes, as registered by a little-considered encounter between Ransom and Adorno in the pages of the *Kenyon Review* in 1945, Adorno's essays significantly influenced some late-career turns by Ransom, and the nature of the influence also reflects the subtle and unexpected "affinities" between Ransom's and Adorno's lines of cultural critique. Robert Archambeau observes in his essay that, given the New Critics' opposition to instrumentalism, "in a meaningful sense, the New Critics are . . . Adorno's cousins"; Wilson illuminates other specific ways in which Ransom's and Adorno's ideas crossed paths.

CHAPTER ONE

Aesthetics as Ethics

One and a Half Theses on the New Criticism

ROBERT ARCHAMBEAU

I F I HAD BELIEVED everything that I was told about the New Critics when I was in graduate school, I suppose I would have been more or less prepared to conclude that they were a nefarious crowd of reactionaries, yearning for the good old days of a slaveholding American South while tuning out the wailings of the oppressed in order to relish a particularly convoluted irony, paradox, or poetic ambiguity. Among other things, I was told that the New Critics disdained Romanticism in favor of the complex ironies of the Metaphysical poets; that they were aesthetes, concerned with form but not with ethics; and that they had nothing in common with Continental literary theory, which spoke to our current condition in a way the New Critics simply could not. Such representations were not without an element of truth to them, of course: Eliot's downgrading of the Romantics in favor of Donne & Co. was real enough, as was the turn to text over context in W. K. Wimsatt's *The Verbal Icon,* and no one would confuse the political dreams of the Fugitives with those of the Frankfurt School (or, for that matter, the prose of Robert Penn Warren with that of Theodor Adorno).

Contrary to what I was told, though, it turns out that the New Criticism is in fact part of a long tradition of ethical thinking, a tradition that, in an apparent paradox, is ethical not despite, but because of, its insistence on aestheticism. Moreover, in an irony of a different kind than that so savored by the authors of *Understanding Poetry,* this tradition is fundamentally Romantic in its origins and characteristic gestures of thought. So my first thesis here is that the New Criticism, contrary to received opinion, is an ethically based criticism. My second thesis, which is really only a half a thesis, deeply provisional in recognition of how much further work needs to be done before it could be fully embraced, is that New Critical thinking may prove to be an important kind of ethical thought for our time.

"N.C. = formalist"

If the ideas about the New Criticism I'd encountered in graduate school were so distorted, how did they become so widespread? I'm inclined to believe there's some truth to Mark Bauerlein's assessment in his article "What We Owe the New Critics." Bauerlein contends that the generation of American critics emerging in the wake of the 1966 Johns Hopkins conference on structuralism—the conference that so famously awakened the American academy to Continental models of criticism—still held the New Critics in some esteem, even when they disagreed with them. By 1980, however, the next generation of American critics "looked not directly at the New Critics, but through the eyes of their mentors, the first-generation theorists, and they assumed only the negative side of their mentors' critique." Where critics such as Frank Lentricchia and Geoffrey Hartman had known the New Criticism at first hand, and taken it seriously even as they rejected its tenets, "for younger readers the message lay all in the titles" of Lentricchia's *After the New Criticism* and Hartman's *Beyond Formalism* (B6). One need not engage the benighted New Critics directly, or so it seemed to a generation of graduate students ready to embrace a newer, hipper, and more European set of thinkers. As Bauerlein points out, direct and detailed knowledge of the New Criticism fell so much out of favor that, by 2001, the editors of *The Norton Anthology of Theory and Criticism,* ever-sensitive to market demand, released an edition of their book "whose 2,624 pages do not contain anything by the main originator of New Criticism, [I. A.] Richards, one of the greatest and most influential literary theorists of the century" (B6).

Given the apparent lack of interest in exposure to Richards's primary texts, it is worth considering what one would learn about Richards if one got one's ideas about him chiefly from secondary sources during the last two decades of the twentieth century. The same holds true for the New Critics for whom Richards was such a formative influence. Though we must tread carefully here, being mindful of the important divergences not only among the work of the New Critics themselves but also of the more significant ways in which they, individually and collectively, departed from Richards, we nevertheless find the same pattern of misreading. Indeed if we take three such secondary sources—the entries on the New Criticism in M. H. Abrams's *A Glossary of Literary Terms* and Roger Fowler's *A Dictionary of Modern Critical Terms* and the section on the New Criticism in Terry Eagleton's *Literary Theory: An Introduction*—as representative, we find two significant trends. First, all three sources make much of the most formalistic, and least ethical, of New Critical texts (such as Wimsatt and Beardsley's "fallacy" essays); secondly, these sources pave the way for the sidelining of I. A. Richards in *The Norton Anthology of Theory and Criticism* by truncating his theories and depriving them of much of the ethical dimension they pick up from the Romantic tradition of thought about aesthetics and ethics.

Abrams acknowledges the differences between various representatives of the New Criticism, but nevertheless holds the following to be generally accepted principles of the movement: the ideal of aesthetic autonomy, in which "a poem should be regarded as an independent and self-sufficient object"; and the embracing of formalism to the exclusion of ethics, in which critics "eschew recourse" to the poem's "psychological and moral effects on the reader" (117). This last point is important, since it is I. A. Richards's emphasis on the psychology and moral state of the reader, and his linking of these things to the idea of aesthetic autonomy, that most strongly links both him and the New Critics who followed to the Romantic tradition of aesthetics and ethics. While Abrams does present Richards as central to the New Criticism, he doesn't take the "reconciliation of diverse impulses" to be something that happens in the reader, as part of the ethical work of poetry. Rather, Abrams limits this reconciliation to textual matters, relating it to verbal irony and paradox (118). A reader working up his study notes for a mid-1990s graduate exam in literary theory from Abrams's glossary could be forgiven for jotting down something like "N.C. = formalist = text only = not interested in ethics/world beyond text." He might even have gone on to pass the exam with distinction, and perpetuate the misrepresentation at a small Midwestern liberal arts college for several years before discovering the error of his ways.

Malcolm Bradbury, writing for Roger Fowler's *A Dictionary of Modern Critical Terms,* does a better job than Abrams in presenting the Romantic roots of Richards's thought, but in his essay on the New Criticism, he stresses the formalist applications of Richards's thought and truncates the ethical theory that Richards arrived at through the treatment of the psychological effects of poetry:

Richards's development of Romantic theories of form as the systemization and harmonizing of elements in poetry, with its idea of the poem as a complex activity of meaning, inspired many of the key terms and concepts of the New Criticism: ambiguity, irony, paradox, tension, gesture, etc. However, Richards's attempt to locate this complexity in the psychological *effects* of poetry, rather than the linguistic structure of the work, had failed to produce immediately useful descriptive attitudes and terminology. (160)

With so much else in the Bradbury's entry confirming the main hypothesis of a nonethical, formalist New Criticism, it doesn't seem likely that this passage would much alter the notes of our hypothetical grad student as he feverishly crammed for his exam in his library carrel.

But what of Eagleton? In that *ne plus ultra* source of conventional seminar-room wisdom of the late twentieth century, *Literary Theory: An Introduction,* Terry Eagleton does acknowledge, albeit briefly, an ethical dimension to the thought of Richards and the American critics who studied his work. The way Eagleton depicts Richards's ethics, though, hardly recommends them. The New Criticism "stopped short of a full-blooded formalism," says Eagleton, because of the interest Richards and others took in the effect of the text on the reader. "The literary text, " says Eagleton, "for American New Criticism as for I. A. Richards . . . was also to induce in the reader a definite ideological attitude to the world—one, roughly, of contemplative acceptance" (47). The ethos of the New Criticism, as rendered by Eagleton, is particularly passive and, in the face of the moral urgencies of the world, rather loathsome. Our grad student may well have snorted derisively at the irresponsibility of Eagleton's New Critics, before adding "reactionary/quietist" to his notes.

Particularly striking about this flattening out of our image of the New Criticism is how persistent it has been. Even the small number of younger critics who have begun, in the last few years, to advocate revisiting the New Critics tend not to look to them for ethical thinking, but for formalism. Bauerlein, for example, lauds Garrick Davis's anthology *Praising It New: The Best of the New Criticism,* without any mention of the ethical dimension of the New Critical movement. He chooses instead to stress formalism, and Davis's sensitivity to the New Critical "focus on a poem's verbal detail" (B6). In a similar vein, Rónán McDonald praises the New Critics in *The Death of the Critic,* but without significant reference to the ethical dimension of their thought. His characterization of the New Critics bears a strong resemblance to the Abrams–Bradbury–Eagleton version:

> The central plank of the New Criticism was focusing on the text-as-text, without befuddling the issue with any appeals to authorial intention (let alone biography), historical background, or reader response. The classic exposition of the New Critical rebuttal of the author's intention and the reader's response are recorded in two essays by W. K. Wimsatt and M. C. Beardsley, "The Intentional Fallacy" and "The Affective Fallacy." (97)

It is all there: the centrality of the highly formalist Wimsatt and Beardsley, the emphasis on text alone, and the downplaying of any reader-response dimension. With friends who see it only in these terms, perhaps the New Criticism needs no enemies.

Affairs of the Moral World

An advocate of the New Criticism who wished to go beyond the (certainly worthwhile, but just as certainly limited) emphasis on form would do well to place the New Criticism in the context of its intellectual tradition. That tradition, in its broadest compass, extends back as far as Lord Shaftesbury's response to the thinking of Hobbes and Locke, but for our purposes Schiller's *Letters on the Aesthetic Education of Man* and Coleridge's *On the Constitution of Church and State* may be taken as the foundational texts of a tradition of thinking about aesthetics as ethics, a tradition that finds its way into the work of I. A. Richards and, after him, many of the New Critics via Matthew Arnold's *Culture and Anarchy.*

When Schiller composed the letters that made up *On the Aesthetic Education of Man* in the mid-1790s, he had good reason to doubt the relevance, even the decency, of so apparently trivial and amoral an endeavor as a study of aesthetics. These were tumultuous times, in which the reign of terror and its aftermath in France seemed to render mere formal and aesthetic matters irrelevant. "Is it not at least unseasonable to be looking around for a code of laws for the aesthetic world, when the affairs of the moral world provide an interest that is so much keener?" he asks near the beginning of his inquiry (25). He provides an answer almost immediately, though, telling us that aesthetics are no mere frivolity in times of revolutionary bloodshed, because "we must indeed, if we are to solve that political problem in practice, follow the path of aesthetics, since it is through Beauty that we arrive at Freedom" (27). In addition to his political anxieties, Schiller was motivated in his aesthetic thinking by a sense that modern commercial and industrial society's division of labor would damage the human psyche. New labor conditions, Schiller wrote, would cause "whole classes of human beings" to develop "only a part of their capacities" (38), a state of affairs that would reduce a manager or a laborer to nothing more than "the imprint of his occupation" (40). Only a disinterested approach to art, he argued, could give free play to all our faculties and save us from such an attenuation of our human wholeness. A powerful ethics, one that could ameliorate the modern political and economic condition, would open up to us from within an aesthetics.

Schiller approaches this aesthetics-as-ethics in *On the Aesthetic Education of Man* through a theory of a two-sided human nature. The first part of our nature consists of what Schiller calls the *Stofftrieb* or *Sinnestrieb,* a kind of sense-oriented self-interest, a collection of appetites and desires. The second part of our nature is the *Formtrieb,* something like our reason, but more specific: it is our drive to impose order on our experience, to create moral and conceptual systems. Neither of these parts of our nature should be allowed to dominate the other, lest we become imbalanced creatures. An excess of *Stofftrieb* without *Formtrieb* would either reduce us to mere appetites (think of Charles Dickens's image of the industrial workers of *Hard Times* as nothing but hands and stomachs), or turn us into monsters of self-interest, exerting a Nietzschean will to power over our rivals. For a creature of *Stofftrieb* all is interest and nothing disinterest: something exists for him "only insofar as it secures existence for him; what neither gives to him nor takes from him, is to him simply not there" (113). If we become creatures of *Stofftrieb,* we may be curbed from dangerous behavior by the agents of law, but we will experience this law "only as fetters," neither understanding the law's rationale nor respecting its agents when we can avoid or overpower them (118).

The inverse situation, in which we have an excess of *Formtrieb* without sufficient *Stofftrieb,* is no better. Without an appreciation for the senses and the particularities of the material world, the man of *Formtrieb* becomes "a stranger in the material world" (42). Worshipping only his abstract system, he will be a figure as disconnected from quotidian existence as the scientists of Laputa in Swift's *Gulliver's Travels,* and a monster as ruthless as the Robespierre who so terrorized the opponents of his revolution during the years when Schiller composed *On the Aesthetic Education of Man.* One imagines Schiller may have had Robespierre and the other bloody-handed *philosophes* of France in mind when, describing the man in whom *Formtrieb* triumphs over *Stofftrieb,* he wrote that such an "abstract thinker very often has a cold heart" (42).

For Schiller, human development tends to follow a tripartite pattern, in which we leave our initial unselfconscious life as creatures of *Stofftrieb,* pass through a phase when we are overly governed by *Formtrieb,* and finally become fully integrated creatures, in whom both urges are fully developed and fully reconciled. We are capable of such a reconciliation only through the cultivation of a third drive, the *Spieltreib* or play instinct. Man is "only Man when he is playing," writes Schiller (80), because it is only play that allows for a full recognition and engagement of both the senses and the urge for rules and order. The whole person is recognized and fulfilled in play. And play is most fully available to us through art, because the "cultivation of beauty" will "unite within itself" the "two contradictory qualities" of our nature (55). Art will, by its sensuous embodiment in its medium, "secure the sense faculty against the encroachments of its freedom" by the *Formtrieb*'s desire to reduce everything to definitive order (anyone who has ever felt that a poem must not mean but be, or that a painting is not reducible to its description, has lived a Schillerian moment). Conversely, art will by virtue of its orderliness or engagement with pattern rescue us from "the power of sensation" alone (69). For Schiller, we become our whole selves through making or appreciating works of art.

For art to function as the reconciler of our divided nature, it must be autonomous. That is, art that seeks to make a particular moral or ideological point, or serve some particular useful purpose—be it ecclesiastical, financial, didactic, or political—cannot be the site where we reconcile our divided drives. "Beauty gives no individual result whatever . . . it realizes no individual purpose, either intellectual or moral," writes Schiller, "it discovers no individual truth, helps us perform no individual duty" and when we have appreciated it, nothing specific has been accomplished except that the appreciator "has had completely restored to him the freedom to be what he ought to be," an integrated being (101). Content itself should be of no importance in the work of art, because

> In a truly beautiful work of art the content should do nothing, the form everything; for the wholeness of man is affected by the form alone, and the individual powers by the content. However sublime and comprehensive it may be, the content always has a restrictive action upon the spirit, and only from the form is true aesthetic freedom to be expected. (106)

It is in fact form that reforms man: the work of art's inner balance is more important than any specific goal, statement, or function. The formalistic appreciation of an art free of specific purpose gives us the opportunity to balance our drives, and so distances us from both cold reason and blind self-interest.

The experience of the aesthetic is, in Schiller's view, of vital ethical importance, in that it constructs a subjectivity fit for the modern world of democracy and industrial specialization. Aesthetic experience can prepare us to be citizens of a democratically reformed state because aesthetic experience is the surest means of enabling us to ameliorate the individual material self-interest represented by the *Stofftrieb;* and also the surest means of enabling us to temper the systematic excesses of the *Formtrieb.* If he is to choose freely to enter into a democratic state, the cultivation of the whole or balanced man is absolutely necessary. "This much is certain," says Schiller: "only the predominance of such a character among a people can complete without harm the transformation of a State according to moral principles, and only such a character too can guarantee its perpetuation" (31). Aesthetic experience, it turns out, supplies the precondition for citizenship.

Aesthetic experience also saves us from the truncation of experience forced upon us by modern industrial specialization. Whereas in ancient Greece (as imagined by Schiller) each citizen could "become a whole in himself," the modern specialized world gives us a situation of specialized functions, "a more rigorous dissociation of ranks and occupations" in which "the essential bond of human nature" is torn apart and "a ruinous conflict sets its harmonious powers at variance." While Schiller was not blind to the overall benefits of specialization, he was also cognizant of how in "confining our activity to a single sphere we have handed ourselves over to a master who is not infrequently inclined to end up by suppressing the rest of our capacities" (39). To divide the economic functions was to risk dividing the human psyche and rendering the ethical life difficult, if not impossible.

Aesthetic Subjectivities: *Bildung,* Clerisy, Best Self

The path from Schiller's Romantic aesthetics-as-ethics theory to Richards and on to the New Criticism runs through Coleridge, who brought so much of German idealism to the Anglophone world. When, in his *On the Constitution of Church and State,* Coleridge calls for educational practices that support "the harmonious development of those qualities and faculties that characterize our humanity," he is importing Schillerian thinking to England (67). Balanced subjectivity is in danger of being lost in a world of specialization and commerce, and for Coleridge as for Schiller, rescue will come in the form of an aesthetic education or *Bildung,* a process Coleridge is the first in England to call "cultivation" (Williams, 61). Where Coleridge differs from

Schiller, though, is in the degree to which he foresees an institutionalizing of aesthetic education. Although Schiller wrote of aesthetic education as a prerequisite for citizenship in a peaceful state, he did not write extensively about the creation of institutions to support such education. With Schiller, the autonomous aesthetic became a path for individual cultivation in a world of specialization, a kind of personal salvation and a prerequisite to citizenship. Coleridge, however, dreamed of a national institution devoted in large measure to disinterested knowledge and aesthetic contemplation and of the creation of a whole new class of people, the clerisy. He called, in *On the Constitution of Church and State,* for the national "support and maintenance of a permanent class or order" devoted to cultivation (76). As D. J. Palmer has argued, Coleridge's idea of the clerisy presaged state education in the humanities, particularly literature, and would eventually give "impetus and shaping spirit to English studies" (40). With Coleridge, we are well on our way to the establishment not only of New Critical thinking, but of the kind of academic department that would, for decades, provide the New Critics with a home and an audience.

The person who would do the most to take Coleridge's ideas and make them central to an education system was Matthew Arnold. If Coleridge was a dreaming prophet of culture, Arnold was, in Ian Hunter's memorable phrase, "the prophet of culture armed" (15). Arnold felt that individual integrity and the safety of his society could be preserved only by the creation, via education, of a group of people who could cultivate a disinterested "best self." Without such a disinterested class, all would fall into a Hobbesian war of clashing self-interest, "for we have seen how much of our disorders and perplexities is due to the disbelief . . . in a paramount best self" (202). As Lionel Trilling put it, "given divergent interests and conflicting parties" in the Victorian class struggle, Arnold's goal was to "create a perfectly fair umpire . . . to deal reasonably and for the good of all" (230). What was needed was a disinterested umpire subjectivity without strong prejudice toward any side in the struggle.

How could such a disinterested umpire class come into being? The Arnoldian proposition is deeply reminiscent of Schiller's ideal of aesthetic education: for both thinkers disinterest comes about as the realization of the whole person and all of his faculties, and involves the study of aesthetic objects (including works of literature) conceived of as autonomous. For Arnold as for Schiller, "culture" is no mere collection of polite knowledge. Rather, it is an ongoing action, a deliberate cultivation that fulfills an urge toward the development of "all sides of our humanity" (11). True culture works toward this without regard to knowledge's utility or potential for advancing our particular interests (6). The kind of study Arnold advocates would, he hoped, create a "disinterestedness" and an "independence of machinery"—that is, independence from instrumental reason—in the student (33). The subject of Arnoldian culture, like that of Schiller's *Bildung*, will be able to distance his understanding from his appetites, interests, and desires, "subduing" the "great obvious faults of our animality" (57).

With Arnold as with Schiller, autonomous aesthetic objects and disinterested appreciations of the aesthetic—particularly of literature—play central roles in the creation of a relatively disinterested subjectivity. Arnold realized that the pursuit of aesthetics for its own sake may seem frivolous in the utilitarian climate of Victorian England, saying "it cannot but acutely try a conscience to be accused, in a practical country like ours, of keeping aloof from the work and hope of a multitude of earnest-hearted men, and of merely toying with poetry and aesthetics" (96). But such apparently useless study is a matter of the utmost social urgency, says Arnold, for "we find no basis for a firm State-power in our ordinary selves"—but the disinterested study of aesthetic objects can lead us to "our *best self*," the version of ourselves to which we may entrust the State (96). Indeed, Arnold comes to see poetry, the most apparently autonomous of literary forms, as the exemplary bearer of the standard of autonomous beauty that will push us in no particular ideological direction, and serve no particular useful purpose, other than helping us develop a fully balanced "character of human perfection" (54). For Arnold poetry can, in fact, serve as a model for culture as a whole, for "culture is of like spirit with poetry, follows one law with poetry" in its anti-utilitarian, anti-instrumental autonomy (54).

The Romantic tradition of aesthetics-as-ethics launched by Schiller and Coleridge and developed by Arnold makes such apparently unsocial things as disinterest, aesthetic autonomy, and formalism central to the creation of a subjectivity capable of distancing itself from mere appetite and self-interested instrumental reason. While all this represents (to take up Terry Eagleton's phrase) "a definite ideological attitude to the world," it certainly is not an attitude "of contemplative acceptance" (47). It is more like an attitude of contemplative vigilance, such as a good administrator of a state regulatory agency or an officer of the law is meant to take toward those who would bend or break social regulations to advance their self-interests. Eagleton, of course, wasn't describing Schiller or Coleridge or Arnold: he was describing the New Critics. But the New Criticism that he so casually dismissed embodied, in some of its most influential works, exactly the Romantic tradition we have been examining.

Avatars of Schiller

As he took up these strands of the Romantic tradition, I. A. Richards, like Schiller, saw disinterested, formalistic literary study and the autonomous aesthetic experience as leading to a balancing of our various drives—a balancing act with ethical and even political implications. Perhaps it shouldn't be surprising to find this Romantic strand in the weave of Richards's thought: he did, after all, write a book on Coleridge, and his first book, *The Foundations of Aesthetics,* contains a précis of Schiller's *Letters on the Aesthetic Education of Man.* That summary is quite sympathetic, with the caveat that Schiller, lacking access to the cognitive tools of modern psychology, gave a "too simple" description of the different inner drives that formalist contemplation would balance (though Richards also notes that theorists of modern psychology would benefit from an appreciation of Schiller's aesthetics) (84–86).

In some respects, Richards's theories are very much in line with the kind of representation given them by commentators such as Abrams, Bradbury, and Eagleton. The attention of the reader, for example, is to be focused largely on formal matters, and "the intellectual examination of the *internal* coherence of the poem" is the method by which Richards suggests the critic proceed (*Practical Criticism,* 261). Matters of form, for Richards as for Schiller, are more fundamental than matters of content—a condition he finds just as prevalent among general readers as among critics:

> [I]t would seem evident that poetry which has been built upon firm and definite beliefs about the world, *The Divine Comedy* or *Paradise Lost,* or Donne's *Divine Poems,* or Shelley's *Prometheus Unbound,* or Hardy's *The Dynasts,* must appear differently to readers who do and readers who do not hold similar beliefs. Yet in fact most readers, and nearly all good readers, are very little disturbed by even a direct opposition between their own beliefs and the beliefs of the poet. (255)

"Doctrine," to use Richards's term for the ideological content of literature, fades into near irrelevance here. But nowhere does Richards sound more like the stereotype of the New Critic than when he tells us that irony "consists in the bringing in of the opposite, the complementary impulses . . . that is why irony itself is so constantly a characteristic of [first-rate] poetry" (*Principles of Literary Criticism,* 250).

As in the Romantic tradition initiated by Schiller, however, this appreciation of internal coherences and ironies is connected with the creation of an ethical subjectivity distanced from its own most immediately self-interested impulses. Richards's thinking involves a kind of mirroring (with modifications) of Schiller's theory of the balancing of opposed drives in the experience of art. Aesthetic experience tempers what Richards calls emotional belief with intellectual belief in a process much like the interplay of *Stofftrieb* and *Formtrieb* in Schiller. Without such tempering, says Richards, we would behave as primitives, indulging self-interest and bending truth to fit our desires:

> In primitive man . . . any idea which opens a ready outlet to emotion or points to a line of action in conformity with custom is quickly believed. . . . Given a need (whether conscious *as a desire*) or not, any idea which can be taken as a step on the way to its fulfillment is accepted. . . . This acceptance, this use of the idea—by our interests, our desires, feelings, attitudes, tendencies to action and what not—is emotional belief. (*Practical Criticism*, 258–59)

Without a balancing of intellect and emotion, we're left with little more than a crude will to power.

By contrast, the aesthetic experience, for Richards, harmonizes our conflicting interests. The results are very much in the tradition of Schiller, since an engagement of a broader spectrum of our urges and impulses moves us toward a balanced subjectivity: "the equilibrium of opposed impulses" in "aesthetic responses," Richards notes in *Principles of Literary Criticism*, "brings into play far more of our personality than is possible in experiences of a more defined emotion." Our appreciation of the world becomes broader than it would have been had we made our perception and thought instrumental to self-interest: "more facets of the mind are exposed and, what is the same thing, more aspects of things are able to affect us" (251–52). Moreover, and in a further parallel to Schiller and the Romantic tradition, Richards envisions this process as leading us to a state of disinterestedness:

> To respond, not through one narrow channel of interest, but simultaneously and coherently through many, is to be *disinterested* in the only sense of the word which concerns us here. A state of mind which is not disinterested is one which sees things only from one standpoint or under one aspect. At the same time, since more of our personality is engaged the independence and individuality of other things becomes greater. We seem to see 'all round' them, to see them as they really are; we see them apart from any one particular interest which they may have for us. Of course without some interest, we should not see them at all, but the less any one particular interest is indispensable, the more detached our attitude becomes. And to say that we

are impersonal is merely a curious way of saying that our personality is more completely involved. (252)

Richards—whose experience of the broad variety of lamentable responses to literature is famously documented in his analysis of student responses to de-contextualized poems in *Practical Criticism*—is not, of course, so naive as to believe that exposure to aesthetic contemplation will necessarily lead to this result. But in the end he shares much of the qualified optimism of the Romantic tradition, writing that appreciation of formal balance in "the construction of the work of art" may well "predispose [us] to," even if it is "not necessarily followed by, equilibrium" (*Foundations of Aesthetics*, 87).

This kind of thinking is by no means marginal to Richards's work: arguments of this kind receive full-chapter treatments in *Foundations of Aesthetics*, *Practical Criticism*, *Principles of Literary Criticism* and in *Science and Poetry*. Even the treatment of emotive and referential meaning in *The Meaning of Meaning* reinforces the Schillerian-Romantic tradition. As John Constable has pointed out, Richards's argument in *The Meaning of Meaning* is part-and-parcel of his later articulation of a theory of aesthetic experience bringing "as many of an individual's appetencies (i.e., their interests, their desires) into as harmonious a balance as is possible" (Constable).

Richards isn't alone, either: the Romantic tradition permeates New Critical thinking itself, perhaps more thoroughly than we have been able or willing to acknowledge. Consider René Wellek and Austin Warren's position in their grand synthesis of New Critical thought, *Theory of Literature:*

> When the work of literature functions successfully, the two 'notes' of pleasure and utility should not merely coexist but coalesce. The pleasure of literature, we need to maintain, is not one preference among a long list of possible pleasures but is a 'higher pleasure' because pleasure in a higher kind of activity, i.e., non-acquisitive contemplation. (31)

Whatever one may think of their hierarchy of pleasures, one has to admit that the idea of mingling two kinds of urges in aesthetic experience—one more appetitive, the other more rational—echoes the Romantic tradition, as does the creation (in the form of "non-acquisitive contemplation") of a disinterested subjectivity that eschews instrumental reason. Their thinking is, to a surprising degree, ethical—not through any emphasis on what they dismiss as a mere "helpful moral lesson" gleaned from the content of the work of art, but from a kind of contemplation that creates a new ethos in the reader (31). While Wellek and Warren may consider literature to be "pure of practical intent (propaganda, incitation to direct, immediate action)" (239), they see the aesthetic itself, and the formalist engagement of the work of art, as fundamentally ethical. Apostles of *Being and Time* may be surprised to hear echoes of Heidegger's opposition to instrumentality via poesis in Wellek and Warren's advocacy of an aesthetically conditioned subjectivity, a subjectivity that doesn't "endeavor to . . . appropriate or consume" (241). For that matter, those who derive their ethics and politics from Horkheimer and Adorno's critique of instrumental reason in *Dialectic of Enlightenment* may be surprised to find allied strands of thought in the New Criticism. Had the origins of New Critical thinking in German Romanticism been kept more in the foreground, of course, such surprise would be unwarranted: in a meaningful sense, the New Critics are, in fact, Adorno's cousins.

The political positions of the various New Critics, of course, don't much resemble those of Heidegger, nor do they bear much resemblance to those of Adorno. But their political positions are not, as is often assumed, extrinsic to their literary theory. The anti-modern, anti-industrial agrarianism of the Fugitives, for example, is predicated on the same kind of anti-instrumentalism we see in so much New Critical aesthetic theory. When, for example, John Crowe Ransom defines the enemies of his agrarian political program in *God without Thunder* as "Work, Power, Activity, Business, Industry, Production" (177), his principles are as profoundly anti-instrumentalist as those of any Frankfurt School thinker—he merely follows the vector of such ethics in a different political direction. Similarly, when I. A. Richards defines a just society in liberal terms as "one in which no faction, no pressure group, no self-interested power-seeker, can push the rest of the citizens around," by seeking the "aggrandizement" of self-interest, he too derives his politics from the Schillerian ethics of balance and disinterest (*Speculative Instruments*, 107–8).

There are, of course, instances where New Critics limit their thinking to formalism. Indeed, the emphasis on the balancing of opposites as a merely textual matter in, say, Cleanth Brooks's "Irony as a Principle of Structure" may be taken as a kind of truncation of the Romantic tradition. But to privilege this abridged version of the New Criticism over the version more fully in touch with the ethical dimensions of its Romantic roots is to give oneself a straw-man version of the New Criticism to attack.

Canonicity, Dialogism, and the New Criticism

Of course not all attacks on the New Criticism are attacks on straw men. I know of no more powerful detractor of the New Critics than William V.

Spanos, whose criticisms carry weight in no small measure due the fact that he is one of the few detractors to attack New Criticism on the level of its oft-overlooked ethical base. Even these attacks, however, have their weaknesses, and it is in the face of these weaknesses that I venture to advance my second thesis, or half-thesis. My tentative hypothesis is this: the Romantic tradition as manifested in the twentieth-century Anglo-American academy by the New Criticism) is worth taking seriously, not only as a formalism, but as an ethics.

Spanos is to be applauded for his understanding of the Romantic and ethical roots of the New Criticism, and for placing the thought of Richards in the context of Matthew Arnold. But the two main arguments Spanos levels against I. A. Richards and the New Criticism in his enormous article "The Apollonian Investment of Modern Humanist Education" are both fundamentally flawed. The first (and the less significant) argument is based on links between disinterest and exclusive notions of canonicity—links that turn out to be accidental rather than essential. The second (and far more profound) argument is predicated on what I take to be a fundamental misunderstanding of the ethical dimension of disinterest.

The first argument maintains that inquiry aiming at formal disinterest will necessarily serve as a screen for received prejudices about what counts as a work worthy of canonical status. Advocates of disinterest, says Spanos, merely reaffirm "the abiding 'touchstones' of the logocentric humanistic mind—'the best that has been thought and said in the world' (by which, as the omission of reference to any other makes clear . . . means the Western world)." Critics committed to disinterested inquiry will always end up seeking a cultural "re-centering," a "restoration of a common body of knowledge" (19–20) based on old ideas of a Western high-art canon. Assertions of this kind are easy enough to refute by citing empirical evidence, and such evidence is easy enough to come by. Here, for example, is the testimony of poet and critic Stephen Burt, looking back on his graduate education in the 1990s:

> [T]hose of us who follow both older kinds of art well-treated within the academy (e.g. written poetry in English) and newer kinds that have yet to find secure homes there . . . have had the odd experience of seeing "close reading" and structural analysis attacked by would-be authority figures who cover the older kinds, even as close attention to how works of art are made, and what happens "inside" them, are ever more in demand as regards the newer kinds. Ten years ago twenty-somethings in top graduate programs were being taught (wrongly) to look down on an influential book called *Understanding Poetry* even as they were reading, and recommending (rightly), a then-new book called *Understanding Comics*, a book (itself

in comics form) that remains the foundation for the arguments about that
art . . . (Burt)

The facts, it seems, are against Spanos—though perhaps we can forgive him,
given that he made his argument several years before the "odd experience"
Burt describes took place.

A much more serious argument against the New Criticism (and, indeed,
the whole tradition behind it, going back to Arnold and Schiller) concerns
the relationship between dialogism—with all of its ethical and political connotations—and disinterest. For Spanos, Richards's commitment to disinterestedness and the balance of inner drives implies a normative subjectivity
and, along with it, a monologic ethos. "The structure of balanced inclusion,"
writes Spanos,

> constitutes Richards's (and, however unevenly developed, the New Critics')
> ideal model for psyche, poem, culture, socius, state, etc. All these sites are
> implied in some degree or other in any particular one of his texts, whether
> such a text is centrally about psychology, the principles of literary criticism,
> the pedagogy of literary interpretation, the idea of the university, culture, or
> national or international politics. Further, Richards's account of the ideal
> poem (and society) is an up-dating of Arnold's "disinterestedness," his Apol-
> lonian commitment against intellectual provincialism, to seeing life steadily
> and seeing it whole. (54)

Intellectual provincialism, here, refers to knowledge motivated by self-interested advocacy or (in Spanos's own somewhat unfortunate phrase) "prejudiced knowledge." Spanos would "rehabilitate or de-colonize prejudice, i.e.,
as the interest which activates inquiry" (55). That is, Spanos sees disinterest as a way of excluding dialogue and dismissing views that can be labeled
"interested." His language devolves into a bit of a thicket, but the point can
still be gleaned from passages such as this:

> Richards . . . categorically dismisses as inevitably activating intellectual war-
> fare precisely what, given the contemporary demystification of the binary
> logic of metaphysics, now appears to the postmodern counter-memory to be
> the most suggestively valuable possibility in Plato's discourse: an originative
> thinking or, more specifically, a hermeneutics of understanding as antago-
> nistic dialogue, which is 'grounded' on and emerges from the acknowledged
> uncertainty of the decentered occasion of human 'being.' The oxymoron I
> am invoking is, of course, Mikhail Bakhtin's. (61)

"Understanding as antagonistic dialogue" is the key phrase here: for Spanos, Richards's emphasis on disinterest implies an exclusion of the clash of viewpoints. As the invocation of Bakhtin makes clear, Spanos is charging Richards (along with the other New Critics and, behind them, the tradition running back through Arnold to Schiller) with monologism.

This, however, involves a fundamental misunderstanding of what is meant by disinterest. When Richards wrote of disinterested aesthetic response as proceeding "not through one narrow channel of interest, but simultaneously and coherently through many," he was advocating a state of mind open to exactly the kind of Bakhtinian dialogue Spanos has in mind. One need not listen too hard to hear the echoes of Bakhtin when Richards says "a state of mind which is not disinterested is one which sees things only from one standpoint or under one aspect," or when he tells us that with disinterest "we seem to see 'all round' [things] . . . we see them apart from any one particular interest which they may have for us (*Principles of Literary Criticism*, 252). This is very much in line with the dialogic inter-illumination of different languages Bakhtin had in mind when he wrote of how "languages throw light on one another: one language can, after all, see itself only in the light of another language" ("Epic and Novel," 12). The disinterested mind, as Richards defines it, *is* the dialogic mind. It is the self-interested mind, the antagonistic mind of the will to power, that is monologic. Bakhtin maintains that a "unitary language" works in tandem with "sociopolitical and cultural centralization" ("Discourse in the Novel," 271) and that the reverse is also true—that dialogue (and here I would include the internal dialogue of disinterested inquiry advocated by Richards) points toward a liberal pluralism. This, of course, is the very politics Richards called for when he described the ideal society as "one in which no faction, no pressure group, no self-interested power-seeker, can push the rest of the citizens around" (*Speculative Instruments*, 107).

It seems beyond question to me that the work of Richards, along with that the New Critics who take their cue from them is, contrary to much opinion, deeply rooted in a long tradition of aesthetic and ethical thought. Moreover, the form of ethics we see most powerfully and persistently articulated in the works of I. A. Richards need not be linked with political reaction, nor is it anathema to pluralism of thought or of politics, as the most forceful thinker to criticize the ethics of the New Criticism has maintained. A rather perilous leap would be involved in proceeding from these conclusions to a general embrace of the New Criticism as a form of ethical thought. But in an environment where the New Criticism is still either dismissed outright, or advocated only for its formal techniques of close reading, it is important to begin a reappraisal of the New Critical heritage as both an aesthetics and an ethics.

Bibliography

Abrams, M. H. *A Glossary of Literary Terms*. 4th ed. New York: Holt, Rinehart and Winston, 1981.

Arnold, Matthew. *Culture and Anarchy*. Ed. J. Dover Wilson. Cambridge: Cambridge University Press, 1954.

Bakhtin, Mikhail. "Discourse in the Novel." In *The Dialogic Imagination: Four Essays,* trans. Caryl Emerson and Michael Holquist, 259–422. Austin: University of Texas Press, 1981.

———. "Epic and Novel." In *The Dialogic Imagination: Four Essays,* trans. Caryl Emerson and Michael Holquist, 3–40. Austin: University of Texas Press, 1981.

Bauerlein, Mark. "What We Owe the New Critics." *The Chronicle Review* 54.17 (December 2007), B6–8.

Bradbury, Malcolm. "The New Criticism." In *A Dictionary of Modern Critical Terms,* ed. Roger Fowler, 160–61. New York: Routledge, 1987.

Burt, Stephen. "Against Argument." *Columbia University Press Blog* (website). 17 April 2008 <http://www.cupblog.org/?p=185>.

Coleridge, Samuel Taylor. *On the Constitution of Church and State*. Princeton: Princeton University Press, 1976.

Constable, John. "I. A. Richards." *The Literary Encyclopedia* (website). 28 October 2000 http://www.litencyc.com/php/speople.php?rec=true&UID=5183.

Eagleton, Terry. *Literary Theory: An Introduction*. Minneapolis: University of Minnesota Press, 1983.

Hunter, Ian. *Culture and Government*. London: Macmillan, 1988.

McDonald, Rónán. *The Death of the Critic*. London: Continuum, 2007.

Palmer, D. J. *The Rise of English Studies*. London: Oxford, 1965.

Ransom, John Crowe. *God without Thunder: An Unorthodox Defense of Orthodoxy*. New York: Harcourt, Brace, 1930.

Richards, I. A., with C. K. Ogden and James Wood. *The Foundations of Aesthetics*. New York: Lear, 1925.

Richards, I. A. *Practical Criticism: A Study of Literary Judgment*. New York: Harcourt, Brace, 1929.

———. *Principles of Literary Criticism*. New York: Harcourt Brace, 1947.

———. *Speculative Instruments*. London: Routledge and Kegan Paul, 1955.

Schiller, Friedrich. *On the Aesthetic Education of Man*. Trans. Reginald Snell. New Haven: Yale University Press, 1954.

Spanos, William V. "The Apollonian Investment of Modern Humanist Education: The Examples of Matthew Arnold, Irving Babbitt, and I. A. Richards." *Cultural Critique* 1.1 (Autumn 1985): 7–72.

Trilling, Lionel. *Matthew Arnold*. New York: Noonday, 1955.

Wellek, René, and Austin Warren. *Theory of Literature*. 3rd ed. New York: Harcourt, Brace and World, 1956.

Williams, Raymond. *Culture and Society, 1780–1950*. New York: Columbia University Press, 1983.

CHAPTER TWO

Eliot, the Agrarians, and the
Political Subtext of New Critical Formalism

ALASTAIR MORRISON

A S IT IS usually remembered, New Critical formalism evokes no adjective so powerfully as "stifling." The focus upon "the poem itself" is generally understood to have come at the cost of personal meaning, and more to the present purpose, of political insight. Marianne DeKoven remembers an undergraduate confrontation with a New Critically minded supervisor:

> When I tried, in 1969, to write my senior honors thesis on the detectability of fascism in T. S. Eliot's form, I was told that I could if I really wanted to, and if I didn't mind risking a lower grade, but why not write instead about something truly important. I ended by writing, what else, a stylistic analysis, a close reading of Murder in the Cathedral which subordinated the question of the politics of form to the truly important question, its own politics still well concealed, of whether or not the structure of the play is indeed organically unified. (679)

In a case like this, there is little disputing that the New Criticism *was* politically suffocating, and undoubtedly, such episodes were common. Yet we would be mistaken in assuming—as DeKoven, to her credit, does not assume—that the seminal commitments which underlie this anecdote in any way constituted political neuter.

Political neuter can be both broadly and narrowly defined. As it figures in William Cain's 1984 *The Crisis in Criticism,* the New Criticism flourished specifically against the backdrop of international Communism. In this context, Cain asserts, it was "apolitical," and as such, a redoubt against a "painful, intimidating political era" (5). Mark Walhout, meanwhile, grants the New Criticism a much more politically agentive role, arguing that it "popularized the skills of language analysis necessary for the successful conduct of geopolitics in the Cold War" (87). This is, in a sense, only a more robust version of the same thing; in both accounts, the New Criticism is a defense mechanism against threatening political transformation, albeit with different degrees of active force. As descriptions of eventual classroom praxis, I take no direct issue with either claim. Parts of them are even appropriate to the New Criticism as it was in its early years in the late 1930s and early 1940s. The genteel cluster of Southern literary men who initially theorized it surely did experience their political era as painful, and it seems unlikely that the dead hand of Marx, any more than the living ones of Stalin and Khrushchev, helped to assuage their pain. But by ascribing to the New Critics merely the reactionary anti-communist default of the mid-twentieth century, we miss the expansiveness with which the inceptive documents of the New Criticism deplored their historical moment.

The reading of these documents as political neuter, as suppressing dissent in either the active or the passive sense, would be more credible had they represented a dominant ideology in any way. And they, or at least their associated textual practices, have sometimes been taken to represent just such an ideology. Terence Hawkes suggests, for instance, that the New Critical methodology's assumptions about the autonomy of reader and text are grounded in "liberal humanism" (155), and the adjective Peter Brooks uses to describe the foregrounding of the "text itself," and the marginaliation of more obscure variables, like history and intertextuality, is "democratic" (512). Again, in the schoolroom actuality to which the New Criticism gave rise, Brooks's adjective is justified, provided that by "democracy," we mean the populistic rather than the liberal or constitutional sort. There is, after all, the affective fallacy to be avoided; the student is not entitled to think what she likes about a given text, as DeKoven's example ably demonstrates. But the ideological direction of the New Criticism at its genesis is another matter altogether.

Depoliticization is a strategy more appropriately ascribed to the Cold Warrior than the nascent New Critic: checking dissent is a perfectly sensible activity for those who represent the political status quo, however theoretically committed to "the free exchange of ideas" that status quo may be. This may explain the enthusiasm of classical humanists like Allan Bloom for reading books "as they are." But it cannot explain the New Critics, whatever they may have thought of international communism. The figures behind the New Criticism were, in Raymond Williams's terms, essentially residual in their ideology, and addressed the society around them with more than implicit hostility. It will be the work of the present essay to demonstrate, first, that New Critical formalism was intended as an ideologically subversive movement, and furthermore, that its most meaningful descendants understood themselves as equally, if differently, subversive.

A date of convenience for this subversive beginning is 1941, the year John Crowe Ransom published the collection entitled *The New Criticism*. But as Mark Jancovich notes, the political stripe of Ransom and his colleagues is most evident in work older than this. The notable text is the 1930 Southern Agrarian manifesto *I'll Take My Stand*, which bore the signatures of Ransom, Robert Penn Warren, and Allen Tate, among others. And upon this eleven year interval I would like to overlay another critical career. I will follow it to 1934, when an address at the University of Virginia the previous year was first published as *After Strange Gods*. It begins with a bravura series of critical essays, which begin to emerge around 1919. The career, of course, is that of T. S. Eliot.

As critic no less than as poet, Eliot was invoked by the Agrarians as a kind of patron saint. The confident postformalism of the last few decades of the twentieth century has suggested that it is conservative New Critical taste, rather than simple unambiguous greatness, which explains Eliot's imperial preponderance in the poetic canon. This relationship works the other way as well; as formalist criticism anoints Eliot's verse, it depends genetically on his prose. The debt is evident on a number of levels; at the stage of specific critical proposition, the objective correlative of 1919 predicts the affective fallacy of 1946. In more general attitudinal terms, Cleanth Brooks's heresy of paraphrase points back to Eliot's sworn adherence to "poetry and not another thing" in the second edition of *The Sacred Wood* (viii). And in the more broadly political arena, there was an equally unmistakable hearkening to Eliot.

What Jancovich has noted in *I'll Take My Stand* can only be reinforced by an association with Eliot: that is, the fundamental illiberalism of the New Critics. *I'll Take My Stand* opposed the rapaciously utilitarian technocracy of the modern world—and specifically, of the Northern states—as well as a legalistic, rational individualism which was eroding authentic community and faith. By 1933, Eliot had read the manifesto, and in the lecture which became *After Strange Gods*, he responded to it enthusiastically. It is from this address that we get the infamous statement that, in the defense of a "traditional society," the imperatives of "race and religion combine to make any large number of free-thinking Jews undesirable" (20). Whether Eliot disliked Jews per se is, to say the least, a matter of debate, but his opposition both to free thought and to cultural diversity is self-evident. It was in this spirit that Eliot turned south, pursuing "tradition, such as the influx of foreign popula- tions had almost effaced in some parts of the North" (15). "I have been much interested," his speaking text runs, "since the publication a few years ago of a book called *I'll Take My Stand,* in what is sometimes called the [A]grarian movement in the South" (15).

Authentic tradition to the exclusion of freedom of thought, and of cosmo- politanism of any kind—hardly the advertised values of the American Cold Warrior. But how much can such illiberal, subversive ideals have counted? When Ransom wrote that "the philosophical critic" was interested only in a poem's "being" and always "in revolt against the tyranny of ideas," was he not, necessarily, segregating the cultural arguments he had made in 1930 from the literary work he would do thereafter, thus ceding ground fertile with subversive potential to ascendant liberalism (*World's Body* 111)? When Eliot pledged to focus his critical prose on "poetry and not another thing," was he not at the same time pledging not to argue against social pluralism? Are these not promises to check subversive baggage at the literary or critical door?

There were, certainly, other organic formalists with more explicitly trans- formative agendas. We might consider another self-styled apostolate of Eliot's, the Cambridge critics who consolidated around the journal *Scrutiny* in the 1930s. Many contemporary commentators have treated the English and American groups as essentially the same. Gerald Graff, for example, clas- sifies I. A. Richards as a New Critic (*Literature against Itself,* 134). Graff is pointing out a valid connection, but for the present purpose I will not include the Scrutineers in the New Critical category. In stark contrast to their Ameri- can cousins, this earlier group was frankly political in its use of literature.

In a muscular summary near the beginning of *Literary Theory,* Terry Eagleton criticizes a lack of directness in the Cambridge critics' political agenda. It is no doubt true that they were less openly partisan than Eagle- ton—indeed, their politics made politicization of the Eagletonian kind abhor- rent. F. R. Leavis once declared his willingness to consider "some kind of communism as the solution of the economic problem," so long as it was not attended by the philistinic instrumentalism with which Marxist thought approached the arts ("Benzonian," 167). Although, as Eagleton observes, the Cambridge critics were generally of "lower-middle-class" origins, "noncon- formist, provincial, and hardworking" (31)—this in contrast to the landed- gentry origins of the Agrarians—critics such as Richards, F. R. Leavis, and

Q. D. Leavis joined in lamenting the loss of "the organic society." And while they never actually "read for politics," or engaged literature as rhetorical or partisan, they certainly asserted a strong connection between aesthetic experience and socialization. I. A. Richards, taking a proto-behaviorist approach to the psychology of reading, was quite frank about his desire to use literature's affective capacity to stimulate social change. Poetry could direct "affective-volitional attitudes" (*Principles,* 90). While Richards was against "message hunting," he did assert that "in subtler ways the intellectual influence of the arts is all-pervasive," and could even create "an improvement of [moral] response" (181, 186). In other words, the ideal society would not instrumentalize literature, but literary critics could use literature's very non-instrumentality to help bring that society about. And more to the point, the Cambridge critics admitted they were doing so.

Though their social values were markedly similar to those of the Cambridge group, both Eliot and the American New Critics were more circumspect. This has nothing to do with the creation of a Cold War "safe space," in which political vexations could be put out of mind. Part of it must be situational having to do with the fact that these writers found themselves in a marginal and residual position; there is something distinctly unenviable in arguing, from a minority position, against social difference, in dissenting against the right to dissent. This is the unhappy inverse of the Cold Warrior's position, which Herbert Marcuse, in a position oddly analogous to that of the Agrarians, called "repressive tolerance." But a more essential reason has to do with organicism itself. If the Cambridge critics proposed an instrumental application of non-instrumental values, neither Eliot nor the New Critics would countenance even this degree of systematic intervention. Rather than a ceding of ground, this refusal was in fact an all the more stringent degree of devotion to the "organicization" of society, though one which significantly narrowed the avenues of critical agency.

There are, it is true, moments when this restraint was less than perfect. In readings of Eliot's own poetry, the New Critics could not always resist the tempting "use value" of topical content, probably because that content— rootless paranoia in "Prufrock," social decay in "Gerontion," antipathy to the modern world almost everywhere—was so attractive to them. In his 1953 book *The Forlorn Demon,* for instance, Allen Tate offered an eloquent, characteristic reading of *The Waste Land* as an assertion of schizophrenic decline, and provoked Northrop Frye's memorably derisive epithet about a "Great Western Butterslide" (444). On this point, Eliot was more consistent than his followers; confronted with this ideological reading, he told an audience at a Harvard lecture that while "various critics have done me the honour to interpret [*The Waste Land*] in terms of criticism of the contemporary world . . . to me . . . it was just a piece of rhythmic grumbling" (qtd. in Davies, 954). But on other occasions, contradiction bit the other way. In his benchmark reading of Keats's "Ode on a Grecian Urn," Cleanth Brooks expresses displeasure at having to chastise Eliot for the comment that the poem "makes a statement which is untrue." Poems, Brooks insisted, didn't state anything but themselves (*Urn*, 152–54). Perhaps the most humorous instance is that of Archibald Macleish's highly didactic poem "Ars Poetica," whose ultimate line, "a poem should not mean but be," Monroe Beardsley and William Wimsatt unthinkingly reproduce in "The Intentional Fallacy" as a statement of their own position. Perhaps it is moments like these that Graff has in mind when he calls the New Critics "reluctant" formalists (146).

But more revealing than these occasional formalist faux-pas, and more important in the New Critical and Eliotic social strategies, are the actual imperatives they urged on readers—the very imperatives which kept them from more direct forms of social intervention. I will observe two fronts of engagement. The first is "impersonality." Against a society they saw standing for self-determination, self-expression, and privacy, both material and subjective/psychological, the new literary-pedagogical establishment prescribed a radical cult of unity.

This effort begins with Eliot's famous early essays. In "Tradition and the Individual Talent" (1919) we are instructed that great works of art do not stand on their own, but instead participate in a kind of continuum, almost a chain of being, stretching back at least as far as Dante. Eliot calls his canon "the mind of Europe," with the at-least-metaphorical implication of even more than harmonious union of parts—a single, irreducible intelligence. "The Metaphysical Poets" (1921) makes a comparable requirement of affective function. Successful poetry, according to Eliot, affects not only the heart, but also "the cerebral cortex, the nervous system, the digestive tract," sublimating the rational and extra-rational components of the observer (66). And upon this proposed unification of the reader hangs an oblique argument for a more political kind of unity. The essay posits a historical volta; whereas a poet like Donne felt a thought "as immediately as the odour of a rose," today we suffer from a "dissociation of sensibility" whose advent Eliot finds in the work of Milton and Dryden (64). When Eliot notes that the writers he admires are those "up to the Revolution," it is in the manner of a passing remark, but one can hardly help concluding that the two he castigates are an inevitable product of English Civil War, of the end of theoretically unconditional monarchial rule, and the disestablishment of the state church to which Eliot would adhere so fervently later in life. The sleight of hand here is astonishing. While remaining strictly "literary," Eliot has more or less told us that constitutional government is a bad thing.

Last and perhaps sneakiest is the young Eliot's case for a homogeneity of feeling between readers. The now-notorious objective correlative is proposed with such nonchalance in Eliot's "Hamlet" (1919) that one might miss its massive implications. The essay's highly confrontational expository argument, that Hamlet is entirely an "artistic failure," makes this even more likely. Eliot's criticism is that Shakespeare has failed to justify his protagonist's emotions to the audience, by failing to demonstrate their source. Provocative as it may be, this is in fact a fairly straightforward objection, which could have been made in any number of already-available terms: Hamlet lacks adequate "characterization"; we are unable to "sympathize" with him; he has not been given "plausible motivation"; and so on. Why Eliot felt the need to theorize a "set of objects, a situation, a chain of events which shall be the formula for (a) particular emotion" (48), inevitably and in everyone, which Shakespeare had overlooked, is not immediately clear. Unless, that is, Eliot wanted to posit this universal code by which human emotion is evoked for more general reasons, and wanted the much louder claim about Hamlet as cover. The allegation that there is no natural reason for affective idiosyncrasy, made on its own, would be exactly the sort of positivist thesis, born of intellectual and professional segregation—in this case, probably the domain of clinical psychology—that Eliot would find distasteful and "un—literary," even though its actual truth might please him. It would be, in other words, precisely the difference between Eliot and I. A. Richards. But here, Eliot appears to come upon it by accident, with no motive outside his business as a critic of poetry.

This, however, is only Eliot. In fact, the approaches of the American New Critics clash with Eliot's recommendations on more than one of the preceding points. Eliot's comment about the virtues of treating poetry "as poetry and not another thing" appears in the 1928 Introduction to the second edition of *The Sacred Wood*. It was offered retrospectively, as an explanation of the attitude in which he had first published these essays. But by 1928 (perhaps more than coincidentally, the year after his conversion to Anglo-Catholicism) he wanted to nuance this position; the new preface admits that "poetry certainly has something to do with morals, with religion, and even with politics perhaps" (viii). By the 1933 publication of *The Use of Poetry and the Use of Criticism*, he had settled on the opinion that "Every poet would like . . . to think that he had some direct social utility," but that while "The doctrine of 'art for art's sake' is a mistaken one," it "contained this true impulse behind it, that it is a recognition of the error of the poet trying to do other people's work" (152).

From this series of statements, it would be fair to generalize an under-standing of literature as a special institution which is completely different from other, more topical kinds of utterance, an indeed not subject to their rules, but which cannot be reified and segregated absolutely because it is a part of a shared culture. When, in "Criticism, Inc.," Ransom maintained that English should regard itself as "entirely autonomous" from the claims of moralists, historians, and political radicals, he seems to have meant some-thing more abstemious (1112).

For if the Cambridge critics outdid Eliot in the directness with which they pursued their social objectives, the New Critics were even more reserved than he. New Critical analysis is by its very nature atomizing; the literary text is to be approached as a discrete artifact, precluding any assessment of its participation in a "mind of Europe." Nor is a New Critical reading likely to make ambitious claims about what organs, mind, digestive tract, or oth-erwise, a poem will stimulate. Wimsatt and Beardsley specifically disallowed such "affective fallacy." To muse, as Eliot had, that the failure of Hamlet resides in Shakespeare's having felt something he couldn't explain, was to commit the other of the two famous sins these critics proposed, the "inten-tional fallacy." Such refusals, and the clinical reserve which motivated them, may have prompted Eliot's quip that his colleagues across the Atlantic prac-ticed a "lemon squeezer criticism" ("Frontiers," 113).

But apparent disagreements are in fact only more pessimistic and self-lim-iting attempts towards the same goals. The cult of unity is the same, though differently realized. Take the affective fallacy, which arises from the same impulse—a dislike of idiosyncratically subjective art appreciation—as the objective correlative. The difference is that Eliot appears to have believed that he could convince people that they ought not to feel outside of a shared rubric of meaning. Wimsatt and Beardsley made no such attempt. They merely sought to demonstrate that anything so individual as personal feeling was irrelevant to the proper understanding of a shared text. Eliot sought to fight affective individualism via literature; Beardsley and Wimsatt, though they belittle such individualism as much as possible, resign themselves to fighting it only on the subject of literature, by developing a criticism separate from the inevitable "relativism" of "psychological effect" (345). Eliot, of course, dis-liked self-seeking in criticism as much as anywhere else: Goethe had "made of Hamlet a Werther," he quipped, just as Coleridge had "made of Hamlet a Coleridge" ("Hamlet," 45).

Like its affective cousin, the intentional fallacy is a more timid, more strictly literary continuation of a highly Eliotic impulse. "Tradition and the Individual Talent" opposed overly individualistic understandings of the artistic creator, just as "Hamlet" suggested a unified and collective readership. Much as the reader had been told to respect the objective correlative and avoid cultivating private irregularities of response, the author was here instructed to engage in a "continual surrender of himself" to the greater totality of literary history (40). And just as the affective fallacy, without actually denying that readers' emotions are unpredictable and individual as per Eliot, nevertheless concluded that such individuality was irrelevant to criticism and even vaguely embarrassing, the intentional fallacy admits, and simultaneously jettisons from literary analysis, the unique interiority of the creative artist. Wimsatt and Beardsley allow that A. E. Housman's account of his own composition process—"drink a pint of beer, relax, go for a walk"—is the advice "the young poet might well take to heart as a practical rule," though it is evident they find his suggestion at least a little ridiculous (338). But comments like this are absolutely not to be treated as "criticism of poetry." If Housman is any indication, the private silliness of authors may be inevitable. It has, however, no bearing on literature itself, for after the text is produced, it becomes "no longer the property of the poet," but of that uniform collective, theoretically pure of the actual idiosyncrasies of its members, called "the public."

Both of the arguments just summarized—the banishment of both reader's and writer's personality from the realm of the literary via the affective and intentional fallacies—have direct Eliotic precedents. There is one final "unity" asserted by the New Critics, one more definitely of their own creation, though Eliot would likely have approved at least of the impulse behind it: that is, the unity of the text itself. Since questions of the kind Kenneth Burke called "extrinsic"—What ideals does the text endorse? What kinds of thinking or behavior does it valorize?—were off limits, the critic was to evaluate the "structural unity" of a text, its "balance," "irony," "tension," even its "organic" connectedness.

It is from this imperative, more than anywhere else, that the New Criticism gets its reputation as ideologically staid. Take the anecdote from Marianne DeKoven with which I began. It would be unsurprising had the student in such a case concluded that New Critical methodology was utterly apolitical, or even mean-spiritedly opposed to new ideas. DeKoven, however, makes a subtler observation; the compulsion to assess the text's organic unity forestalled her own political interests, she notes, while leaving "its own political implications totally opaque" (679). And what are New Criticism's political implications? Does not a preference for unified texts align with a desire for an integrated, pre-capitalist society? And in training readers to bring about unity in highly fragmented texts, are we not also subtly encouraging them to value that unity in a larger sense? This is not, of course, an overt call to politics, but neither is it a merely a defense of the textual status quo from revisionist opinions. The work of art, self-contained but perfectly balanced and cohesive within itself, stands as metonym for the institutions around it.

A frequent misapprehension about these critical practices, and the near-architectural readings they made possible, will bring me to my second observation about the covert social and political agenda of formalism: the ascription to literature of irrational, or at least extra-rational, characteristics, its opposite signification to forms of literal knowledge. In some lights, this will seem discordant with the collectivist or communitarian tendencies I have been asserting. An emphasis on reasoned or objective truths is sometimes seen as essential to the establishment of consensus, and personal subjective freedom, as per the Romantic and Nietzschean traditions, as its enemy—thus the common conjunction of "socialist realism."

Frank Lentricchia may be the only commentator to accuse the New Critics of Stalinism (5), but the perception of the group's methods as technocratic and "anti-subjective" is fairly widespread. Gerald Graff, in "What Was New Criticism?" makes an impressive list of commentators who have attacked the New Criticism as "forcible seizure" or "rape," and accused it of imposing a disciplinary violence on readers and texts (131). It is certainly true that the New Critics styled themselves as empirical and impersonal analysts, and the texts they analyzed as concrete and self-contained artifacts in need of measurement and explication. Ransom used the word "scientific" to describe what he hoped criticism could become. But is the New Critical model of the literary text, mysteriously continent as the Keatsian urn, really the rationalist's position? A really rationalist criticism—Graff's own work serves as example—would treat texts as positive statements. Such a style of reading would have opened up significant space for the articulation of oppositional, Agrarian agendas. And yet the New Critics avoided it absolutely.

Some part of their disinterest in such explicit argument comes, once again, from their ironic minoritarian/anti-minority position, but the more fundamental problem is with the positivistic statement itself. Scientific reason, after all, is significantly to blame for the collapse of the organic society the New Critics favored. In *The World's Body* (1938), a work of which certain essentialist strands of modern ecocriticism might make some major capital (or by contrast, by which they might be effectively embarrassed), Ransom described science as an act of violence upon a natural universe meant to be savored in more phenomenological terms. It was scientific liberalism, which Ransom as Southerner associated with Northern aggression, that was guilty of rape. Cleanth Brooks, even more revealingly, wrote that,

Love is the aesthetic of sex; lust is the science. Love implies a deferring of the satisfaction of the desire; it implies a certain asceticism and a ritual. Lust drives forward urgently and scientifically to the immediate extirpation of the desire. (Modern Poetry, 147–48).

To love the text, therefore, was to de-instrumentalize it. In imagining the poem as a constellation of paradox, an object on its own terms, we give up the right to mine it for political payload (even in the service of a broader anti-instrumentalism, though again, the poem becomes an implicit metonym for how we should approach the world in general). Since, as Graff writes, New Criticism "identified personal self-expression with technological reason," the communitarianism noted earlier actually serves this irrationalist/ anti-instrumental purpose (138). The sin of the idiosyncratic reader hails from the same domain as that of the avaricious sexual partner or the rapacious scientist.

Eliot is again at the nascence of this trend. The poet, he wrote in "The Use of Poetry" in 1933, should not "meddle with the tasks of the theologian, the preacher, the economist, the sociologist or anybody else," and this is not a sentiment the soon-to-be New Critics would have had trouble absorbing, opposed as it is to topically didactic uses of literature (154). When Brooks corrects Eliot about the "truth" of Keats's poem in 1947, he has really only taken Eliot's idea to its ultimate point. Thus Brooks's castigation of the paraphrase of a text's "message" as "heretical," and his argument that poetic texts are made of paradox—and accordingly, that the better they are, the less likely they are to say anything comprehensible in abstraction. Eliot's lesser compunctiousness allowed him to profess an even bolder irrationalism. "The Use of Poetry," as well as offering views on the separateness of art and economics, disclosed that its author "should like an audience which could neither read nor write," and that there was more to fear from "the half-educated and ill-educated" than the uneducated (152). Princeton historian Lawrence Stone once remarked that, "If you teach a man to read the Bible, he may also read pornography or seditious literature; put differently, if a man teaches a woman to read so that she may know her place, she may learn that she deserves his" (qtd. in Kaestle, 27).

Stone, the Whig historian, meant this positively. Eliot, the Tory, seems to have been conscious of the same principle, but he must have reflected rather differently on its appeal. What, after all, would have been more pleasing to the "organic" sensibility than the compact between pious peasants, content to treat the work of art with hushed sensualism, and the enlightened aristocrat or cleric who ministers mysteries? And what would have been more disruptive of this state of affairs than the bad middle-class habit of demanding literal understanding?

The New Critics followed Eliot's lead, though they were more timid—or in another light, more absolutely dedicated. Class literacy is a fairly positivistic thing to be caught discussing, whatever one feels about it. If, by contrast, we are limited to sensual close reading, we are forbidden from considering more abstractly "factual" variables, like a text's impact upon given readers, or its relation to its author, or its historical circumstance. The original New Critics may not have intended to make these questions quite as impossible as they actually became for students like DeKoven—in his late essay "The Formalist Critics," Brooks allowed that that biography and the history of taste "may well be worth studying" (23)—but they certainly did hope to segregate them from that which was "truly" literary.

Such marginalizations may be the consequence of any robust formalism. But formalism as practiced by the New Critics promoted two more peculiar irrationalisms. The first is a marked preference for verse over prose. Eliot's "Use of Poetry" considered only that form of literature; "The Intentional Fallacy" focused exclusively on poets; *The Well Wrought Urn* was subtitled "Studies in the Structure of Poetry," and the methodology it outlined, the one which became synonymous with the New Criticism, was tailored expressly to verse; the celebrated textbook which Brooks created with Robert Penn Warren in 1938 was *Understanding Poetry*. A second text, *Understanding Fiction,* was published in 1943, but its secondary date and lower general esteem may say something about the demoted position of the novel in New Critical taste. Finally, while several of the Agrarians published poetry, Penn Warren is unique among them as a writer of significant prose fiction.

There is nothing innately extra-rational about verse; Chaucer used iambic pentameter just as lucidly to instruct readers in the use of the astrolabe as to render the passions of lovers. But, for a number of reasons, the cultural position of poetry has become more fixed since Chaucer's fourteenth century, and especially since the Romantic period. No adequate history of poetry's associations will fit into the present essay; suffice it to say that for "some time" (the early nineteenth century at very least), the lyric mode of poetry has assumed a default status.

This is not as simple as saying that poetry comes to be "about feelings" and prose about facts. From the New Critical perspective, such a claim would assign poetry a dangerously confessional, individualized function. Indeed, it would miss the general atmosphere of modernist poetic formalism in which the New Criticism flowered. For William Carlos Williams, one of the foremost American figures of this phenomenon and a vigorous defender of de-instrumentalized language, the opposite was true: "poetry liberates words from their emotional implications, prose confirms them in it. . . . Poetry has to do with the crystallization of the imagination, the perfection of new forms" (Spring, 140, 145). But however "impersonal" this formulation may be, it leaves no room for functional referentiality. There were, of course, a number of major verse epics undertaken in this period, some of which, like Pound's *Cantos,* were New Critical favorites. But they are favorites in fairly direct proportion to the reader's ability to ignore their content. Sigsmundo Malatesta, the meta-historical hero of the *Cantos,* was of great topical importance to Pound, but one needs relatively little knowledge of this Italian mercenary's actual life to read the poem successfully—the kind of knowledge one does need, for instance, to have of Napoleon in *War and Peace.* Whether we understand the poem as an "overflow of powerful feelings," as "collective dreaming," or as an ontological object defined above all by its form, we tend more and more not to understand it as referential, as explicative, as telling a story in any literal sense.

The novel, by contrast, is in many ways uncomfortable ideological territory for the organic or Agrarian perspective. Its rise, since it cannot be easily memorized or recited, coincides with that of mass literacy, and it has been linked, by Mikhail Bakhtin, Ian Watt, and many others, to the rise of political liberalism. Most vitally, we tend to hold novelists more accountable for the telling of stories, for the highlighting of language's instrumental function in the communication of fact, than we do poets. Any number of novels have been written to disappoint or even bait this assumption, but it continues to operate.

But for their preference to have been significant, the New Critics would have to have had a *choice* in their material, and it could be protested that formalism gravitates towards poetry by methodological necessity. This depends, however, on what we mean by formalism. It is certainly true that a careful analysis of syllabic accent or a search for relationships between sound effect and visual imagery will be more fruitful with Swinburne than with Dickens. If, however, we mean "formalism" to include everything that is contained entirely within the text as aesthetic product, everything "intrinsic" in Kenneth Burke's terms, then prose fiction offers the formalist a great deal. Classical narratology, for instance, need not violate New Critical dogma about the separateness of the text or the intentional fallacy, though it attends to different formal nuances than New Criticism: *Bleak House* need no more have been a statement of actual fact, or of opinion, than Keats's poetic claims about truth and beauty—but it does call more attention to language's function in stating facts and opinions.

In other words, the social attributes of prose fiction are no reason why the New Critics could not have focused on it. They nevertheless seem to have been reasons why they did not. "Formalism," supposedly an approach devoid of ideology, thus enfolded a discrimination which was profoundly ideological in its effect, and very likely in its intent. It did not simply de-instrumentalize the text, or ignore its function as argument. It preferred, and encouraged the study of, texts which themselves represented anti-argumentative and anti-instrumental values.

The second, and perhaps the more revealing irrationalistic tendency of New Critical formalism is the investment of literature, especially poetry, with ceremonial significance. Richard Foster, a dissenting contemporary of the New Critical ascension, wrote in 1959 that in light of their affiliations with fundamentalist Christianity, the "ritualistic" manner in which the New Critics read poetry was ironic; secular verse, as Foster saw the New Critics approaching it, was filling in for worship, and this confirmed Matthew Arnold's prophecy that poetry would come to replace religion in Western society (232). Both the observation about ritual and the proposed Arnoldian connection are astute. But this is less of a problem than Foster imagined. Arnold was equivocal about his own religious convictions; Eliot was not. His considerable devotional poetry (*Ash Wednesday, Four Quartets*) and verse to be used for liturgical services (*Choruses from the Rock*), make it clear that he agreed with Arnold's assessment of poetry's spiritual potential, but his art was supplement to, rather than replacement for, organized religion.

In proper irrationalist fashion, the supplement takes the form of affective persuasion rather than of theological apologetics. In the introduction to *The Sacred Wood,* Eliot wrote that "Poetry certainly has something to do with religion," but in "The Use of Poetry," "the theologian" appeared on the list of professions in whose business the poet was not to meddle (*Wood,* viii; *Poetry,* 154). With a typical Eliotic audacity, however, this preference for feelings of piety over doctrinal argument in poetry spills over into religion in general. Theism can also be rationalist; indeed, rationalized theism is one of the conditions of the dissociation of sensibility laid out in "The Metaphysical Poets." The modern man "falls in love, or reads Spinoza, and these two experiences have nothing to do with each other," Eliot reasons, the implication being that religious experience, as provided by Spinoza, ought to be more sensual, more like smelling a rose, than it is in modernity (64). Eliot does not fault Spinoza personally for the modern man's propensities, but his selection does not seem entirely coincidental. Spinoza's theism was archetypally reasoned and unorthodox. What better incarnation could there be of the free-thinking Jew?

Eliot's devotional poetry proceeds along very different lines. The "three white leopards" of Ash Wednesday are written not to prove to readers the existence of a deity, but to dazzle with their strangeness. The "Lady of silences / calm and distressed / torn and most whole" cannot justify the ways of God to Man (Milton being as much a free thinker as Spinoza), but is excellently suited to prompt reveries on the koanic mystery of the Christian cosmos (62). Again, the duplicity is impressive. On the one hand, Eliot the poet is simply adhering to what Eliot the critic has said the role of poetry should be. On the other, Eliot the sermonizer (remembering the quantities of his writing which were intended for, and used by, high Anglican service), gives necessary flesh to the collective/sensualist doctrine arrived at by Eliot the ideologue.

The New Critics, less overtly ideologues, had little to say about how "modern man" experienced things, and were not, with the partial exception of Allen Tate, active spokesmen for specific religious institutions. Nevertheless, the approach to poetry they codified required "receptive" readers, rather than suspicious ones, just as Eliot produced mysterious texts. To Foster's charge of ritualism partial exception must be taken. The best close readings, like Brooks's, are perceptive and surprising accounts, in no way conducted mechanically or by rote, though they do remain within the realm of dumb sensualism. But for the average student, Foster's diagnosis is keenly appropriate, at least at the metaphoric level. The freshman close-reader runs obediently through a catechism of rhyme, meter, and metaphor, but is allowed to remain as mystified as to what the poem says topically as vernacular laity in a Latin Mass.

If these were indeed the founding motives of the New Criticism, their defeat (in the academy, at least) is undeniable. This defeat is a tragedy to few; it was certainly none to those who perceive the New Criticism as what it sometimes later became—a technocratic discipline imposed by liberal hegemony. It is, oddly enough, precisely this turn of mind in which we most echo the original New Critics. I want to conclude with a parallel between the New Criticism and, rather than anti-communism, a certain kind of anti-anti-communism. In his 1968 Pulitzer Prize winning *The Armies of the Night,* Norman Mailer asked, "When was everyone going to cut out the nonsense and get to work, do their own real work? One's own literary work was the only answer to the war in Vietnam" (9). The book is a definitive instance of creative nonfiction; the imposition on "real work" that Mailer resents is the October 1967 march on the Pentagon, in which he ends up participating. Sean McCann and Michael Szalay, who begin their 2006 introduction to the *Yale Journal of Criticism* with this quotation, read Mailer as exemplary of a counterproductive gravitation towards symbolic politics in the American Left, a tendency they categorize as "libertarian"—not a term with much analogy in the New Criticism. There is certainly a self-centered note in Mailer's hypothesis (though his narrative demonstates awareness of this), and McCann and Szalay's broader observation is a crucial one. I want to observe a difference, however, between the rationalist libertarianism evident in certain erstwhile leftists—Christopher Hitchens, Jerry Rubin—and the kind belonging to literary figures like Mailer and the others whom McCann and Szalay name.

Mailer's recalcitrance, for instance, was premised less on a claim of autonomy than on a horror of systematization. Troubled by the planned post-Vietnam utopia discussed by his hosts at a party, he laments that "Liberal academics had no root of a real war with technology land itself, no, in all likelihood, they were the natural managers of that future air-conditioned vault where the last of human life would still exist" (15). And, atypically in a libertarian story, the egghead prison guards of the future are to go around removing restrictions. For people like Mailer's hosts, "guilt was invariably so irrational—for it derived from the warped burden of the past" (25). In an unmistakable if mutated echo of Cleanth Brooks, Mailer countered that "Guilt was the existential edge of sex. Without guilt, sex was meaningless" (24).

Though he sought re-enchantment through transgression rather than forbearance, Mailer was as uncomfortable with instrumental modernity as the New Critics. And it is his position, not that of the progressive academics, which comes to define anti-Vietnam protests. To the dismay of many of its organizers, the demonstration at the Pentagon becomes a pantheistic rite, approvingly designated by Mailer as "the cutting edge of primitive awe," rather than a coherent piece of propaganda or intervention (123). Perhaps the Dionysian qualities of this scene strain its association with Agrarianism. Certainly, they clash with the icily punctilious personal associations of T. S. Eliot. But lest these differences obscure the relation altogether, we should note that New Left anti-instrumentalism could also take the form of evasive literary cattiness. Mailer recalls a letter he wrote during a spat with Old Left sociologist Paul Goodman, which, while not deigning to engage with Goodman's arguments in favor of social reform, "did nonetheless feel competent to comment on the literary experience of encountering Goodman's style," which "was not unrelated to the journeys one took in the company of a laundry bag" (23).

In *Professing Literature,* Gerald Graff proposes a trajectory of "rags to riches to routine," whereby the formalism developed by the Agrarians, quietly radical at its inception, was gradually co-opted by the political and institutional default. Consequently, it may sometimes have underwritten the doctrines of liberalism Terence Hawkes associates with it. It may, as Cain suggests, have been palliative against the "politically painful" Cold War, or, in as Walhout's counterargument, may have been used to train people against Communism. But if we allow such methodological hijackings to characterize the movement, we risk missing a major tendency in American literary and political thought, a tendency which does not stop at the borders of academic close reading. The riddle of literature's "anti-instrumental potential" may in large part be the legacy, in Eliot and the Agrarians, of an essentially residual, feudal worldview. But it has gone on to belong equally to the left and to the right. If McCann and Szalay are correct, it is alive and well today.

Bibliography

Brooks, Cleanth. *The Well Wrought Urn.* New York: Harcourt Brace, 1947.

———. *Modern Poetry and the Tradition.* New York: Oxford University Press, 1965.

———. "The Formalist Critics." In *Literary Theory: An Anthology,* ed. Julie Rivkin and Michael Ryan, 22-27. 2nd ed. Malden, MA: Blackwell, 2004.

Brooks, Peter. "Aesthetics and Ideology: What Happened to Poetics?" *Critical Inquiry* 20.3 (1994): 509–23.

Cain, William. *The Crisis in Criticism.* Baltimore: Johns Hopkins University Press, 1984.

Davies, Norman. *Europe: A History.* London: Pimlico, 1997.

DeKoven, Marianne. "The Politics of Modernist Form." *New Literary History* 23.3 (1992): 675–90.

Eagleton, Terry. *Literary Theory.* Minneapolis: University of Minnesota Press, 1996.

Eliot, T. S. *After Strange Gods.* London: Faber and Faber, 1934.

———. *Ash Wednesday: The Complete Poems and Plays, 1909–1950.* London: Harcourt Brace & Co., 1952.

———. "The Frontiers of Criticism." In *On Poetry and Poets,* 103–18. London: Faber and Faber, 1957.

———"Hamlet." In *Selected Prose of T. S. Eliot,* 45-49.

———. The Sacred Wood: Essays on Poetry and Criticism. 2nd ed. London: Methuen, 1928.

———. "The Metaphysical Poets." In *Selected Prose of T. S. Eliot,* 59-67.

———. *Selected Prose of T. S. Eliot.* Ed. Frank Kermode. New York: Harcourt Brace Jovanovich, 1975.

———. *The Use of Poetry and the Use of Criticism.* London: Faber and Faber, 1933.

———. "Tradition and the Individual Talent." In *Selected Prose of T. S. Eliot,* 37-44.

Foster, Richard. "The Romanticism of the New Criticism." *The Hudson Review* 12.2 (1959): 232–46.

Frye, Northrop. "Review: The Ministry of Angels." The Hudson Review 6.3 (1953): 442–49.

Graff, Gerald. *Literature against Itself: Literary Ideas in Modern Society.* Chicago: University of Chicago Press, 1979.

Hawkes, Terrence. *Structuralism and Semiotics.* Berkeley: University of California Press, 1977.

Jancovich, Mark. *The Cultural Politics of the New Criticism.* Cambridge: Cambridge University Press, 1993.

Kaestle, C. F. "Studying the History of Literacy." In *Literacy in the United States: Readers and Reading since 1880,* ed. C. F. Kaestle, H. Damon-Moore, L. C. Stedman, K. Tinsley, and W. V. Trollinger, Jr., 3-32. New Haven, CT: Yale University Press, 1991.

Leavis, F. R. "Under Which King, Benzonian?" In *A Selection from Scrutiny,* ed. F. R. Leavis, vol. 1, 166-74. Cambridge: Cambridge University Press, 1968.

Lentricchia, Frank. *Criticism and Social Change.* Chicago: University of Chicago Press, 1983.

Lodge, David, ed. *Twentieth Century Criticism: A Reader.* New York: Longman, 1972.

Mailer, Norman. *The Armies of the Night: History as a Novel, the Novel as History.* 1968. New York: Plume, 1994.

Ransom, John Crowe. "Criticism, Inc." In *The Norton Anthology of Theory and Criticism,* eds. Vincent Leitch et al, 1108-17. New York: Norton, 2001.

———. *The World's Body.* New York: Scribner's, 1938.

Richards, I. A. *Principles of Literary Criticism.* London: Routledge, 1967.

Walhout, Mark. "The New Criticism and the Crisis in American Liberalism: The Poetics of the Cold War." *College English* 49.8 (1987): 861–71.

Williams, William Carlos. *Spring and All: Imaginations.* Ed. Webster Schott. New York: Directions, 1970.

Wimsatt, William and Monroe Beardsley. "The Affective Fallacy." In *Lodge,* 345–59.

———. "The Intentional Fallacy." In *Lodge,* 334–44.

CHAPTER THREE

Androgyny and Social Upheaval

The Gendered Pretext for John Crowe Ransom's
New Critical Approach

AARON SHAHEEN

J OHN CROWE RANSOM's essay "Criticism, Inc.," included in his volume *The World's Body* (1938), reads in many respects as a manifesto for the New Criticism that he was in the process of developing: "[I]t is from the professors of literature, in this country the professors of English for the most part, that I should hope eventually for the erection of intelligent standards of criticism. It is their business" (328–29).[1] These professors, he suggests, will be armed both with a poet's knowledge of technique and style and a philosopher's understanding of abstractions and themes. By the end of the essay, Ransom outlines several tendencies that such critics should avoid, including paraphrasing the text in lieu of analysis as well as providing "personal registrations," which describe the "effect of the art-work upon the critic as reader." But perhaps most importantly, critics should refrain from literary analysis that stresses historical context or political moralizing at the expense of close examination of the text itself (342–45).

As a number of critics, including Michael Kreyling and Paul Bové, have noted, this last directive at first glance appears odd coming from Ransom.[2] After all, in the years before his development of the New Criticism, in works such as *God without Thunder* and the Agrarian symposium *I'll Take My Stand,* both published in 1930, Ransom concentrated his literary energies on cultural/historical criticism and theology—all pursued directly or indirectly in defense of Southern traditionalism. Bové and Kreyling argue that the New Critical method allowed critics to bypass the messiness of history, especially when that history was deeply immersed in issues of race and slavery. Moreover, such "political quietism" gave these critics a chance to resist the forward lurch of time and the recognition of modernity, just as the essays comprising I'll Take My Stand did by setting forth an economic and cultural program based on precapitalist agrarianism (Bové, 115). Striking a somewhat different chord, Mark Jancovich insists that the New Critical approach never intended to divorce itself from history and culture, though he concedes that the New Criticism was the logical intellectual extension of agrarianism, not Southern nationalism: "[I]t was not Ransom, [Allen] Tate, and [Robert Penn] Warren who abandoned their Agrarian ideals. They merely felt that their position had become overidentified with the South as a region and their shift to the New Criticism was a way of refocusing attention on their criticisms of modern society" (27).

Despite their differences, these assessments of the historical and cultural context in Ransom's New Critical method largely overlook issues of gender, though gender is perhaps the one cultural/political issue that retained its visibility throughout the Agrarian *and* New Critical phases of Ransom's career.[3] During the Agrarian phase, Ransom's concern about gender upheaval in general and androgyny in particular was part and parcel of his brooding about the modernizing South. The blurring of gender roles that seemed to characterize the end of the late nineteenth and early twentieth centuries provided Ransom with a point of departure for discussing a wider range of threats, including Southern acquiescence to industrial capitalism, the emergence of a Soviet-style welfare state, the evisceration of traditional Southern social customs, and even the breakdown of a notion of a racially cohesive organic Southern community.

Thus in one sense androgyny was a symptom of a modern world that had lost its historical and cultural moorings. At the same time, however, androgyny for Ransom also served as a prescriptive measure to anchor humans to the landscape, to God, and to each other. In this latter prescriptive form, androgyny functioned for Ransom as it did for fellow modernist T. S. Eliot, whose The Waste Land uses the hermaphroditic Tiresias to embody poetic unity and historic continuity. Likewise, Ransom sought a synthesis of his "masculine" intellect and "feminine" sentiment as the means to create a myth of an organic Southern community, ironically based on clear social distinctions between men and women.

Though Ransom abandoned the South and Southern nationalism by the late 1930s, many of his gender formulations simply found amplification through aesthetics. In sorting out the differences between the two competing versions of androgyny, he was able to codify and articulate the type of gendered dualisms that would constitute the backbone of his later New Critical methodology. Perhaps without his realizing it, Ransom's deployment of gendered paradigms beyond the sexed body into the realm of aesthetics betrays a larger point about gender itself. As theorists Judith Butler and Thomas Laqueur have suggested, gender does not depend on the sexed body for meaning; rather the sexed body has been made to fit preconceived notions of gender.[4] Controlling the world of men and women during a time of tremendous social upheaval first meant controlling the discourses by which masculinity and femininity were defined.

Angered by the ridicule the South suffered in the wake of the 1925 Scopes "Monkey" Trial in Dayton, Tennessee, Ransom (then an English professor at Vanderbilt University in nearby Nashville) turned his intellectual energies from poetry to religious and cultural criticism (Jancovich, 22). Better known today for his contributions to *I'll Take My Stand*, Ransom also wrote a full-length study of Christianity, *God without Thunder: An Unorthodox Defense of Orthodoxy*. In it he questions how modern western society—which he calls the Occident—interprets Christianity. In its quest for material acquisition and scientific knowledge, the Occident has chosen to put its faith in a God without thunder—that is, a benevolent God who loves His children so much that He opens up the secrets of the universe for them to exploit for their own scientific and commercial gains: "[T]he new religion," cautions Ransom, "presents god as a Great Man with all the uncertainties left out: a Great Man whose ways are scientific and knowable and whose intention is amiable and constant" (20). Ransom consequently believes that the West is bent on self-destruction, and he exhorts his readers to understand God as the "Orientals" (i.e., the premodern Church or the Jews of the Old Testament) once did, as a jealous God of contingency, one who could be "capable of evil as well as good" (301). Furthermore, he explains, "When God was pictured in the likeness of a fabulously Great Man, of marvelous technique and uncertain favor, it was fairly difficult for one to be at ease in Zion; for his fiat was unaccountable and unpredictable; and man worshiping him was necessarily humble, and for the time being neglectful of the ordinary routine of practical life as a very vain thing" (20). Though Ransom was never a devout believer himself,[5] he felt that only by living in fear of God as "the Orientals" once did could the West reverse the course of industrial capitalism's tendency to fragment traditional communities, lay waste to arts and social customs, and bring humans into interminable warfare with their natural environment.

At the center of this book stands a Godhead who has been largely understood in the Occident as implicitly male, but who in Ransom's opinion should be seen as androgynous. Remarkably, the gendered construction of Ransom's irascible Oriental god has gone unnoticed over the years, even though it has everything to do with the book's basic thrust. The God of Thunder that Ransom would like to reinstate in western culture is not the Trinitarian deity commonly worshiped in traditional Christianity; Ransom believes that Christ is merely a demigod, and thus the two remaining components of the Trinity are the true and supreme components of the Godhead.[6] Ransom calls these coequal figures the Mother and the Father:

> God is the Father, the masculine, cosmic, and rational Creator. But the material is the Mother, who is feminine, anarchical, and irrational. (We would add, with Plato's permission: The Father is the personification of Quantity, and the Mother is the personification of Quality.) It is upon such a Mother that God [the Father] must beget his children, the objective creatures which we now know on earth as nature. They partake of the being of both parents; and so far as biology can generalize them, in equal degrees. (*God without Thunder*, 300)

The Mother is for Ransom what has otherwise been known as the Holy Ghost. "It is a significant fact," he says, "that the Holy Ghost for the Old Testament authors, and for Christ himself speaking in his native Aramaic, was of the feminine gender. But this was the right gender for defending the demonic and irrational aspect of his being" (304). These musings make for a heady proclamation. In short, Ransom asserts that nature (of which humans are a part) is the metaphysical or cosmological product of a masculine and feminine Godhead. Ironically the Godhead's phallic thunderbolts come from the feminine, irrational side of its being. This configuration may very well be what Ransom had in mind when he claimed later in *The World's Body* that the male poet is an "intellectualized woman": he partakes of both the Father's spirituality and the Mother's mutable, sensual materiality (77).

The Southern soil, which is at the ideological, spiritual, and imaginative core of *I'll Take My Stand*, likewise partakes of the Father and Mother. On one level the soil exists as a certain quantity of atoms that can be represented by the rational—that is, masculine—abstraction of a molecular compound. Yet simultaneously the soil elicits a certain amount of sentiment from its cultivator. Through daily toils on the farm the agrarian establishes a personal relationship with the soil, something that cannot be represented merely by a chemical equation. The poem "Antique Harvesters," published in Ransom's 1927 book of poetry *Two Gentlemen in Bonds*, invokes the landscape's feminine aspect. In the first stanza the poet asks: "What shall this land produce?" The answer, which comes at the end of the poem, is an image of a "Proud Lady" who "hath not stooped" (50–51). As the poem suggests, physical matter such as the soil possesses its own personality that people can experience in infinite varieties. The Proud Lady, though old, *is* the primordial landscape, and the (presumably male) Antique Harvesters, made in the Godhead's androgynous image, are in touch with their feminine sides enough to experience the soil in more than just scientific or "masculine" ways. This distinction would prove instrumental in the development of the New Criticism in the 1940s.

As a mythical object of homage, the Proud Lady becomes what Anne Goodwyn Jones has called the symbolic Confederate woman who dutifully wears Dixie's diadem. "Rather than a person," Jones remarks, "the Confederate woman is a personification, effective only as she works in others' imaginations. Efforts to join person and personification, to make self into symbol, must fail because the idea of Southern womanhood specifically denies the self" (4). Ransom sees androgyny as a form of male prerogative. Male poets, alongside their agrarian brethren, mystically in touch with both their masculine rationality and feminine sensibility, cultivate a female art object. As a result the Proud Lady is displaced from politics and the marketplace, standing still eternally, never disrupting the patriarchal order. In fact she becomes the very symbol of that order. In this sense, then, the Proud Lady's advanced age is not a sign of temporal decay, but an embodiment of the sweep of (white) Southern myth and tradition.

Ransom's religious vision reflects a larger modernist interest in androgyny. For example, William Faulkner, H. D., James Joyce, and Virginia Woolf all entertained the notion that the imagination was made up of masculine and feminine faculties that, when combined, could produce remarkable artistic achievements (Rado, 7). No doubt this affirmative version of androgyny was what T. S. Eliot's *The Waste Land* sought in its depiction of Tiresias. "[T]hrobbing between two lives / Old man with wrinkled female breasts," the aged prophet is, as Eliot's "Notes" to the poem explain, "the most important personage in the poem, uniting all the rest. . . . [S]o all the women [in the poem] are one woman, and the two sexes meet in Tiresias" (38, 50).

Yet in "Reconstructed but Unregenerate," his contribution to *I'll Take My Stand,* Ransom addresses a dystopian version of androgyny heralded by a capitalist economy that has the power to uproot familiar gender and social structures. Though the essay rarely mentions religion, the principles of *God without Thunder* obviously serve as the essay's philosophical basis. Placed at the opening of the symposium, the essay is in many ways the most general. While Ransom claims not to miss the Old South per se, he at least misses the leisurely approach (white) Southerners supposedly took to life—one that allowed them to experience the aesthetic pleasures of the quotidian. Since the Civil War, industrial capitalism had encroached upon the South's traditions and ripped them apart.

Yet beneath Ransom's worry about capitalism was a deeper brooding about socialism. The Agrarians believed, for example, that it was through the crisis in capitalist overproduction that the economy would slump and labor would organize to the point of applying government directives to the modes of production. Thus the Agrarians ironically believed in the Marxist dialectical narrative of history but certainly did not condone its ends. As the United States was sinking deeper and deeper into the Great Depression while the Soviet Union was reporting a surge in its economy under the first Five Year Plan, the Agrarians no doubt felt they had legitimate reason for concern. It is little wonder that Allen Tate originally proposed calling the Agrarian manifesto *Tracts against Communism* (Murphy, 63). The manifesto's "Statement of Principles," which Ransom had a direct hand in drafting, touches on these threats, arguing that a band of "super-engineers" will "adapt production to consumption and regulate prices and guarantee business against fluctuation: they are Sovietists. . . . [T]he true Sovietists or Communists—if the term may be used here in the European sense—are the Industrialists themselves" (*I'll Take My Stand,* xxiii).

As "Reconstructed but Unregenerate" makes clear in later passages, the modern age of industrial capitalism distorts the "orthodox" view of androgyny *God without Thunder* so earnestly delineates. Here Ransom speaks of masculine and feminine forms of ambition that operate symbiotically, yet destructively, in the modern world. The masculine form of ambition manifests itself in a war against nature, and its bottom line is production. Ransom worries that men have used their intellectual grasp of chemistry, physics, and engineering to promote a pioneering spirit of progress that sees no end to this conquest. This war is sustained in large measure by an insatiable consumption:

> If it is Adam's curse to will perpetually to work his mastery upon nature, it is Eve's curse to prompt Adam every morning to keep up with the best people in the neighborhood in taking the measure of his success. There can never be stability and establishment in a community whose every lady member is sworn to see that her mate is not eclipsed in the competition for material advantages. ("Reconstructed," 9–10)

Ransom also presents here a variation on what current-day critic Christophe Den Tandt refers to as "corporate androgyny." For Den Tandt this concept describes male protagonists in early-twentieth-century American fiction "whose willingness to develop a supreme sense of masculinity paradoxically involves the appropriation of feminine features. . . . [They] derive their heightened power from an ability to bracket off their sense of individuation and to merge with entities modeled as feminine bodies—the urban market, the corporation" (640). Clearly there are some differences between Den Tandt's and Ransom's concepts, yet both recognize that women—either as consumers or more abstractly as symbols of corporate entities—held a stake in the American marketplace that businessmen could not afford to overlook. As a further indication of androgyny's centrality to the modern American economy, Ransom states that Adam may become a consumer alongside Eve. Any strict dichotomy between masculine production and feminine consumption, he observes, "may not be without the usual exceptions" ("Reconstructed," 9).

Furthermore, the blurring of the masculine and feminine impulses emerges through the irrational fears of cultural emasculation men feel in response to the demands of their wives. In fact as *God without Thunder* explains, the impulse to consume so preoccupies men that readers might forget that consumption had historically been understood and depicted as an innately feminine activity—as Eve's activity. In this sense corporate androgyny leads not to "a supreme sense of masculinity," as Den Tandt would have it, but to a debilitating self-consciousness. Thus the male consumer becomes subject time and again to the irrational sense of lack that contemporaneous Freudian theory ascribed to women.

The feminine sense of ambition goes well beyond turning men into castrated individuals who fulfill their lack through consumption. As "Reconstructed but Unregenerate" further explains:

> The feminine form is likewise hallowed among us under the name of Service. The term has many meanings, but we come finally to the one which is critical for the moderns; service means the function of Eve, it means the seducing of laggard men into fresh struggles with nature. It has special application to the apparently stagnant sections of mankind, it busies itself with the heathen Chinee, with the Roman Catholic Mexican, with the "lower" classes in our own society. Its motive is missionary. Its watchwords are such as Protestantism, Individualism, Democracy, and the point of its appeal is a discontent, generally labeled "divine." (10–11)

In essence Ransom suggests that the feminine bourgeois devotion to "Service"—a common term in the contemporaneous discourse of the New Woman—evolves slowly but surely into the modern welfare state. At first glance one might suspect that Ransom would be relieved if "laggard" men could find work; a strong employment rate, after all, might keep workers from organizing and rebelling. Yet Ransom is also mindful that the industrial economy will always have a surplus labor force that women will thus enjoin the state to employ. "Along with the gospel of progress goes the gospel of Service," he explains. "They work beautifully as a team" ("Reconstructed," 8). As Ransom later explained in response to Stringfellow Barr's indictment of *I'll Take My Stand,* "The old Southern instinct which identifies [socialism and communism] is perfectly right in the long run. . . . Big business, which [Barr] accepts, and which every day becomes bigger business, will call for regulation, which every day will become more regulation. And the grand finale of regulation, the millennium itself of regulated industrialism, is Russian communism" (Davidson, 49).

In fact, in positioning the "feminine form" of ambition as a key instigator in a specific historical sequence beginning with the Protestant Reformation and ending with the establishment of secular democracies, Ransom shows the extent to which modern women have ventured beyond the mythological parameters of his ultrafeminine Proud Lady. The reforms established in the Progressive era and 1920s were largely fueled and populated by women activists, such as settlement house founders Jane Addams and Lillian Wald, Women's Christian Temperance League president Frances Willard, feminist Charlotte Perkins Gilman, and National Consumers League general secretary Florence Kelley. Not surprisingly, many of these women not only promoted a broader base of gender and social progressivism (if not outright socialism), but had come under fire for being mannish and aggressive.[7]

By looking at the deeper gendered implications of Ransom's writings of the 1930s, one might find that the status, power, and legitimacy of the postwar New Woman was still very much at issue. With one foot in the bourgeois world of mass consumption and another in the world of social reform, the New Woman was anathema to conservative Agrarianism. Just as American men lived out the "pioneer doctrine" in their never-ending battles with nature, so did women in their striving to ameliorate the inevitable effects of those battles ("Reconstructed," 11).

Thus it would seem that Ransom had been hailed by cultural currents that regarded social amelioration in general as an oddly gendered ideological construct. As social historian Daniel J. Walkowitz notes, the 1920s proved a key decade for women who sought to make social work a viable career option. Women social workers effected changes in society through the adaptation of scientific methods for treating clients. And "because objectivity and rationality were conventionally associated with male professional culture . . . , the scientific model created its own tensions for female social workers." The woman social worker not only had to play the Good Mother; she "had to adopt attributes of passionlessness and objectivity generally associated with men, traits that easily allowed others to stereotype her as desexed and androgynous" (1051–56).[8] By the time *I'll Take My Stand* was published at the start of the new decade, social work had changed so much as a result of the "male" scientific principles it accepted that it had adopted its own manual for scientific research. The 1930 census, moreover, reported employment of 31,241 social workers with seventy-six different job titles; eighty percent of the profession was female. By 1932 social work had moved into the university curricula of twenty-five different graduate degree-granting schools (Brown, 142–43).

The androgynously constructed Service impulse also threatened Ransom because it could abstract the South well beyond the mystical organic community he so devoutly envisioned. Using Benedict Anderson's famous term, Michael Kreyling understands the Agrarians' South as an "imagined community" (3–6).[9] Yet the insidiousness of the welfare state makes that cohesive community nearly impossible to imagine because feminine Service uses the masculine sense of intellect and rationality to carry out its program of uplift and reform. Under such positivist guises as sociology, history, anthropology, demography, and social work, the encroaching welfare state would demystify the South's cultural "unity," which had relied mainly on myths of white supremacy and religious conservatism to keep the bond strong.

Scholars of Southern literature have noted the ideological rift between the conservative Vanderbilt Agrarians led by Ransom and the liberal academics at the University of North Carolina led by sociology professor Howard Odum.[10] This rift developed in large part because Odum and his Chapel Hill colleagues attempted to ameliorate the poverty and racism of the South by first assessing them through the use of different empirical and abstract methods. Thus industrialism and the various "-ologies" would not only create the pretext for a proletarian state in Ransom's view, but would also use masculine modes of science to connect seamlessly the North and the South culturally, economically, and racially. Through scientific and economic abstraction, the nascent welfare state would create an androgynous and miscegenated social body by incorporating the worst of modern masculine and feminine ambitions.

The perceived racial implications of feminine Service wedded to masculine rationality were far-reaching for Ransom. At the heart of the Agrarian movement was a cultural nationalism that was very much in keeping with the romantic primordialism of Johann Gottfried von Herder and Giuseppi

Mazzini (Reed, 52–53). The Agrarian emphasis on primordialism might explain, for example, Donald Davidson's reluctance to include Robert Penn Warren's essay "The Briar Patch" in *I'll Take My Stand* because it spoke of blacks' participation in the Southern agrarian tradition. Ransom himself is guilty of the same discomfort when it comes to the place of African Americans in the South. His essay awkwardly glosses over the issue of slavery, absurdly suggesting that the peculiar institution was "monstrous enough in theory, but, more often than not, humane in practice" ("Reconstructed," 14). Ransom concerns himself primarily with the "vegetative aspect" of a person, which he asserts is the impulse to settle permanently on a piece of land, but which also implies in quasi-Herderian fashion that white Southerners spring up from their native Southern soil. Of course he fudges the lines of descent in his assumption, and perhaps Warren's "Briar Patch" met such resistance among his colleagues because it reminded them that white Southerners were no more indigenous to the land than the first slaves who arrived in Virginia from west Africa in 1619 ("Briar," 246).

The inherent contradictions between Ransom's religious and dystopian visions of androgyny are, I argue, an integral part of his eventual turn away from Agrarianism. On the one hand, androgyny was the dreadful result of modernity, for as the American industrial economy slumped further, it necessitated a governmental intervention that put masculine rationality in the service of feminine uplift. Yet on the other hand, androgyny in its orthodox, spiritual manifestation provided the antidote for a nation-state's ills, not only involving a belief in a Godhead half-male and half-female, but also enjoining individuals to see themselves as a part of the Godhead's world; like the natural world itself, humans are both material and spiritual, intellectual and sentimental. In both forms of androgyny, masculine intellect and feminine sentiment are present, but Ransom could never articulate just how these two constitutive elements veered off in such dangerously different directions. In other words, where was the line between artistic creation on the one side and social amelioration on the other if both required the use of masculine rationality and feminine sentiment?

When Ransom turned away from Southern nationalism and religious criticism by the late 1930s, the larger theoretical implications of this disjuncture haunted him. By the end of the 1930s, he was no longer even a Southerner. Unable in 1937 to agree on a sufficient salary and contract with the English department at Vanderbilt, Ransom uprooted to Kenyon College in Gambier, Ohio, and took on a dual role as professor and founding editor of the *Kenyon Review*. By this point in his career, Ransom had moved so far from his previous promotion of religious orthodoxy that he often found himself in the middle of the religious idealist and the secular "realist" camps between which William James tried to negotiate in his famous essays on pragmatism (Quinlan, 68–87).

With this change came Ransom's deeper ambivalence about the cultural legitimacy and economic viability of the agrarian South. The shift appears in his 1936 essay entitled "What Does the South Want?," which was included in *Who Owns America? A New Declaration of Independence,* a companion piece to *I'll Take My Stand.* This essay already marks some acquiescence to the welfare state as it had developed during the first four years of Franklin Roosevelt's New Deal. Ransom recognizes the incredible devastation the Great Depression has wreaked upon the South, and he admits to the need for a number of improvements that only a technologically advanced and centrally cohesive federal government can provide. Almost as though laughing about his militancy during the earlier Agrarian years, he remarks: "The Agrarians have been rather belabored both in the South and out of it by persons who have understood them as denying bathtubs to the Southern rural population. But I believe they are fully prepared to concede the bathtubs" (248). In fact he accepts the need for fairer income distribution, backup employment, hospitals, paved roads, parks, and dependable plumbing, all of which are "urged nowadays by the welfare workers." One might be shocked to see just how much Ransom acclimated himself to the idea of the welfare state. Once deriding social scientists for breaking up the organic community, he now admonishes them much more humbly: "But I should be a little wary of the professional welfare workers, and not let them drill the population too hard in playhabits and social functions. I should give the labor community its rights and let it make the most of them" (251). In other words, he exhorts the social workers to shape up the Southern laborers, but still to be gentle and let them save face by keeping some of their regional-based leisure habits.

Ransom's essay "Poets without Laurels," also included in *The World's Body,* serves as a farewell to his overtly political phase of the early and mid-1930s. In it he argues that modern poets, needing to adapt to the alienation of modern life, have chosen to write poetry about subjects that are largely divorced from the political arena. The modern poem "has no moral, political, religious, or sociological values. It is not about 'res publica,' the public thing. The subject matter is trifling" (59). Among these trifles are those Wallace Stevens made famous, such as a blackbird, a Key West seascape, or a jar atop a hill in Ransom's home state of Tennessee (Malvasi, 79). Not surprisingly, the critical theory that would spring from his *The New Criticism* (1941) and related writings was one that would champion such poetry, removed as it was from politics, history, and authorial intention.

But androgyny did not disappear from Ransom's later writings. By the late 1930s he had found a way to rechannel it back toward the aesthetic program suggested in *God without Thunder.* For example, in his essay "The Woman as Poet," a review of Edna St. Vincent Millay's poetry that is included in *The World's Body,* he remarks:

> A woman lives for love, if we will but project that term to cover all her tender fixations upon natural objects of sense, some of them more innocent and far less reciprocal than men. Her devotion to them is more than gallant, it is fierce and importunate, and cannot but be exemplary to the hardened male observer. He understands it, from his "recollections of early childhood," or at least of youth, but has lapsed from it; or rather, in the best case, he has pursued another line of development. The minds of man and woman grow apart, and how shall we express their differentiation? In this way, I think: man, at best, is an intellectualized woman. Or, man distinguishes himself from woman by intellect, but he should keep it feminized. He knows he should not abandon sensibility and tenderness, though perhaps he has generally done so. (77)

This distinction gets at the very heart of certain gender dynamics that reside just under the surface of Ransom's earlier writings. Good poets, Ransom suggests, are those who find the right balance of sentiment and intellect. In this case Ransom shows no anxiety about women social workers whose masculine rationality threatens to override their femininity. Rather, he frets about those such as Millay, who allow their feminine poetic sentiment to override their masculine sense of discipline and precision. Likewise, he expresses concern for the overly rational man, who gets no love from poetry and invests all his energies in the corporate or scientific world: "[N]ow that he is so far removed from the world of the simple senses, he does not like to impeach his own integrity and leave his business in order to recover it. . . . He would much prefer if it is possible to find poetry in his study, or even in his office, and not have to sit under the syringa bush" (77–78).

In 1941, the same year *The New Criticism* was published, Ransom published "Criticism as Pure Speculation" in *The Intent of the Critic,* a volume of essays edited by D. A. Stauffer. Here Ransom dichotomizes poetry into structure and texture. Likening these two components to a fully furnished home, he explains that the structure consists of the "beams and boards"—that part of a poem that can be transcribed or paraphrased seamlessly into prose. The structure of the poem therefore consists of its abstract theme or argument. The texture of the poem, however, is "the paint, the paper, the tapestry"—

those formal elements such as imagery, rhyme scheme, meter, enjambment, or caesurae that provide the poem with its feel, its particularities. As Ransom explains, "The intent of the good critic becomes therefore to examine and define the poem with respect to its structure and its texture. If he has nothing to say about its texture he has nothing to say about it specifically as a poem, but is treating it only insofar as it is prose" (111). This dichotomy sounds suspiciously close to masculine spirituality and feminine materiality, the two components of Ransom's orthodox Godhead articulated in *God without Thunder*. As the thematic core of the poem, the structure is the masculine thematic abstraction—perhaps love, happiness, dejection, anger, or jealousy—that is given its character by feminine texture.

In *The New Criticism* Ransom again explains the difference between the structure and texture of a poem, adding to his explanation the remark that understanding the tension between structure and texture gives way to a sense of resolution and order:

> The composition of a poem is an operation in which the argument fights to displace the meter, and the meter fights to displace the argument. It would seem that the sacrifices made on both sides would be legible forever in the terms of peace, which are the dispositions found in the finished poem, where the critic may analyze them if he thinks it furthers the understanding of poetry. (295)[11]

Should my suspicions about the genders of the structure and the texture prove tenable, I suspect as well that Ransom attempts to do in poetry what he could not do in the world of time and space: find a creative means of controlling the rivalry between masculinity and femininity. The productive tension of the androgynous poem supplants the androgynous Godhead as Ransom's new object of reverence. True, Ransom labels poetry fraught with tension between texture and structure as "impure," but he concedes that "[t]he World of Appearance (or opinion) seemed to Plato inferior to the World of Pure Being (or reason), but he acknowledged that the former was the world which our perceptions took hold of, and indeed was the world of nature" (328). The "pure" poetry made up of structure alone is too close to masculine rationality. Unchecked by feminine texture, the structure has the character—and perhaps the potential destructiveness—of a scientific theorem.

Though New Criticism resisted didacticism at all costs, Ransom subtly, albeit undeniably, makes a case for applying his method beyond the classroom or the study. In his essay "Forms and Citizens," also found in *The World's Body*, he makes a general plea for the preservation of social custom and ritual, though he concedes that the informality of the modern world seems to have the upper hand in the matter. In his defense of custom he creates the hypothetical example of the man who wishes to possess a woman sexually. In this example structure and texture take the respective forms of the man's intention and the various rituals he performs to woo her. Ransom suggests that, given the lack of pretense in the modern era, the man might be able to simply approach the woman straightaway and engage her in (presumably consensual) sexual play. "If our hero, however, does not propose for himself the character of the savage . . . he must approach her with ceremony, and pay her a fastidious courtship. . . . The form actually denies him the privilege of going the straight line between two points, even though this line has an axiomatic logic in its favor and is the shortest possible line" (*World's Body*, 33). In other words, the "structure" of the situation is tempered by the logically unnecessary but nonetheless satisfying "texture" of the courtship ritual.

The hypothetical woman's sexuality is made more enjoyable for the man willing to travel a circuitous route to take her: "But the woman, contemplated in this manner under restraint, becomes a person and an aesthetic object; therefore a richer object" (33). The sexism in this statement is made all the more curious by the contention that the woman somehow becomes more of a person by achieving the status of aesthetic object—a poem in the flesh. But it is also worth remarking that in treating the man's plight as an androgynous trajectory made up of masculine argument and feminine ritual, Ransom's narrative arrives at gender stability: men court; women are courted—and then enjoyed for their sexual richness. His concentration on fixity mirrors a statement he made eight years earlier in *I'll Take My Stand*: "The arts of the [South] . . . were the eighteenth-century social arts of dress, conversation, manners, the table, the hunt, politics, oratory, the pulpit. These were the arts of living and not arts of escape; they were also community arts, in which every class of society could participate *after its kind*" ("Reconstructed," 12, emphasis added). Poetry is like any other formality in that it provides boundaries, hierarchies, and stasis.

As an example of a culture that has already "rationaliz[ed] and economiz[ed] its citizens down to their baser instincts, Ransom cites Soviet Russia, where "there is less sex-consciousness . . . than anywhere in the Western world" (*World's Body*, 37). Though by 1938 Ransom had come to embrace much of the New Deal's welfare programs, he nonetheless preserved some of his earlier Agrarian reticence about the destructive form of androgyny. In heralding the "New Soviet Woman," Russian feminists such as Lenin's wife Nadezhda Krupskaya and Alexandra Kollontai seriously questioned what, if anything, constituted difference between men and women. Kollontai was one of the most vocal of Soviet feminists, even publishing opinions in the *Baltimore Sun* in the early decades of the twentieth century. She was particularly outspoken in her advocacy of a Soviet culture that would abolish the notions of gender distinction promoted by the bourgeois patriarchal family. "In the place of the individual and egotistical family," she argued, "there will arise a great universal family of workers, in which all the workers, men and women, will be above all workers, comrades" (Stites, 351).

Ransom seems to suggest the same thing, though reluctantly. "I suppose," he continues, "that the loyal Russians approach the perfect state of animals, with sex reduced to its pure biological business" (37). In other words, while he may believe that the differences between genders are the result of convention, they are nonetheless necessary for sustaining an enjoyment of life. Here he readily acknowledges the relative inconsequence of sex distinctions between males and females in comparison to their gender distinctions, which are governed by culture and habit. In the absence of divinely or culturally enforced gender codes, men and women must *choose* to be different just as in an earlier moment Ransom was willing to submit to an irrational god in whom he did not personally believe. Here Ransom concedes a larger point made by Judith Butler that gender is performed "in an exterior space through a stylized repetition of acts" to perpetuate the illusion of immutability (140). In preferring "efficient animality," which recognizes sex but not gender differences, humans are bound for a life of "perfect misery" (38). While Jancovich believes that "[i]t would be wrong to suggest that Ransom is egalitarian in his sexual politics," he states nonetheless that Ransom's ideas evolve "from a profound discomfort with the distinctions between masculinity and femininity" (39). I argue the opposite, however: androgyny as Ransom defines it—insofar is it is made up of masculine and feminine components—is essentially a conservative formulation, for it implies that there is a clear distinction between the two, even if the distinction is grounded in culture and not biology. Ransom's aesthetic comfort, then, comes from his ability to articulate those differences if for no other reason than to keep them in a proper balance. Through keeping the distinctions clear he is able to conclude that the hyperfeminine Millay is just as flawed as the hypermasculine New Soviet Woman.

For John Crowe Ransom the process by which poets create poetry is essentially no different than the Southern yeoman who finds in the landscape a substance imbued with both abstract and material qualities. In both cases the blending of masculine and feminine attributes provides not only a better understanding of the world's complexity but also a sense of order and control. As the South joined the rest of the nation in experiencing the breakdown of nineteenth-century gender barriers and the rapid increase in industrialization, Ransom came to realize that yearning for a Southern yeomanry was fruitless; but via his New Critical method he was able to articulate the boundaries of masculinity and femininity in ways that helped him make order of a dynamic and sometimes hostile world.

Notes

1. A substantially different version of this essay appears as part of the chapter entitled "Reactionary and Radical Androgyny: Two Southerners Assess the Depression-Era Body Politic," in Aaron Shaheen, *Androgynous Democracy: Modern American Literature and the Dual-Sexed Body Politic* (Knoxville: University of Tennessee Press, 2010).

2. See Bové and Kreyling.

3. Jancovich does acknowledge the intersection between gender and criticism in Ransom's writing, but he only devotes two paragraphs of his book to this intersection. See chapter 4, "John Crowe Ransom: The Social Relations of Social Activity."

4. See Butler and Thomas Laqueur.

5. See Watkins, Hiers, and Weaks. Unlike T. S. Eliot, who found personal refuge from the fragmentation of modernity in Anglo-Catholicism, Ransom remained fairly agnostic throughout his adult life. Talking with Robert Penn Warren in 1931, he made a curious remark about *God without Thunder*: "I found it very odd that I who am not a religious man, should write such a book; but I had to write it for the truth that was in it" (*Talking with Robert Penn Warren*, 382). The apparent "truth" for this son and grandson of Methodist preachers was the cultural efficacy, though not the verifiable reality, of the wrathful Christian God.

6. In Ransom's orthodoxy, Christ plays a different role. Now relegated to the inferior position of "demi-god," he does not command nearly the authority that he does in the Trinitarian tradition. For Ransom, Christ was "*The Demigod who knew he was a Demigod and refused to set up as a God*" (*World's Body*, 305; italics in original). In other words, Christ, being male and partially divine, was an emanation of the Godhead's rational masculine principle, what Ransom calls the "Logos."

7. For analysis of Kelley's and Addams's purported androgyny, see the chapter entitled "The New Woman as Androgyne" in Smith-Rosenberg.

8. Equally at issue in Ransom's writings was the so-called "social gospel," a doctrine of Christian-sanctioned progressivism that caught up many reform-minded men and women in its evangelical sweep. Middle- and upper-class Christians worked through established church organizations and also created new outlets for reform, such as the Young Women's and Young Men's Christian Associations. This latter institution Ransom lumps in with "welfare establishments, fraternal organizations, and Rotary" as "philanthropic societies with a minimum of doctrine about God" (*God without Thunder*, 5).

9. See also Anderson.

10. See, for example, Chapter 3 in Hobson.

11. In later years Ransom would back away from these claims, arguing that such unity was really another term for the domination of the abstract over the particular. (See Ransom, "Art Worries the Naturalists," 282–99).

Bibliography

Anderson, Benedict. *Imagined Communities: Reflections on the Origin and Spread of Nationalism.* London: Verso, 2000.

Bové, Paul A. *Mastering Discourse: The Politics of Intellectual Culture.* Durham: Duke University Press, 1992.

Brown, Esther Lucile. *Social Work as a Profession.* New York: Russell Sage Foundation, 1935.

Butler, Judith. *Gender Trouble: Feminism and the Subversion of Identity.* New York: Routledge, 1990.

Davidson, Donald. "Counterattack, 1930–1940: The South against Leviathan." In *Southern Writers in the Modern World.* Athens: University of Georgia Press, 1958.

Den Tandt, Christophe. "Amazons and Androgynes: Overcivilization and the Redefinition of Gender Roles at the Turn of the Century." *American Literary History* 8.4 (1996): 639–64.

Eliot, T. S. *The Waste Land and Other Poems.* San Diego: Harcourt, Brace and Co., 1962.

Hobson, Fred. *Tell about the South.* Baton Rouge: Louisiana State University Press, 1983.

Jancovich, Mark. *The Cultural Politics of the New Criticism.* Cambridge: Cambridge University Press, 1993.

Jones, Anne Goodwyn. *Tomorrow Is Another Day: The Woman Writer in the South, 1859–1936.* Baton Rouge: Louisiana State University Press, 1981.

Kreyling, Michael. *The Invention of Southern Literature.* Jackson: University Press of Mississippi, 1998.

Laqueur, Thomas. *Making Sex: Body and Gender from the Greeks to Freud.* Cambridge: Harvard University Press, 1990.

Malvasi, Mark G. *The Unregenerate South: The Agrarian Thought of John Crowe Ransom, Allen Tate, and Donald Davidson.* Baton Rouge: Louisiana State University Press, 1997.

Quinlan, Kieran. *John Crowe Ransom's Secular Faith.* Baton Rouge: Louisiana State University Press, 1989.

Rado, Lisa. *The Modern Androgyne Imagination: A Failed Sublime.* Charlottesville: University of Virginia Press, 2000.

Ransom, John Crowe. "Art Worries the Naturalists." *Kenyon Review* 7 (Spring 1945): 282–99.

———. "Criticism as Pure Speculation." In *The Intent of the Critic,* ed. D. A. Stauffer, 91–124. Princeton: Princeton University Press, 1941.

———. *God without Thunder: An Unorthodox Defense of Orthodoxy.* 1930. Hamden, CT: Archon Books, 1965.

———. *The New Criticism.* Norfolk, CT: New Directions, 1941.

———. "Reconstructed but Unregenerate." In Twelve Southerners, *I'll Take My Stand,* 1–27.

————. *Two Gentlemen in Bonds.* New York: Knopf, 1927.

————. "What Does the South Want?" 1936. In *Who Owns America? A New Declaration of Independence*, ed. Herbert Agar and Allen Tate, 233–52. Wilmington, DE: ISI Books, 1999.

————. *The World's Body.* 1938. Baton Rouge: Louisiana State University Press, 1968.

Reed, John Shelton. "For Dixieland: The Sectionalism of *I'll Take My Stand*." In *A Band of Prophets: The Vanderbilt Agrarians after Fifty Years,* ed. William C. Havard and Walter Sullivan, 41–64. Baton Rouge: Louisiana State Press, 1982.

Smith-Rosenberg, Carroll. *Disorderly Conduct: Visions of Gender in Victorian America.* New York: Oxford University Press, 1985.

Stites, Richard. *The Women's Liberation Movement in Russia: Feminism, Nihilism, and Bolshevism, 1860–1930.* Princeton: Princeton University Press, 1991.

Twelve Southerners. *I'll Take My Stand: The South and the Agrarian Tradition.* 1930. New York: Harper, 1962.

Walkowitz, Daniel J. "The Making of a Feminine Professional Identity: Social Workers in the 1920s." *The American Historical Review* 95.4 (1990): 1051–75.

Warren, Robert Penn. "The Briar Patch." In Twelve Southerners, *I'll Take My Stand*, 246–64.

Watkins, Floyd C., John T. Hiers, and Mary Louise Weaks, eds. *Talking with Robert Penn Warren.* Athens: University of Georgia Press, 1990.

CHAPTER FOUR

The Fugitive and the Exile

Theodor W. Adorno, John Crowe Ransom, and
The Kenyon Review

JAMES MATTHEW WILSON

I N 1945, Theodor W. Adorno published two short essays in the spring and autumn issues of John Crowe Ransom's *Kenyon Review*. Ransom indirectly responded to the first in the same issue, and he directly reacted against Adorno's ideas in the second. This marks an improbable moment in modern literary history, at which the practical genius of the academic institutionalization of American letters in the New Criticism and the anti-discursive polymath of the Frankfurt School crossed intellectual paths. Their essays testify to the subtle affinities between the literary and cultural criticism exemplified by the New Critics in the middle decades of the twentieth century and the ideology critique that came to dominate the center of academic literary–critical activity at the end of the century. An account of the meeting on the page between the founding editor of *The Fugitive* and *The Kenyon Review* and the exiled savant of Frankfurt offers more than the novelty of intersection between academic fashions past and present. Crucially, Ransom's encounter with Adorno's anti-teleological, western Marxism provoked him to abandon publicly most of the agrarian, religious, and aesthetic theories he had developed in the 1930s.

Gerald Graff, John Guillory, and most recently, Stephen Schryer have made compelling arguments that the career of Ransom, as the exemplary New Critic, does not merely mark the decline of an ambitious but consciously "traditional" mode of cultural criticism into a hermetically sealed institutional form of literary pedagogy.[1] As Schryer rightly emphasizes, the shift in Ransom's career from that of an Agrarian agitator in *I'll Take My Stand* (1930) and a defender of southern Christian fundamentalists in *God without Thunder* (1930) to an advocate of a professional, philosophically consistent and "purely" literary criticism in *The World's Body* (1937) and *The New Criticism* (1941) was not one from politics to culture, nor from social forms to poetic ones.[2] Rather Ransom's and his colleagues' loyalties moved from the region to the academy as "the critic's primary object of identification" (Schryer, 670). In *God without Thunder,* Ransom had argued that poetry and religion (itself a collective concretization of poetry) were the necessary check on science and the totalitarian impulses of practical human action. *I'll Take My Stand* contended that traditional southern culture was the form of society that best expressed the proper balance among poetry, religion, science, and praxis; that form should be adapted to current conditions and restored to its place of honor. Ransom's later two books were primarily—though by no means exclusively—concerned with defining the proper nature of poetry and the proper practice of literary criticism. Schryer highlights the continuity between these projects, while observing that Ransom's turn to the latter would eventually result in his abandonment of his earlier, anti-modern and anti-industrial regional politics. He would come to accept the division of labor because, as his essay "Criticism, Inc." notes, only through a process of professionalization could criticism achieve its proper levels of academic sophistication and credibility (Schryer, 673). In fact, Ransom's gradual abandonment of his earlier politics in concession to a modernity that granted him institutional and aesthetic autonomy would have more causes than just an emergent academic loyalty. The most startling and direct of those causes would be the provocation of Adorno's two essays. And yet no full account of this brief, important episode in the history of the New Criticism has been given until now.

Adorno's essays reflect his experience as a German intellectual in exile, living in a United States he finds culturally barbarous, while a more lethal barbarism devastated his native land. The first, titled "A Social Critique of Radio Music," offered challenging and pessimistic insights on the dynamics of American mass culture. Here Adorno observed that the democratization of orchestral or "classical" music was in fact merely its mass commodification and fragmented distribution, and so fundamentally changed art itself into "entertainment." Such reflections stemmed from his work on the Princeton Radio Project, an engagement lasting several years in which Adorno studied and measured, by various empirical means, the effects of music and radio on the American public (O'Connor, 8).

The second essay, "Theses upon Art and Religion Today," was briefer and more elliptical. Indeed, aside from its unwavering and specific focus, the "Theses" offers an early example of the organization of ideas into a spatial constellation rather than a specifically linear-temporal mode of composition: a style of which the dialectics of Adorno's posthumous *Aesthetic Theory* remains the best example. Unlike the "Social Critique," this later essay follows the typical Adorno style of avoiding the presentation of empirical evidence. And yet, the "Theses" may be even more historically embedded, more concerned with the environment of its production than its predecessor, for in it Adorno challenges the interdependence, even the association, of religion and art as either intrinsic or even possible in contemporary western society. Almost certainly, Adorno was responding to the conditions of Anglo-American modernism, which, as Perry Anderson has noted (84), was considerably more conservative in its ideological and formal practices than was its Continental counterpart. A significant factor in that conservatism was the persistence of a nebulous point of intersection between art and religion (a variously defined phenomenon), even a conflation of the two, that had been ever more anxiously theorized since the days of Cardinal Newman and Matthew Arnold. Adorno's expressed contempt for American mass culture in particular may have been not only part of a larger pessimism about mass culture per se but also part of a general distaste for the way in which modernism and the avant-garde were developing in the American grain. In any case, both essays mark a significant, indeed formidable, intervention into American critical discourse.

The appearance of both essays in *The Kenyon Review* seems oddly appropriate, given Ransom's use of that journal to ponder the interaction between the social and the aesthetic spheres. In the first instance, Ransom's essay— perhaps coincidentally—directly follows Adorno's; "Art Worries the Naturalists" in no obvious way functions as a commentary on Adorno's "Social Critique." The "Theses," however, are more explicitly linked to Ransom; they are gathered as the second contribution to a tripartite "Speculation" in which Ransom, exercising editor's privilege, has the last word. His "Art and the Human Economy" is in substantial part a direct response to Adorno's essay. It again marks a moment of transition, not in this instance one of critical methodology but rather of political conversion. Adorno's essay and that of a more regular contributor, W. P. Southard, prompted Ransom to "renounce" (Young, 449) his wary advocacy of Agrarianism, the very architectonic of political, social, religious, and aesthetic concerns that had initially made his important criticism possible. He also thereby gave up, or at least radically attenuated, his career-long struggle to establish art as an ultimately triumphant form of knowledge that could challenge the mere naturalism of science, even from its marginalized position in the secular industrialized world. As Mark Jancovich has noted (112–13), this essay marks the practical end of Ransom's writing career. What has gone unexamined until now is the way in which the two essays in tandem suggest the provinciality of Anglophone modernism and, within it, of the ascendant American variety typified by the Agrarians and New Critics. While both Adorno and Ransom always appeal to a form of objectivity in their critical work, these essays reveal a deep rift between their different forms. Adorno's criticism is predicated on an attentive phenomenology of "the whole objective structure of society" (*Aesthetic Theory*, 212), whereas Ransom's is based on an act of what Adorno would dismiss as "hypostatization." Whatever the similarities between them, and there are many, Ransom's concept of objectivity, and the epistemological security it affords, is always theo-ontological, appealing as it does alternately to a transcendent absolute outside of time and to a narrative of history that describes an ideal, normative social condition—what he would call a proper "human economy."

"A Social Critique of Radio Music" and "Art Worries the Naturalists"

Adorno's "Social Critique" provides a spectacular example of the close interpretation of a particular phenomenon facilitating the presentation of a larger sociological vision. The essay commences as a counterdialectic to that posed by "administrative" and "market" analyses of the broadcasting of music and the demographic it reaches. Rather than asking "how can good music be conveyed to the largest possible audience," Adorno poses a range of epistemological and phenomenological questions that interrogate how music is listened to, and also, how it is transformed by wireless transmission and the very methods of presentation that the radio stations and disc-jockeys structure.

As a means to such inquiry he offers four axioms: a) that society has been fully, or almost fully, commodified; b) society operates on a trend toward standardization; c) the ideological tendency of an increasingly complex society is to maintain a status quo; and d) there is an antagonism wherein the forces of production are fettered by the relations of production (210–11). Within the complex of these axioms, Adorno is able to distill certain features of radio music as it functions within its American social context. Music becomes a product to be consumed. The new or avant-garde is rejected as orchestral music in favor of "classical" music, meaning that which was composed before the advent of radio and so carries with it a Benjaminian aura of high culture that the masses cannot penetrate, comprehend, or judge even as it becomes the significant quality that drives consumption. This "classical" music serves as an anodyne, or to be vulgar, an "opiate" for the masses—convincing them that economic modernization, which works materially to their disadvantage, is desirable because it is masked by cultural democratization: "Toscanini compensates for low market prices for farm products," Adorno notes (212); "compensatory" functions of art, like "cathartic" ones, are not effects of art at all, but of ideologies external to, and obscuring of, it. And finally, apropos of this last point, Adorno details the way in which music on the radio ceases to function as art at all, reduced by a plethora of ideological delusions to subjective "infantile" emotivisms (213). American listeners in "The Middle West," he notes with scorn, are incapable of mustering the slightest incidental judgment *about* orchestral music; they can only write to the radio stations to confess an appreciation that, in fact, merely reproduces the intentions of the station's administration in its banal "public service" announcements. Adorno cites as evidence the piles of "fan letters" written to a particular station: "It widens my musical horizon and gives me an ever deeper feeling for the profound qualities of our great music. I can no longer bear the trashy jazz which we usually have to listen to" (214). The supposed democratization of high-culture music has not accomplished (and probably cannot accomplish) what its advocates claim: the medium of distribution and the intellectual paradigms the listeners have available to them ensure that this mass audience has an experience that may have any number of qualities, but is almost certainly nothing like the experience of the competent musician nor of the attentive and elite audience that traditionally filled concert halls. Adorno observes that they listen for isolated strands of melody in a symphony rather than grasping its total orchestration. They listen to quotations as if these were complete "songs," and they listen for a flute solo in the same way they might listen to a sax solo in a Charlie Parker tune. Their interpretive ear is not inadequate by degree but rather deaf to the necessary *kind* of listening. And so they experience symphonies as entertainment, as a commodity, rather than as a measured and, in some sense, dialectical encounter: "Entertainment may have its uses, but a recognition of radio music as such would shatter the listener's artificially fostered belief that they are dealing with the world's greatest music" (217). Adorno insists that it is the disparity and contradiction between American radio listeners' conception of what they are experiencing and the actual form of their perceptions that make orchestral musical "classical" for them. Their listening practice remains untransformed even as their sense of that practice reconceptualizes it by means of a vocabulary of class and moral elevation. Adorno diagnoses listeners as experiencing a combination of vague feelings and programmed responses; they lack the knowledge necessary to *experience* music in any active sense: "Music is not a realm of subjective tastes and relative values, except to those who do not want to undergo the discipline of the subject matter. As soon as one enters the field of musical technology and structure, the arbitrariness of evaluation vanishes, and we are faced with decisions about right and wrong and true and false" (216). Such sentential remarks in Adorno's work elide the difference between empirically objective and objective ethical and aesthetic categories of knowledge, while his historicism refuses the "objective" as a metaphysical category.

It is instructive to note how Adorno's concern with "right and wrong" listening and interpretation touches on the work of the predecessor to the American New Critics, I. A. Richards—specifically to his psychological theory of literary interpretation set forth in *Principles of Literary Criticism* (1924) and *Practical Criticism* (1929). In these works Richards reads the proper interpretation of a text, and the refusal of "stock" responses, as signs of a healthy intellect.[3] Ransom criticizes Richards's "psychologism" in *The New Criticism* on ontological grounds (11–12), suggesting that it lacks objectivity. When one reduces aesthetic experience to psychological or biological phenomena, Ransom emphasizes, one loses the reality of the object causing the experience in the first place and settles for vague notions of feeling. He protests Richards's "psychologism" with specific reference to music:

> There are not two schools of musical appreciation, one instructing our feelings and attitudes, the other, perhaps staffed by intellectual snobs, instructing our intellects. There is one school, and its method is the study of musical composition, as in 'harmony' or 'counterpoint,' by analysis of the objective sound-structures in their own terms, and it does not need to say a word about emotions. (20)

By refusing categories of the subjective and psychological as adequate to understanding music or art in general, Ransom insists, one comes to the ontologically objective reality of the work itself *as a thing*. Adorno, meanwhile likewise insists on objectivity, but his version of it is historical and dialectical rather than ontological; he refuses "essentialism" without accepting subjectivism. This improbable effort to argue according to categories of the "real" without admitting the language of realist metaphysics proceeds by Adorno's, first, analyzing the specificity of a medium—music—and its context, and second, his insistence that such specific analysis serves as an exemplum for larger social phenomena. Once Adorno's investigation has homed in on a particular subject, it magnifies out, by suggestion and implication as much as by clear statement, to a general critique of modern society. This magnification proceeds by way of homology: the cause of poor music apprehension (not to say enjoyment) in the American Midwest is also the cause of "deafening" processes of reification in modern life as a whole.[4] Adorno's method does not allow him to specify the ultimate cause, but only the forms of action it undertakes, as outlined in his four axioms.

Ransom's counterpart essay in the same issue of the *Review,* "Art Worries the Naturalists," pursues a similar movement from specificity to more general social commentary based on implicit homology. However, its success in so doing remains far more ambiguous. It begins as something of a review of the minutiae found in various recent books on aesthetics by pragmatic and naturalist philosophers, who offer what Ransom viewed as an urbane and carefully limited attempt to understand aesthetic experience by means of the categories established by the natural sciences. By the time Ransom wrote this particular essay, of course, he had been reading the works of the American Pragmatic philosophers for many years. This helps to explain why the ontological criticism he defined in *The World's Body* and, more explicitly, in his chapter "Wanted: An Ontological Critic" in *The New Criticism* (republished in *Beating the Bushes*), does not simply hypostatize an opposition between science and poetry, but inadvertently takes natural science as the standard, and more importantly *the form,* of all knowledge even as it struggles to establish a place for criticism and poetry beyond the compass of that science. When Ransom attempted to understand poetry or religion (or anything threatened by the utilitarian and empirical movements of modern science and philosophy), his efforts went into making that supposedly ineffable phenomenon of poetry comprehensible and acceptable to a presumed hostile scientific audience. At the beginning of "Art Worries the Naturalists," he confesses that the "apologist of the arts cannot do otherwise than refer the question of their strange kind of activity to the current philosophies; therefore, in these days, to naturalism" (*Beating the Bushes,* 93). Hence the need to establish poetry ontologically was not one exclusively grounded in his prior acceptance of metaphysical realism; for that matter, Ransom's prose but little suggests that he had rejected his early education in the idealism of F. H. Bradley for realism.[5] Rather, the persistent ontological focus of Ransom's criticism seems to have been formed primarily in reaction to an American variety of nominalism and positivism that denied the reality of ideas, save those which perfectly corresponded to material facts.[6] He wanted to establish the objective attributes of poetry's *being* to prove to his hostile audience that in fact poetry possessed some kind of existence that merited attention independent of the slush and subjectivity of vague feelings somehow adhering to nonsense.[7]

Adorno had no compunction about asserting the objectively assessable qualities of music. Although the equally assessable attributes of verse—rhyme, meter, metaphor—were available to Ransom, they only tentatively satisfied him as evidence that poetry had some objective existence, that it had a structural integrity as poetry, as more than the sum of its parts. However, he sometimes felt compelled to rebel against the very empirical ontology he advocated by leaping into the irrational. Often, he pandered to the specters of his insecurity—naturalist philosophers such as John Dewey—by attempting to harness their discourse to prove what he nonetheless asserts is unverifiable within its bounds. In "Art Worries," however, this strategy is inverted. Here, he will not convict science of limitations whose lines of demarcation poetry exceeds and "worries." Rather, he optimistically suggests that Dewey's naturalism is richer than that of his younger colleagues and might mature beyond the reductive vision characteristic of that school of philosophy. Unlike that of his colleagues, Dewey's writing exhibits "a tangle of bold philosophical speculations which are religious as well as aesthetic, and do not yield any firm or demonstrable results" (97). If his naturalism only continues to evolve it will move beyond the material and the empirical to the "supernatural" and the speculative. Ransom does not observe that it would then cease to be naturalism.

Ransom does confess, however, that this optimism replaces a former hostility—and this shift in thinking marks the distinctive importance of the essay and suggests the role Adorno's cultural criticism played in his intellectual development. Years of effort suddenly begin to unravel. In a subtle apology for his early *God without Thunder,* where his suspicion of science reached its most indignant pitch, Ransom notes the need for "supernaturalists" to bone up on their "naturalist" philosophy before speaking. "If it seems impertinent in me to say this," Ransom interrupts himself, "let me remark that I have myself come down a long and rather absurd hill. Like my preceptors I used to regard naturalism as a specially malignant heresy, if not an abomination unto the Lord" (*Beating the Bushes,* 94). After nearly fifteen years of combating, while making concessions to, the reductive nature of modern science and philosophical naturalism, Ransom's only intellectual option left was a strategic surrender to the naturalists, in hopes that by admitting their terms of debate he might coax some margin of the field of "knowledge" to be left for poetry to till.

Ransom's essay makes no mention of Adorno's "Social Critique of Radio Music" appearing in the same issue, yet Ransom's retraction of his early defense of southern Christian fundamentalism seems to be provoked by Adorno's pessimistic vision of the American Midwest as a landscape desolate of proper aesthetic understanding. As *Aesthetic Theory*'s occasional dives into American slang would later hint, Adorno's characterization of rationalized, administered society finds its unhappy apotheosis in the America he came to know as an exile. When Adorno explains in "Social Critique" that music has "ceased to be a human force and is consumed like other consumers' goods," he observes,

> This produces "commodity listening," a listening whose ideal is to dispense as far as possible with any effort on the part of the recipient—even if such an effort on the part of the recipient is the necessary condition of grasping the sense of the music. It is the ideal of Aunt Jemima's ready-mix for pancakes extended to the field of music. (211)

The move into particularity—a particular brand, a particular product—is not incidental. The "society of commodities" that Adorno generally discusses with conscientious abstraction is revealed as the home of instant pancake mix, Benny Goodman, of "giving the people what they want" (216), and a "mass-culture" incapable of hearing Bach (213) or articulating its experience of music except in prefabricated, stock terms (215). In short, Adorno's "Social Critique" of mass-culture is specifically one of American culture, of flatlands rural and primitive in appearance but commodified in fact.

Ransom's apologia of a mature philosophical naturalism likely responds to this attack on his country. Adorno's essay impugns two ideas precious to Ransom. His suspicion of popular "taste" undermines Ransom's democratic populism, a belief which had led Ransom to write *God without Thunder,* an "unorthodox" defense of Southern Christian fundamentalism, and to organize the symposium, *I'll Take My Stand,* in defense of Southern culture against Northern industrialism. Second, Adorno insists that all efforts to disseminate serious music, or great art in general, are futile, because the mode of dissemination transforms the attributes of the work (217) and the categories of perception under which it is received. This last assault would have struck Ransom as particularly threatening, because he was already in the process of abandoning his religious and cultural populism in favor of a democratic theory of the professionalization of literary criticism and education. Ransom had already prepared, *in nuce,* a response to such strikes against his two cardinal ideas. In *The New Criticism,* just before demolishing I. A. Richards's "psychologism," he defends the naturalist, positivist, and skeptical methodology behind it. He finds Richards's methods to "suit a sort of pioneering, start-at-the-bottom Americanism, and are an excellent strategy for us, as I idealize our national temper and prospects of knowledge" (6). Whatever his anxieties over the method, he admits it is appropriate to the American "empirical" character. So too, in "Art Worries," he abandons the anti-rationalist defense of fundamentalism in his earlier writing to laud the suitable, even patriotic, character of philosophical naturalism: "If there is anywhere a philosophy indigenous to our local climate, it is naturalism; whereupon, even if America were not my country, I think I should not care to convict this philosophy of inherent viciousness, but at most of an immaturity" (94). As many intellectual historians at home and abroad had already claimed, naturalism was the "American Philosophy." Ransom's theory of poetry had largely been geared toward proposing art as beyond the grasp of science and as resisting the rationalism of "northern industrialism." This shift towards the naturalism he had previously reviled reconfigures Ransom's aesthetic and critical theory so that it appears concerned with finding a suitable "indigenous" philosophy for the American psyche—one that is national rather than regional in character. Surely this change is rooted in Ransom's departure from the South for Kenyon College in the late 1930s, and in a felt imperative of patriotism imposed during the Second World War, which ended the same year Ransom wrote the essay. No less likely, Adorno's double alienation—exile from Germany in consequence of the war, and repulsion by the American cultural landscape in which he was forced to abide—prompted the scathing attacks of "Social Critique." These provoked Ransom, in response, to take up an intransigently American apologetic for even those aspects of American culture he had once found most threatening. If immature naturalism seemed reductive to him, it nonetheless seemed a philosophy that gave Americans what they "wanted."

Ransom's new sympathy for naturalism required intellectual compromise on both sides. Particularly, Ransom's mature naturalism had to avoid the positivist reduction of knowledge to science, and the definitive naturalist reduction of reality to matter. Again, Dewey's philosophy makes "a tangle of bold philosophical speculations which are religious as well as aesthetic" (97). Ransom succeeds (if that is the right term) in luring the naturalists into his own native territory. The writers to whom he replies seem to have formulated in the language of biology, indeed with a literal use of the concepts of biology, an argument for the organic unity, or "fusing," of works of art (103). Ransom out empiricizes the empiricists by arguing that the artwork is not a unity of any kind. Against this naïve claim of organicism, Ransom argues that artworks are the product of "funding," a word he finds expressive of the central axiom of his poetic theory that a poem consists of a logical structure overloaded with "irrelevant textures" of meaning and meter. He urges that the naturalists are saying what he has always said. His exemplum and metaphor is that of a Christmas tree:

> . . . I will risk some absurdity, to suggest that it might be wholesome for us to see [the work of art] as something like a Christmas tree. For, on Christmas morning when the switch is turned on, and the Christmas tree bursts upon our prepared vision in its beauty, we have the almost instantaneous sense of an intelligible object, and we feel such assured satisfaction and completion as may amount to the 'ecstasy' or the 'seizure' which qualitists, from Dewey on, desiderate for their arts. But I think the experience is not too spectacular when examined. There is the strong and steady tree, beneath the lights and ornaments and gifts which are so thickly strung upon it. . . . And at once we sense enough of the frequency and the quality of the accessories to know that the total object is of great magnitude and dimension of its density . . . here is the moral. It is only the sturdy frame of a small cedar which holds everything together to make an object that is technically and sufficiently one, and, looking for the 'unifying principle,' we say comfortably that this framework will do. (111)

Ransom consistently argued for the organic unity of artworks, but that unity referred to a specific logical structure held in tension with a potentially vast series of local textures. Much like Adorno's theory of artworks as constellations, this argument for the "funding" of disparate elements into a complete thing suggests that the ineffable qualities of art reside not in its "organic" analogy to biology or in its *otherness* from science, nor does it lie in some romance of the supernatural, but in the almost supernumerary number of elements operating simultaneously. Science cannot suffice because there is no such thing as "Science": there is biology, physics, psychology, etc., but no one discourse that can embody and articulate the totality of experience. That, for Ransom, is the point: art worries the naturalists because it reminds them that our experience of the world is neither univocal nor mono-vocal. We may try to understand the world by means of discrete disciplines, but we do not encounter it *within* them; they must arise only retrospectively. Ransom therefore recuperates the theory of art he had always maintained, but in a context hospitable to the naturalism he had previously refused. In the process, he abandons his earlier, deliberate "fundamentalist" anti-rationalism, and implicitly his Southern regionalism, for an American national imperative intended to resist the indictment of American culture found in Adorno's dialectical social critique.

"Theses upon Art and Religion Today" and "Art and the Human Economy"

The second exchange between Adorno and Ransom in *The Kenyon Review* was a far more direct confrontation. In the spring 1945 issue, Ransom may have abandoned his defense of Christian fundamentalism, but he maintained a fierce attachment to a necessary link between poetry and religion. The "Theses" testify to Adorno's frustration with just such modernist theories of poetry as a hieratic art form, and target Rilke's poetry in particular because it lingered on deteriorated "religious symbols" (678). Adorno generally excluded the Marxist doctrines of historical necessity from his work, finding its teleological thrust toward totality barbaric, but he evidently preserved a hint of that barbarism in believing that religion was vestigial and that art must abandon its ornaments to reflect accurately the historical truth of the present. Surely his experience in America had taught him that the residual nature of Rilke's religion was not merely "retrograde," but rather exemplary of a typical promise of modernist literature to manifest reality though a symbolism that was at least a "secular" analogy of the Catholic sacraments and at most their consubstantial manifestation.[8] Adorno could scarcely approve what he saw as a project that was retrograde, patronizing, facetious, and of course, hypostatizing.

The theses themselves run as follows:

I) The unity between art and religion was the contingent product of specific historical conditions that cannot be recovered simply because western society has awakened to a crisis "involving individuality and the collectivistic tendencies in our society" (677).

II) The unity of art and religion was never tranquil and is not aboriginal; only romanticism posits a late and unusual break between them; art is a protest of the humane against any and all institutions; the protest would not end by establishing a "right" or religious society any more than that society would be established by the simple reunification of art and religion.

III) Modern artists who add religious content to their work are not *doing the same thing* as artists of earlier periods, but are merely adding futile ornamentation: "It glorifies religion because it would be so nice if one could believe again" (678).

IV) The borrowing of religious forms, such as "the mystery play" is "equally futile," (679) and fails to effect a union between form and content or subject and object.

V)   The loss of a hegemonic or universal religion or philosophy does not mean that their forces "should have passed on to art" (679). Art cannot become the new religion. This kind of reasoning would reconcile religion (or, for that matter, the various religions), philosophy, and art into one eviscerated category—leaving them as mere "cultural goods," a desiccated residue that could no longer be taken seriously by anyone (680).

VI) Nonetheless there was a primeval connection between art and religion, and as a result, art "bears the imprint of its magical origin: a halo that emanates from the artwork's dual claim to uniqueness and the representation of something universal. But to insist upon this magical quality in the artwork itself actually diminishes it: "Today it is only the hit composer and the best seller writer who prate about the irrationality and inspiration of their products" (681).

VII) Artworks function as a Leibnizean monad, representing the universal within their own walls but "without windows" (681). The attempt of the artist to mediate between the specificity of his word and the universal or absolute it represents *in nuce* cannot work. Rather, the most successful artists, like Marcel Proust, will invest in the concretion of experience; only by precise representation will they create a work that, constructed out of the ephemeral details of the world, becomes immortal by touching upon the absolute (682).

The American literary landscape in the high- and late-modernist periods could not but have provoked these observations. Although Adorno only specifically targets Rilke for his opprobrium, T. S. Eliot associated himself with Rilke on numerous occasions, and Eliot was the godfather of the American late modernism that *The Kenyon Review* promoted in its pages. Adorno's theses would have been of immediate interest to Ransom who, following Eliot, made the connection between art and religion a central question of his critical work. Whereas Eliot and Ransom aggressively sought to hypostatize the intimacy of these two entities, Adorno no less aggressively sought to historicize it and dismiss it as obsolete. Theses I and II could apply equally well to the critical works of Ransom and Eliot, along with the then-flourishing masses of neo-Thomists and Catholic converts swelling the ranks of philosophers, aestheticians, and artists up to the late 1950s. Thesis IV almost surely was targeted at Eliot's *Murder in the Cathedral*, although that was only one of myriad attempts to revive the place of mystery in modernist drama. Ransom, for his part, had argued that *Murder* was incompletely poetic because it was insufficiently religious (*The World's Body*, 166–72); a position he later retracted along with his early pretenses of defending Christian orthodoxy (*The World's Body*, 366, 377). Thesis V, harking back to the disciples of Arnold and Santayana, must surely have registered with Ransom as countering the arguments in *God without Thunder*, which he had repented for reasons quite other than Adorno presents here.

In total, the implication of these theses is to exclude the bulk of Anglophone literary modernism from Adorno's canon of truly modern artworks. More than two decades later, these theses would find more subtle expression in Adorno's *Aesthetic Theory*, so it is telling that the modernism defined in that book would take James Joyce and Samuel Beckett as the very prototypes of literary modernism, rejecting by silence the other major figures who composed the modernist canon at mid-century. It is doubtful that Ransom fully grasped the significance of the theses, but he clearly sensed they put under erasure the literary modernism his work as a poet and critic had fostered. Detecting the western Marxist note in Adorno's writing, Ransom observes in his essay responding to the theses, "Mr. Adorno is evidently for collectivism in politics, but not with all the potential ferocity of a partisan, i.e., fanatically. His social ideal has no room for religion yet provides a special asylum for art" (129). Students of Adorno will doubtless recognize the trace of his ideas in this statement, though Ransom has bowdlerized them. Adorno, like the poststructuralist philosophers who followed him, did not critique the "ontology" of art from the position of an empirical rationalist, but from a phenomenological position that was as skeptical of the ideology of rationality as it was of romanticism, as unconvinced by the attempt to boil down the individual subject to a number of material phenomena or nervous impulses as it was of conservative humanist attempts to preserve its unity. Ransom, whose philosophical positions were formed in response to German and English idealism as well as American pragmatism, was unlikely to have warmed to the nuances of a writer featuring negative dialectics.

While Adorno had launched an assault on the inherent relationship between religion and art, in "Art and the Human Economy," Ransom took some such relationship for granted. But he questioned that this relationship could resolve itself into a "unity of culture" within history, because, in his view, art always acts in a dialectical opposition to "culture" rather than as the adhesive bond within it. From *I'll Take My Stand* onward, Ransom had assumed just the opposite; religion and art reminded humanity of its insufficiency, its incapacity to conquer nature absolutely and its responsibility to walk uprightly and fear the Lord. Adorno's second thesis denies the foundational assumption of nearly all of Ransom's writings (including the poetry). Yet, in his response to Adorno, Ransom scarcely registers these attacks. In a stunning reversal of his past position, Ransom instead takes issue with the idea that art can hold even so significant a social role as that of opposition or agitator. Ransom's and Adorno's writings had generally concurred in regarding art as a "check on action." In this scheme, art was at minimum a retarding force, like that of ritual and ceremony, to prevent a merely pragmatic humanity from running into the abyss. Once more embarrassed to find his old Agrarian and New Critical positions overlapping with Adorno's, as they had seemed to in Adorno's "Social Critique," Ransom swiftly abandons his long-maintained position in favor of a patriotic imperative.

For Ransom in 1945, art has ceased to operate as a response to the ideology of everyday life. It becomes for him a mere commemoration of action, not stopping human activities but magnifying them through an ideal image. To be more precise, art for Ransom has become mere consolation, like that found in "Sunday institutions." If one must modernize six days a week, one may at least have one day's poetic rest: "The arts are the expiations, but they are beautiful. Together they comprise the detail of human history" (133). The updated prototype Ransom chooses to define this function is that of the public statue of a general. Art venerates and improves *as an image* of reality; but both these actions are passive and neither continue nor repel action. Or rather, only within the artwork is action checked. The artwork cannot engage society in any kind of active dialectic: "Those who are supposed to commemorate action are commemorating reaction; they are pledged to the Enlightenment, but, even in Its name, they clutter It with natural piety" (135). Rather than an oppositional force to society, art in this view is the compensatory beauty that society requires to continue with the Enlightenment program of modernization, professionalization, and the division of labor. In this new theory, Ransom suggests that Agrarians of 1930 and the Wordsworthian romantics of every generation do not protest against this project, but offer in their poems a patch of pastoral to which one can retreat figuratively while one's literal existence moves forward with the stream of progress.

> We have fallen . . . and henceforth a condition we might properly call 'decadence' is our portion; guilt and repentance, guilt followed by such salvation as can be achieved. In the forms which this salvation takes, we do go back to our original innocence, but vicariously, symbolically, not really. We cannot actually go back. (132)

These comments come as a bemusing anti-climax in Ransom's career. The America of applied science and economic efficiency that Adorno would critique thoroughly in his *Aesthetic Theory* had somehow fought the once "unreconstructed" Ransom to an intellectual stalemate. He had always based his theories on a transcendental absolute and an ideal historical past, all of which were to serve as guideposts for human action; he now left himself with only the images of those things, not the belief in them. Indeed, though his comments appear as a rejection of Adorno's theses, they actually enact the third one with distressing exactitude. Ransom's concept of the religious function of art had been reduced to commemoration, what Ransom himself would call "nostalgia" (134), and what Adorno mocks with the observation that such art "glorifies religion because it would be so nice if one could believe again" (678).

Ransom had abandoned his anti-rationalist theory of religion and art in his previous exchange with Adorno. We see that he severely reduces the connection of art and religion, which had once been a poetic force against modernity, to that of a civil religion "central" to modern life only to the extent that a public statue might be located in the center of a Midwestern town square. These symptoms of Ransom's final acceptance of the division of labor in modern administered society signify his abandonment of the Agrarian cultural theory he had done so much to propagate in the 1930s. He did not leave this abandonment to mere suggestion. Ransom wrote "Art and the Human Economy" with the state of Germany clearly in mind: perhaps Adorno's identity as a German exile partly stimulated his reflections, as surely as his critique of religion and art provoked them. In any case, the recently concluded war directly imposed itself on Ransom's political ideas. Near the end of the essay, he confesses,

> I find an irony at my expense in remarking that the judgment just now delivered by the Declaration of Potsdam against the German people is that they shall return to an agrarian economy. Once I should have thought there could be no greater happiness for a people, but now I have no difficulty in seeing it for what it is meant to be: a heavy punishment. (134)

Caught between antipathy for Adorno's western Marxism and sympathy for Adorno's homeland, Ransom recognizes the religious and political synthesis he had forged in his theory of art could not hold. The work of art must be isolated at once from politics and religion to the extent that a statue—whether representing a general or a god—is so isolated. The dialectic by which art stood in a meaningful, but by no means easy, relation to society now struck Ransom as necessitating political and religious positions to which he could no longer assent. As a tenured professor at Kenyon College, and as editor of a literary review, Ransom found it necessary to abandon those positions and to content himself with poetry alone, with the "commemoration" of a "natural piety" left to worry the margins of the otherwise unstoppable American juggernaut of industrial modernity. Adorno's career reached an impasse no less troubling. As the axioms of his "Social Critique" indicate, however, he had early reconciled himself to the totalitarian direction of modern consumer society. Having abandoned all hope of art's dialectic with society having a direct social function, he was perhaps better prepared to take up an intransigent position, accepting the absence of power that the political and religious pretensions of art seemed to promise. Adorno therefore could wait without hope, preferring to know the truth and see it bowdlerized by ideology, than to seek after a reconciliation with the status quo akin to that Ransom effected in declaring his patriotic admiration for the naturalism of John Dewey and his new aesthetics as one no more troubling than a "stone Bismarck" (135) welcomed in the town square.

Notes

1. See Graff, Guillory, and Schryer.
2. See Twelve Southerners, and Ransom, *God without Thunder, The World's Body,* and *The New Criticism.*
3. Ransom summarizes the psychologistic strain in Richards's theory as reductive much as utilitarian philosophy is reductive:

> The health of the mind depends on its ability to organize its impulses into attitudes, and then to coordinate their operation so that there may be maximum activity and minimum friction among the units, as in the atomic society imagined by Jeremy Bentham. Poetry is needed as a complement to science because it is prepared to give to the emotions, and through them to the attitudes, their daily work-out; science intends to suppress them in order to map the objective world without distraction. (*The New Criticism*, 22)

4. After the fashion of another American New Critic, Yvor Winters, Adorno decries theories of art based on pleasure or enjoyment as forms of subjectivist hedonism: Art works are

> not a higher order of amusement. The relation to art was not that of its physical devouring; on the contrary, the beholder disappeared into the material; this is even more so in modern works that shoot toward the viewer as on occasion a locomotive does in a film. Ask a musician if the music is a pleasure, the reply is likely to be—as in the American joke of the grimacing cellist under Toscanini—"*I just hate music.*" (*Aesthetic Theory*, 13)

5. Francesca Aran Murphy's *Christ the Form of Beauty: A Study in Theology and Literature* (Edinburgh: T. and T. Clark, 1995) situates Ransom's criticism in a tradition

of conceptual realism and theological aesthetics extending from Jacques Maritain to Allen Tate, and continuing on to include William Lynch and Hans Urs von Balthasar. This may in fact be the most fruitful context in which to read Ransom, capturing as it does the realist implications of his poetic theory, despite, as Murphy concedes, the fact that "Ransom's conception of imagination is a partially Kantian one" (73). As it happens, the modernist aesthetics grounded in the conceptual realism of Thomas Aquinas, such as those of Maritain, Tate, and von Balthasar, also splice Kantian idealist aesthetics to their metaphysics; what distinguishes Ransom is the absence of a conscious effort to conceal this debt.

6. Introducing Richards's literary criticism, he notes that its

> bias is deeply *nominalist,* and by that I mean that it is very alert to the possibility that a word which seems to refer to the objective world, or to have an objective 'referent,' really refers to a psychological context and has no objective referent; this bias has governed Richards' conception of poetry, for one thing, almost from that day to this. And with that bias goes—and the combination is a very common one nowadays though almost paradoxical—a *positivist* bias, through which the thinker is led to take the referential capacity of science as perfect, in spite of his nominalist skepticism; and by comparison to judge all other kinds of discourse as falling short. Nominalism and positivism are strange-looking yokefellows for undertaking knowledge, but it must be said that they may work very well together. (*The New Criticism,* 5–6)

7. Ransom would note in *The New Criticism* that poetry in its ontological reality bore certain resemblance to science, but differed from technology, because its being was not immediately subject to uses beyond itself:

> art will seem specially affiliated with science, and further away from technology, in not having any necessary concern with pragmatics or usefulness. But in another sense it is closer to technology and further from science. We recall our old impression, or perhaps recall our knowledge of the Greek Philosophers, to the effect that art, like technology, is concerned with making something, as well as knowing something; while pure science seems concerned only with knowing something. And what poetry makes—and the word means a making—is the poem, which at least in respect to its meter is a discourse with a peculiarly novel and manufactured form, and obviously a rather special unit of discourse. (283–84)

8. Denis Devlin captures the widespread and troubled meeting of Catholic sacramentality and hieratic symbolism in late modernist poetry in his review, "Twenty-Four Poets," in *Sewanee Review* 53 (1945): 457–66. Naturally, the early Robert Lowell and late W. H. Auden provide the scales in which this phenomenon was hung—to Adorno's ironic smile no doubt.

Bibliography

Adorno, Theodor. *Aesthetic Theory.* Minneapolis: University of Minnesota Press, 1997.

———. "A Social Critique of Radio Music," *The Kenyon Review* 7.2 (Spring 1945): 208–17.

———. "Theses upon Art and Religion Today," *The Kenyon Review* 7.4 (Autumn 1945): 677–82.

Anderson, Perry. *The Origins of Postmodernity.* New York: Verso, 1998.

Eliot, T. S. *Christianity and Culture.* New York: Harcourt Brace, 1976.

———. *The Complete Poems and Plays: 1909–1950.* New York: Harcourt Brace & Company, 1980.

———. *Selected Prose.* New York: Harcourt Brace, 1975.

Graff, Gerald. *Professing Literature.* Chicago: University of Chicago Press, 1987.

Guillory, John. *Cultural Capital: The Problem of Literary Canon Formation.* Chicago: University of Chicago Press, 1993.

Jancovich, Mark. *The Cultural Politics of the New Criticism.* Cambridge: Cambridge University Press, 1993.

O'Connor, Brian. "Introduction." In *The Adorno Reader,* ed. Brian O'Connor, 1–19. Oxford: Blackwell, 2000.

Ransom, John Crowe. *Beating the Bushes: Selected Essays, 1941–1970.* New York: New Directions, 1972.

———. *God without Thunder.* London: Gerald Howe Ltd., 1931.

———. *The New Criticism.* New York: New Directions, 1941.

———. *The World's Body.* Baton Rouge: Louisiana State University Press, 1968.

Schryer, Stephen. "Fantasies of the New Class: The New Criticism, Harvard Sociology, and the Idea of the University." *PMLA* 122.3 (May 2007): 633–78.

Twelve Southerners. *I'll Take My Stand: The South and the Agrarian Tradition.* Baton Rouge: Louisiana State University Press, 1977.

Winters, Yvor. *In Defense of Reason.* Athens: Swallow Press, 1987.

Young, Thomas Daniel. *Gentleman in a Dustcoat: John Crowe Ransom.* Baton Rouge: Louisiana State University Press, 1976.

PART II

New Criticism and Modernism

THE ESSAYS of this second section address relations between the New Criticism and the cultural phenomenon of literary modernism, which were significantly intertwined in a number of ways. First, the New Critics, along with their predecessors and counterparts, began their careers in a post–Great War cultural climate in which writers now considered "modernist" were on the rise. Critics associated with the formation of the New Criticism often shaped their work in response to modernist literature, and especially modernist poetry. Cambridge critics such as I. A. Richards and F. R. Leavis, along with the American New Critics who followed their lead, were keenly inspired by T. S. Eliot in particular—both by his poetry, whose iconoclasm caught the imagination of a generation of readers, and his considerable body of criticism. In his landmark *Principles of Literary Criticism* (1924), Richards devotes an appendix to explicating and defending Eliot's poetry; in *New Bearings in English Poetry* (1932), F. R. Leavis showcases the significant impact of Eliot on poetry of the years after the war. In 1939, Cleanth Brooks would position his reading of *The Waste Land* as a centerpiece of *Modern Poetry and the Tradition*. Moreover, as Chris Baldick notes, Eliot set a new agenda for literary criticism of the early to mid-twentieth century. This is not to say that the tenets that came to be associated with the New Criticism were coincident with all of Eliot's critical positions—and in fact, by the late 1950s, Eliot sought to distance himself from the New Criticism, disavowing claims about its having derived from him ("Frontiers of Criticism" [1956]). Nonetheless, several of the pathfinding claims Eliot advanced in his early essays became foundational for what Baldick terms the "period of revolution" in literary criticism between the two world wars—and for much New Critical thought specifically. Concepts such as the "Impersonal theory of poetry" articulated in Eliot's "Tradition and the Individual Talent" (1919), the "objective correlative" from "Hamlet" (1919), and the elevation of John Donne and kindred seventeenth-century poets in "The Metaphysical Poets" (1921)—along with an argument that the canon of English literature needed redefinition according to standards derived from the Metaphysicals—would underpin the new wave in criticism.

More generally, the New Critics and their predecessors were responsive to modern poetry, Eliot's and otherwise, as a watershed movement—and particularly attentive to the "difficulty" associated with modern poetry, on which Eliot had famously commented in "The Metaphysical Poets": "[I]t appears likely that poets in our civilization, as it exists at present, must be *difficult.*" In *Modern Poetry and the Tradition* (1939), whose title echoed Eliot's "Tradition and the Individual Talent," Brooks acknowledged such difficulty as a signature of modern poetry, which was challenging critics to rise beyond their previous standards, zones of comfort, and concepts of poetry.

During the years leading up to the advent of the New Criticism, recognition of the difficulties of modernism brought criticism to the fore as an important source of assistance for the "plain reader" whose usual approaches would be baffled by much of the new poetry. In their *Survey of Modernist Poetry* (1927), Laura Riding and Robert Graves underscored the importance of devising new, more rigorous methods of reading to accommodate the challenges of new poetry such as that of E. E. Cummings. In *How to Teach Reading* (1932), F. R. Leavis called for a new "trained reader." As Bradley Clissold observes, literary modernism served as the dominant "cultural subtext" for Empson's *Seven Types of Ambiguity* (1930), and Empson's techniques proved among the most apt for unpacking the complexities of the new poetry—techniques upon which the American New Critics would draw. As of the late 1930s, the New Critics placed themselves as mentors for a new readership of difficult modern work, through their essays and textbooks reaching a far wider audience than Leavis had imagined. Studies such as Brooks's *Modern Poetry and the Tradition* sought to help readers navigate through the new modern poetry; and textbooks like Brooks and Warren's *Understanding Poetry* set about training college students to engage in what came to be called "close reading"—a technique which, to use Bradley Clissold's phrase, "modernism's experimental poetics explicitly demanded, as well as rewarded."

Aside from Eliot, modern poets featured in New Critical demonstrations of close reading included Pound and Gerard Manley Hopkins (in Leavis's *New Bearings*), Frost, MacLeish, and Auden (in Brooks's *Modern Poetry and the Tradition*), Yeats (in Brooks's *Well Wrought Urn*), Stevens (in Ransom's *The World's Body*), and Crane (in Tate's *On the Limits of Poetry*). New Critics such as Ransom and Tate were themselves poets; their poetry was also sometimes included as exemplary of the new modern poetry. (As Clissold notes, even Empson, albeit problematically, was sometimes grouped among the moderns.) But this is not to say that the New Critics engaged exclusively with modern poetry: classic readings by the New Critics addressed a much wider ambit of poets, including Shakespeare, Donne, Herrick, Milton, Wordsworth, Keats, and Tennyson.

Even as the New Critics were inspired by, and shaped their criticism importantly according to the demands of, the new modern poetry, modern poetry and modern literature more generally were legitimated by the work, criteria, and methods of the New Critics. Critics such as Richards and Leavis advocated for new poets such as Eliot. The American New Critics likewise championed the moderns and brought them to the classroom. As Ransom defended modern poets in the conclusion to *The New Criticism*: "[T]hey find the old practice trite, and ontologically inadequate . . . and therefore they work by taking liberties with the old practice, and irregularize and de-systematize it, without denying it." In his study focused on modern poetry, Brooks credited the moderns with an artistic revolution "of the order of the Romantic revolt" that necessitated a corresponding revolution in critical approaches and standards.

This said, the versions of "modernism" invested in by the New Critics certainly did not encompass all the work developed during the modern period that later critics would find significant: certain poets such as Edna St. Vincent Millay and William Carlos Williams, for instance, were noted among the moderns but not acknowledged by the New Critics as important modernists. Many other writers now read as significant modernists—such as H. D., Mina Loy, Muriel Rukeyser, and Jean Toomer—if sometimes lauded in early-twentieth-century commentary, were not included in the New Critical pantheon. As Adam Hammond suggests, what needs to be recognized are the contours and limits of specifically New Critical conceptions of modernism. Moreover, as Connor Byrne observes, we should also take care not to confuse latter-day caricatures of how the New Critics conceptualized modernism with the ways in which they actually did. His essay and the others in this module aim to enrich understanding of how the New Criticism read modernist literature.

CHAPTER FIVE

No Two Ways about It

William Empson's Enabling Modernist Ambiguities

BRADLEY D. CLISSOLD

> Critics, as "barking dogs," on this view, are of two sorts: those who merely
> relieve themselves against the flower of beauty, and those, less continent,
> who afterwards scratch it up. I myself, I must confess, aspire to the second
> of these classes. . . .
>
> —William Empson, *Seven Types of Ambiguity*

FOR ALL of his talk of close verbal analysis, William Empson was a literary critic of missed opportunity—which is not to take anything away from the fact that he remains a foundational figure in the institutionalization and practice of literary criticism in both the twentieth and twenty-first centuries. In fact, his scholarly contribution to the study of literature and culture is well-documented across an archive that ranges from reviews of his books and Empson's responses to those critiques, to discursive essay entries about him in standard reference texts and a selection of full-length monographs committed to renegotiating Empson's place in the annals of literary criticism. That Empson's name has become synonymous with the use of ambiguity as a literary device is both highly reductive and ironically accurate. In fact, it is this inescapable association of Empson with his privileging of ambiguity as *the* operative term for literary close reading that throws into relief his failure to subject experimental modernist texts to the same types of magnified verbal analysis that he practiced in *Seven Types of Ambiguity* (1930), something that modernism's experimental poetics explicitly demanded, as well as rewarded. This essay attempts to account for both Empson's conspicuous refusal to engage the complex ambiguity in works of modernist literature, and the profound implications of that decision for modernist studies and narratives about the historical development of literary criticism.

If, according to the discourses of addiction theory, enablers are broadly defined as individuals who create environments that support the continued practice of specific types of behaviors, then William Empson must be read historically as an important enabler of literary modernism, both in terms of its production and reception. Specifically, he enabled modernism, first, because he helped to enshrine detailed close reading as a methodological standard for twentieth-century literary studies; and then, ironically, because he did *not* apply this method of analysis to the more difficult formal features of canonical experimental modernist texts. As a result, he further enabled modernism because he did not provide constraining procedural models for successor modernist critics to follow when it came to reading meaning into modernist ambiguities.

As early as 1938, John Crowe Ransom touted Empson as "one of the closest living readers of poetry," but then posed the question that ultimately orients this essay: "What will be the line taken by Mr. Empson when he reviews modern poetry?" ("Mr. Empson's" 91, 104). In his critique of *Ambiguity,* Ransom argues that it is Empson's "manifest destiny" to explicate literary modernism because his "interpretations increase immensely the range of experience, and therefore the density of lines, beyond what the ordinary reader finds of these elements in the poem" (104, 93). However, this obvious critical fit between Empson's methods of close verbal analysis and the aesthetic formal practices of literary modernism serves only to highlight Empson's modernist omissions in *Ambiguity:*

> It is remarkable in Mr. Empson that he turns his subtle critical gifts not upon the modern poets who are professionally obscure but upon the old and established poets whose surface logic is explicit and competent, and whose obscurity lies, if anywhere, below, and behind. Mr. Empson hardly notices the moderns, or not on his usual scale. Other critics have to do it, with prodigious exegesis. (103)

Although reviews of *Ambiguity* would continue to claim that Empson had applied his method of verbal analysis across a range of texts from Chaucer to T. S. Eliot—a misleading if technically accurate statement—Ransom's *where's the modernism?* question cuts directly to the chase. Indeed, Empson's indirect, career-long answer to this question appears in his subsequent critical writings, his correspondence, and his published poetry, all of which attest to Empson's conflicted (perhaps *ambiguous*) attitude towards experimental modernist literature.

In the "Preface to the Second Edition" (1946) of *Ambiguity,* Empson specifically addresses the concerns of his early critics, but his responses continue unwittingly to foreground the applicability of his critical methodology to modernist aesthetics. He claims he wants "ambiguity" to do broadly conceived interpretive work, wherever there are "possible alternative reactions to the [same] passage": "We call it ambiguous, I think, when we recognise that there could be a puzzle as to what the author meant, in that alternative views might be taken without sheer misreading" (x). After he rewrites the sentences at the beginning of Chapter I, he explains in a footnote that his goal in the second edition is to avoid defining ambiguity so broadly that it "becomes almost meaningless," yet paradoxically acknowledges that "the question of what would be the best definition of 'ambiguity' . . . crops up all through the book" (1). In the end, his revised opening statements read just as broadly as the originals:

> An ambiguity, in ordinary speech, means something very pronounced, and as a rule witty or deceitful. I propose to use the word in an extended sense, and shall think relevant to my subject any verbal nuance, however slight, which gives room for alternative reactions to the same piece of literature. (1)

This retrospective desire to maintain a wide breadth of application for literary ambiguity is not new to Empson's *Ambiguity;* in fact, it is evidenced in his seven blurred types of ambiguity that range from puns, allegories, and connotations to ambiguities occasioned by syntax, rhythm, and authorial states of mind (e.g. judgment, doubt, or confusion), as well as in the summary claims he makes for ambiguity as an indispensable tool of literary analysis. Immediately after defining ambiguity as "any verbal nuance" that allows for "alternative reactions to the same piece of literature," Empson argues that "[i]n a sufficiently extended sense any prose statement could be called ambiguous" (1). This new claim effectively cuts across any false distinction between poetic language and prose by positing all language use as a potential site for ambiguity. Although Empson's critical focus in *Ambiguity* is poetry, he repeatedly acknowledges ambiguity as a general linguistic resource for all literary works within a given field of cultural production: "'Ambiguity' itself can mean an indecision as to what you mean, an intention to mean several things, a probability that one or other or both of two things has been meant, and the fact that a statement has several meanings" (5–6).

In Empson's hands, ambiguity becomes an effective tool for literary analysis because it involves an aesthetic "heightening of effect" through "verbal subtleties"; as such, ambiguity is inseparable from both the semantic and formal properties of literary texts. Nouns, verbs, adjectives, adverbs, even prepositions, according to Empson, all become sources of potentially ambiguous meaning such that every word, theoretically speaking, possesses "a body of meaning continuous in several dimensions": "[A] word may have several distinct meanings; several meanings connected with one another; several meanings which need one another to complete their meaning; or several meanings which unite together so that the word means one relation or one process" (5).

Strikingly poststructuralist, as well as distinctively modernist, in its commitment to semantic open-endedness and the linguistic proliferation of multiple meanings, passages like this one clearly situate Empson's arguments within larger twentieth-century philosophical debates and aesthetic experiences. The strong correlation between Empson's claims about literary ambiguity and experimental modernist texts that exploit this "fundamental situation" of ambiguity—whereby "a word or a grammatical structure is effective in several ways at once" (2)—would seem to recommend literary modernism as an obvious testing ground for Empson's explorations of literary ambiguity. Indeed, he repeatedly offers readers modernist-sounding statements like "ambiguity is a phenomenon of compression" (31), and

> Both in poetry and prose, it is the impression that [ambiguous] implications of this sort have been handled with more judgment than you yourself realize, that with this language as text innumerable further meanings, which you do not know, could be deduced, that forces you to feel respect for a style. (28)

However, Empson never directly turns his critical attention to the same, if not more pronounced, aestheticization of ambiguity foregrounded in texts of experimental literary modernism, even though literary modernism provides the dominant contemporary cultural subtext for *Ambiguity*.

When Empson defends his "method of verbal analysis" in the second "Preface," for instance, he ironically cites governing modernist sensibilities as the impetus for his research on non-twentieth-century literary ambiguity: "At the time Mr. T. S. Eliot's criticism in particular, and the Zeitgeist in general, were calling for a reconsideration of the claims of nineteenth-century poets so as to get them into perspective with the newly discovered merits of Donne, Marvell, and Dryden" (viii). Moreover, in prototypical modernist fashion, Empson finds fault with nineteenth-century poets who are too concerned with atmosphere to practice certain types of grammatical ambiguity; and when they do, he argues, they often highlight their use of ambiguity through the "vulgar" italicization of words (20, 28).

In *Ambiguity*, however, he is equally dismissive of modern poetry that foregrounds "straightforward mental conflict" and even critically undercuts such modernist examples as "perhaps not the best kind of poetry, but one in which our own age has been very rich" (ix). For Empson, modern poetry that aped Imagist protocols was too "clinical," a "mug's game" (here he borrows Eliot's terminology). In an almost confessional tone, he admits that "I had not read Hart Crane when I published the book, and I had had the chance to" (ix). Conscious of the fact that he never proffered a sustained interpretive account of literary ambiguity in early-twentieth-century poetry when he had the chance, Empson claims that "if I had tried to rewrite the seventh chapter to take in contemporary poetry I should only be writing another book" (ix). Empson's own awareness of his missed critical opportunity with modernist aesthetics ("I had had the chance to")—here represented by the poetry of Hart Crane—indirectly haunts the margins of his entire critical project. The modernist intellectual climate of the day helped to focus Empson's verbal analysis on the "intentional heightening of paradoxes," but he was much more concerned with such use in already established literary works (xvi). As a result, modernist texts that foreground "ambiguity" and "paradox" as central aesthetic devices selectively make their way into Empson's *Ambiguity*, but only as cursory topics of discussion.

At the end of Chapter III, for instance, Empson detours momentarily into twentieth-century literature when he references Marcel Proust as an example of a less obvious form of ambiguity that effectively blurs the distinctions between types three and four.[1] This is one of the only times in *Ambiguity* that Empson cites a novel—an experimental modern novel at that—thereby suggestively pointing to the applicability of his analysis of literary ambiguity to modernist fiction. His passing reference to Proust's *Remembrance of Things Past* (*À la recherche du temps perdu*, 1913–27), however, is notable because he never specifically names the novel, and never directly cites the corresponding ambiguous passages that highlight the complex interaction of temporalities he foregrounds as "valuable" ambiguity:

> [Y]ou remember how Proust, at the end of that great novel, having convinced the reader with the full sophistication of his genius that he is going to produce an apocalypse, brings out with pathetic faith, as a fact of absolute value, that sometimes when you are living in one place you are reminded of living in another place, and this, since you are now apparently living in two

places, means that you are outside of time, in the only state of beatitude he can imagine. (131)

Empson then glosses his own paraphrase of Proustian modernist sensibilities with the summary statement that "[i]n any one place (atmosphere, mental climate) life is intolerable; in any two it is an ecstasy" (131). In fact, Empson holds up Proust's novel as an example of writing that affords the "formal satisfaction" that comes, not from the modernist "cult of 'style'" (form for form's sake), but from the pleasure of a stylistic formalism that "is continually to be explained by just such a releasing and knotted duality, where those who have been wedded in the argument are bedded together in the phrase" (132). Here literary modernism is temporarily showcased for its strategic use of ambiguity, but only in the form of reductive paraphrase that never engages the specific ambiguities of Proust's actual writing.

Empson, quite simply, had neither the critical desire, nor the energy to explicate works of literary modernism that he did not like. Implicit within all of the dodges of modernism in *Ambiguity* is a strong subjective value judgment about where to draw the formal limits of modernist literary experimentation. For instance, when he does analyze literary ambiguity in the verse of two of the period's more notable figures of innovative modernist poetry, T. S. Eliot and W. B. Yeats, Empson chooses selections from their poetic oeuvre that are not distinctively modernist at all, but instead strongly derivative of earlier, more traditional, poetic styles. In the case of Eliot, Empson turned to *The Waste Land* to illustrate how ambiguity of syntax functions. Rather than interrogating sections from the poem where more fragmented, experimental verse forms produce densely complex semantic ambiguities, he cites the first seventeen lines of "A Game of Chess," which Eliot's own note claims was inspired by and written in a blank verse parody of Shakespeare's *Antony and Cleopatra* (II.ii.190). Empson completes his critical sidestepping of Eliot's more challenging modernist poetics by reinforcing his first example of syntactical ambiguity with reference to three (unacknowledged) ABCB rhyming quatrains from "Whispers of Immortality"—again, not "The Love Song of J. Alfred Prufrock" or "The Hollow Men," but rhymed modern verse that closely resembles Empson's own poetic output (77–79).

His subsequent use of Yeats's verse to explore poetic instances of ambiguity that say "nothing" by way of "irrelevant statements," also sets up unfulfilled modernist expectations. Empson introduces the selection as "One of the finest poems of W. B. Yeats," only to cite (again unacknowledged) the entire two stanza poem of "Who Goes with Fergus?" from Yeats's 1893 collection *The Rose*. In *Ambiguity*, therefore, Yeats is represented as a modern poet of literary ambiguity not with a poem from the strikingly modernist *Michael Robartes and the Dancer* (1921), nor from *The Tower* (1928)—both of which were well known by the time Empson was writing *Ambiguity*— but rather with an early poem (from the late nineteenth century) that sentimentally romanticizes provincial Irish folk traditions. Rather than probing the calculated vagueness and semantic ambiguity in lines from "The Second Coming," "Leda and the Swan," or "Among School Children," Empson concludes the sixth type of ambiguity chapter with an example of modern poetry that is, as is the case with his example from *The Waste Land*, poetically derivative in both its form and subject matter. Unlike Eliot, however, Yeats was not engaging in playful irony.

Empson's revealing omission of literary modernism from sustained critical scrutiny in *Ambiguity* is further highlighted when, in the second "Preface," he specifically credits Robert Graves as the "inventor" of and inspiration for his method of close verbal analysis (xiv). The critical work to which he refers, yet again does not actually name, is *A Survey of Modernist Poetry* (1927); and the specific chapter that captured his attention was the one in which poet-critics Laura Riding *and* Robert Graves analyze an unpunctuated version of Shakespeare's *Sonnet 129*. Incidentally, the chapter is entitled "Wm. Shakespeare and E. E. Cummings: A Study in Original Punctuation and Spelling," so Empson necessarily also read their analysis of Cummings's experimental literary form, which concludes that the poet's "unconventional typography improves the accuracy of the [poem's] description" (85). Although Riding and Graves do what Empson would not—that is, directly engage modernism's more difficult aesthetic forms and productively explicate the significance of unconventional typography (syntax, spelling, punctuation) and alternative word meanings—they ultimately shared with him a belief that modernist poetry in its more experimental forms had effectively divorced itself from the "plain reader" and "common-sense standards of ordinary intelligence" (9). As their title suggests, they were committed to finding critical ways to read the formal challenges of modernist poetry, and they were convinced that understanding literary modernism required close reading methods to interpret its innovative aesthetic practices (258). Empson's 1931 public defense of I. A. Richards's *Practical Criticism* echoes this sentiment, seemingly unaware of the retrospective irony it casts over his work in *Ambiguity*:

> The matter is a topical one nowadays because so much of the best modern poetry is so difficult to read, and so hopeless of finding fit readers. It is for this reason, I said, that it would be useful nowadays, both for the poet and

public, if the "poetical public" had some process of interpretation for the verbal subtleties involved in poetry. (*Letters*, 30)

In 1930, Empson's critical neglect of landmark experimental modernist texts is nothing if not conspicuous.

Like Eliot, Empson was both a modernist critic and poet, but he was highly selective about the types of modernist poetics he valued as actual cultural contributions. If his sparing, misrepresentative use of modernist figures in *Ambiguity* was not statement enough about his preference for modernist verse that appears conservative—when compared to more experimental texts that foreground avant-garde forms and radical ideas—Empson's pointed discussion about elitist modern aesthetics at the end of the book eliminates all ambiguity on this point:

> Not to explain oneself at length . . . is snobbery in the author and excites an opposing snobbery in the reader; it is a distressing and common feature of modern aesthetics, due much more to disorientation and a forlorn sense that the matter is inexplicable (it is no use appealing to the reason of ordinary people, one has got to keep up one's dignity) than to any unfortunate qualities in the aestheticians. That is one of the reasons why the cult of irrationalism is such a bore. (*Ambiguity*, 251)

Empson simultaneously condemns and forgives the more experimental (and disoriented) forays made by modernists into the world of avant-garde aesthetics as poetic misjudgments. Literary movements such as Surrealism, Dadaism, Imagism, and the like, are denigrated collectively under "the cult of irrationalism" and deemed a "bore" because they no longer shock and engage in meaningful ways.

Empson's mixed feelings about literary modernism not only prevented him from engaging modernist poetics fully in *Ambiguity;* he also chose not to make modernism a central part of the textual analysis in either of his two subsequent books of literary criticism that were decidedly shaped by his work in *Ambiguity.* He similarly circumvents literary modernism in *Some Versions of Pastoral* (1935), where prominent figures such as Proust, Faulkner, Kafka, Hemingway, Dostoyevsky, Stein, and Lawrence are considered in passing, but left underdeveloped as examples of writers and literary texts that either pervert or ignore the tradition of pastoral conventions, which Empson delineates in literary production from seventeenth-century poetry to the premodernist novels of Lewis Carroll.[2] Chronologically and strategically, his final chapter stops short of engaging literature from the modernist period, especially because, for Empson, many of its elitist aesthetic commitments stand in ideological opposition to the pastoral intentions of proletarian literature, broadly defined as "by the people, for the people, and about the people" (13). Likewise, *The Structure of Complex Words* (1951), whose very title suggestively evokes the latent multiplicity of meaning characterized by the defamiliarizing aesthetics of literary modernism, ultimately remains dismissive of the modernist examples it cites. "The trouble about the double meanings in *Finnegans Wake*," Empson argues, "is that since they are wholly artificial one cannot tell which way they are meant to go" (65). As a result, he calls Joyce's final novel a "titanic corpse" (66). When Empson returns to *Finnegans Wake*, he negatively compares Shakespeare's overuse of metaphors drawn from the theatre in *Hamlet* to Joyce's "appalling persistence" with puns: "Exactly like Joyce; and the best thing the public can do is avoid noticing it" (68).

Empson's statements on modernist poetry in "Obscurity and Annotation," an unpublished essay that he wrote in 1930—the same year that he published *Ambiguity*—reinforce his troubled relationship with experimental modernist aesthetics:

> Poetry at present is in a difficult position. All the recent good poetry is obscure, and more recent good poetry is more obscure, and becoming more so. . . . [M]ost people will agree that poetry seems, by some inner necessity, to be becoming more difficult to read. (*Argufying*, 70)

From here the essay quickly becomes a throat-clearing defense of authorial annotations, theoretically paving the way for Empson's own inclusion of explanatory notes with his published poetry. "Poets, on the face of it," he argues prescriptively, "have either got to be easier or to write their own notes; readers have either got to take more trouble over reading or cease to regard notes as pretentious and a sign of bad poetry" (70). He labels poetic obscurity "unnecessary pedantry," claiming further that "not to explain a term which competent readers of a poem may have to go and look up *is* an arrogant act" (71, 72).

Not surprisingly, Empson's ambiguous relationship with literary modernism (and its attendant difficulties) is also glaringly evidenced in his insistence that his own poetry be published with extensive notes of explication. Writing to Ian Parsons about the possibility of publishing his poetry in June 1929, Empson qualifies his offer of "about twenty poems" with

> [o]n the other hand I should want to print very full notes; at least as long as the text itself; explaining not only particular references—paraphrasing

particularly condensed grammar, and so on—but the point of a poem as a whole, and making any critical remarks that seemed interesting. And I should apologize for notes on such a scale, and say it was more of an impertinence to expect people to puzzle out my verses than to explain them at the end, and I should avoid the Eliot air of intellectual snobbery. (*Letters*, 6–7)

The allusive use of Eliot's name as an adjective to identify the specific "air of intellectual snobbery" Empson wanted to avoid in his own poetry, at once pays homage to Eliot's landmark contributions to modern aesthetics (even as a model of what not to do) and signals Empson's desire to make his poetry notes function differently from Eliot's: "When Mr. Eliot writes notes to *The Waste Land* so as to imply 'well, if you haven't read such and such a play by Middleton, you had better go and do it at once'—the schoolmaster's tone is an anachronism, it belongs to a time when knowledge could be treated as a unified field" (*Argufying*, 71). Indeed, Empson advocates a strangely tempered modernism that tries to balance the aesthetics of obscurity and complexity with a concern for reader comprehension and accessibility.

More strangely still, Empson himself participated in multiple economies of modernist cultural production and reception. In 1928, the same year he started work on *Ambiguity,* Empson even co-founded and co-edited, with Jacob Bronowski, the avant-garde magazine *Experiment.* The Cambridge-based magazine ran for seven issues until May 1931, and, as its provocative title suggests, was committed to publishing works of modernist experimentation broadly conceived as "all and none but the yet too ripe fruits of art, science, and philosophy" (Haffenden, *Among,* 152). Both Joyce and Eliot wrote letters of praise to the editors acknowledging the magazine's contribution to modernist thought and aesthetic experimentation, and in 1930, Eugene Jolas reprinted a group of modernist pieces first published in *Experiment* in his own Paris-based avant-garde magazine *transition.*

Over the seven-issue lifespan of *Experiment,* the co-editors stayed with their original mandate and consistently published innovative

verse of all sorts, critical essays, fiction, portraits, reproductions, translations, photographs by Cartier-Bresson, paintings by Braque and Ernst, and articles on everything from biochemistry to art and theatre design. Every genre and medium that was new and vital (and very little that could be called phoney with the benefit of hindsight) filled out its pages—and Bronowski even had the cocksureness to reject a proposed submission by Ezra Pound. (Haffenden, *Among,* 152)

According to his biographer, "Empson had editorial control [of *Experiment*] only for the first three issues"; however, even though no longer an official editor for the last four issues of *Experiment,* he still contributed poems and articles to every one of the remaining issues. Ironic, then, that the man who published works like sections of Joyce's *Work in Progress* and Malcolm Lowry's *Ultramarine* in the avant-garde magazine he co-edited at Cambridge should be so dismissive of works like *Finnegans Wake* in his literary criticism. To Empson's credit as an early enabler of modernist works, he helped provide a publication vehicle for a range of experimental literature which he regularly described quite pejoratively as "a collage of logically unrelated images" (*Argufying,* 160).

Empson's reservations about literary modernism are even more perplexing because, at the time, he himself was also considered an important poetic figure of literary modernism. His poetry began appearing in print as early as June 1927, when he anonymously published "Poem about a Ball in the Nineteenth Century" in *Magdalene College Magazine.* However, it was the Hogarth Press publication (by Leonard and Virginia Woolf) of *Cambridge Poetry 1929,* that publicly established Empson's reputation as a modern poet; of the twenty-three contributors, only Empson and T. H. White shared the distinction of having the most pieces (six poems each) published in the collection. In his review of the collection, F. R. Leavis acknowledged Empson's modernist poetics by highlighting his nuanced originality and difficult poetics:

> He is an original poet. . . . His poems have a tough intellectual content (his interest in the ideas and the sciences, and his way of using his erudition, remind us of Donne—safely), and they evince an intense preoccupation with technique. These characteristics result sometimes in what seems to me unprofitable obscurity, in faults like those common to the Metaphysicals. . . . But Mr Empson commands respect. (qtd. in *Complete Poems,* xii)

According to Leavis, the critical chatter around Empson's poetry even led language philosopher Ludwig Wittgenstein—upon his return to Cambridge in 1929—to demand, on one occasion, that Leavis read and explain Empson's poetry to him. When Richard Eberhart nostalgically remembered Empson's status as a poet in 1929, he described his poetry in terms conventionally associated with iconoclastic experimental literary modernism:

> In Cambridge everybody talked about Empson's poetry. His poems challenged the mind, seemed to defy the understanding; they amused and they

enchanted; and even then they afforded a kind of parlour game, whiling away lively hours of puzzlement at many a dinner party. The shock and impact of this new kind of poetry were so considerable that people at that time had no way to measure its contemporary or timeless value. They were amazed by it. Eliot was already enthroned. The "Oxford Group" [led by W. H. Auden] had not yet got under way. And Cambridge was buzzing with activity. (qtd. in *Complete Poems*, xiv)

By the end of 1929, Empson had been transformed into a modern poetic celebrity—at least around Cambridge; Leavis, apparently, had even started citing Empson's poetry in his classes.[3] "The Empson cultus is ubiquitous," wrote one of Empson's contemporaries; "Public readings of his poems are given, as you probably know. Leavis mentions him in every lecture. Some poem of his is to be found in nearly everyone's rooms; even in the possession of people who would not dream of reading the work of an *ordinary* poet" (emphasis mine; qtd. in *Complete Poems*, lii). Modeling his poetry after T. S. Eliot's modernist dictum in "The Metaphysical Poets" (1921) that "poets in our civilization must be *difficult*" (65), Empson's verse is both difficult and erudite.

His conspicuous use of recondite language and densely abstract extended conceits directly links his poetry to both Donne's and Eliot's. In "The Metaphysical Poets" (1921), Eliot called for modern poetry to "produce various and complex results," while commanding poets "to become more and more comprehensive, more allusive, [and] more indirect" (65), and Empson's poetry tried to answer the call.[4] In 1932, when Hogarth Press again published six of Empson's poems in the collection *New Signatures* (along with the likes of W. H. Auden, Julian Bell, and Stephen Spender), the editor, Michael Roberts, made strong revolutionary claims to market the collection, something that J. H. Willis, Jr., in his book on the history of the Hogarth Press, notes and develops further:

> The poems in *New Signatures* vigorously announced the arrival of a second generation of modernist poets on the Hogarth list. The press was once more, if briefly, on the leading edge of modern poetry, a position not enjoyed since the Woolfs had hand printed Eliot's *Waste Land* in 1923. (qtd. in *Complete Poems*, liv)

Such was the modernist company that Empson's poetry kept in the late 1920s and early 1930s, when his poetic output was consistently surrounded by the legitimizing rhetoric of modernist aesthetics. In 1932, for example,

Leavis again included a discussion of Empson's poetry in his "Epilogue" to *New Bearings in English Poetry,* where he compares Empson's verse to that of Donne and Eliot, and then emphasizes the distinctive modernism of his poetics:

> Mr Empson's poetry is quite unlike Mr Eliot's, but without the creative stir and the reorientation produced by Mr Eliot it would not have been written. . . . [H]e has clearly learnt a great deal from Donne. And his debt to Donne is at the same time a debt to Mr Eliot. . . . But it will not do to let this reference to Donne imply a misleading account of Mr Empson. He is very original: not only his ideas but his attitude towards them and his treatment of them are modern. The wit for which his poetry is remarkable is modern, and highly characteristic. . . . [A]ll of Mr Empson's poems are worth attention. He is often difficult, and sometimes, I think, unjustifiably so; but his verse always has a rich and strongly characteristic life, for he is as intensely interested in his technique as in his ideas. (qtd. in *Complete Poems,* xiii)[5]

Empson's first solo collection of poetry entitled *Poems* appeared in 1935 to mixed reviews: "The volume received extensive critical coverage, much of it favorable, though some of the reviewers were perplexed by the density of the verse, and by the allusive obscurity" (Haffenden in *Complete Poems,* xxiv). It is precisely this perception of Empson's "density" of verse and "allusive obscurity" that, for some, places his poetic sensibilities squarely within the characteristic traditions of early-twentieth-century experimental modernist poetry. W. B. Yeats solidified this coterie image of Empson as modern poet when he included one of Empson's poems ("Arachne") in his 1936 *Oxford Book of Modern Verse,* and, in the same year, Michael Roberts again chose to include six of Empson's poems in *The Faber Book of Modern Verse,* claiming "I have included only poems which seem to me to add to the resources of poetry, to be likely to influence the future development of poetry and language" (qtd. in Gardner, 12).

Whether critics liked or disliked Empson's poetry, they consistently argued their positions through his apparent radical modernism. Virginia Woolf's nephew Julian Bell, for instance, criticized Empson's "extravagant" obscurity as lacking "discretion," going so far as to offer the caustic suggestion that "[a]nother use for obscurity, Mr. Empson's, is setting ingenious puzzles for old maids to solve in the *Spectator*" (qtd. in Gardner, 23). In 1930, F. L. Lucas similarly critiqued the distinctively modernist inaccessibility of difficult poets like Empson, but this time in a parody poem entitled "Chorus of Neo-Metaphysical Poets":

> We twist the riddle of things terrene
> Into such a riddle as never was seen,
> And nobody knows what on earth we mean,
> So nobody contradicts us . . . (qtd. in Gardner, 23)

This aesthetic response to Empson's poetry confirms two important things: 1) that Empson was considered a modern poet worth recognizing through parody; and, 2) that his poetry was read as distinctively modernist because of his obscure diction and metaphorically complicated subject matter.

The majority of Empson's poetry was written and published between the late 1920s and late 1930s, which means that he started writing poetry, and continued to do so, during the apex years of Anglo-American modernism. Taken together, the more celebrated critical statements made by contemporary readers about his poems and the publication vehicles that featured his poetry effectively cast Empson as an impressive and influential figure of poetic literary modernism; however, his idiosyncratic versioning of modern(ist) poetics—while reminiscent of, if not directly influenced by the likes of Eliot, Stein, and Pound—was never consistently experimental enough to rank him among modernists who were more conspicuously committed to avant-garde aesthetics. At a time when free-verse experimentation with poetic forms and poetic diction was defining what it meant to be a modernist poet, Empson was still writing verse according to strict rhyme schemes and with an eye to maintaining a consistent iambic pentameter, however loosely. In the *Journal of British Aesthetics,* Empson once baldly declared his poetic preferences: "I am in favour of rhyme and metre in British poetry" (qtd. in Willis, 23). True to his Classicist word, his poetic stanzas are, for the most part, arranged in tightly rhyming quatrains or *terza rima,* and his commitment to elaborate interlocking stanza forms is exemplified in the poems "Villanelle" and "Sonnet," where the practice of form is announced in each poem's self-reflexive, pointedly generic, title. While this juxtaposition of conventional verse forms supplying the material support for Empson's poetic explorations of modernity (such as increased scientific awareness, the ethics of modern warfare, new ideas in psychology, and ever-changing social relations) would, in the hands of more experimental modernist practitioners, become a potential site for contrapuntal irony, Empson intends none.

In fact, Empson's poetic commitment to classical form—in terms of meter and rhyme scheme—makes his poetry sound and appear artificially elevated. His use of traditional verse forms fills his poetry with the poetic archaisms and forced syntactical constructions that were anathema to experimental modernist sensibilities. In order to maintain metrical rhythms in his poetry,

Empson carefully counted feet, and when lines were too long, he resorted to recognizably archaic truncations to excise extra syllables: "ere" ("Dissatisfaction with Metaphysics" and "Rolling on the Lawn"); "ne'er" ("Rolling the Lawn"); "oft" ("Sea Voyage"); and "o'erthrew" ("To an Old Lady"). These efforts were often coupled with Empson's regular use of hyphenated-adjectival epithets to compress his imagery and make it conform to his fixed metrical patterns.[6] However, these are not the only seemingly elevated constructions of fitted syntax in Empson's poetry; consider the forced syntactical inversions in the following lines designed to preserve patterned end-rhymes and rhythms at the expense of lyrical flow: "What though the garden in one glance appears?" ("The Ants"); "Can then go munching on unburst" ("Advice"); "Dwarf seeds unnavelled a last frost has scolded" ("Value Is in Activity"); "Holding it then, I Sanctus brood thereover" ("High Dive"); "(Ambiguous gifts, as what gods give must be)" ("This Last Pain"); and, "It lit, like a struck match, everything by" ("Flighting for Duck"). Because there is no indication from either Empson's verse or his accompanying notes of explanation that such decidedly archaic poetic practices were ironic parody, they read instead as poetic posturing. Against a benchmark of unconventional modernist poetics, Empson seems especially stilted and traditional when he uses dated poetic diction such as "Alas" ("The World's End") and "delighteth" ("Four Legs, Three Legs, Two Legs"), especially when it is completely unwarranted by either metrical or rhyme-scheme motivations.

That said, Empson's poetry does contain individual lines and isolated stanzas that showcase a distinctively experimental modernist poetics. For instance, the last stanza of "High Dive" is driven by an elliptical insistence in tone and noun-verb imagery that is reminiscent of Vorticism and Imagism:

> Leave outer concrete for the termite city
> Where scab to bullet and strong brick has grown;
> Plunge, and in vortex that destroys it, puppy,
> Drink deep the imaged solid of the bone. (*Collected Poems*, 14)

While these lines are suggestively modernist because enigmatically ambiguous, the dangerous "[p]lunge" inward that leads to destruction described in them employs diction that directly recalls specific modernist avant-garde movements: Vorticism ("vortex") and Imagism ("imaged"), even as its compression also recalls uses of language associated with these movements. Isolated lines of his poetry, like "Your well fenced out real estate of mind" ("Legal Fiction"), "This is the Assumption of the description" ("Doctrinal Point"), and "Delicate goose-step of penned scorpions" ("Plenum and Vacuum"), similarly reveal Empson's strong modernist tendencies towards playful semantics, condensed syntax, elevated diction, and conceptual Imagism. In spite of his carefully measured syntax and rhyme schemes, then, such lines still express a characteristically anti-traditional modernist style and attitude.

One poem of Empson's in particular stands out for its formal experimentation, and its opening stanza is worth quoting at length to highlight the rare innovative stylistics he was more than capable of producing. Ironically, it was the very first poem Empson ever published, albeit anonymously, and its title, "Poem about a Ball in the Nineteenth Century," strategically juxtaposes obsolete Victorian content (a nineteenth-century ball) with radically experimental modernist form:

> Feather, feather, if it was a feather, feathers for fair, or to be fair, aroused. Round to be airy, feather, if it was airy, very, aviary, fairy, peacock, and to be well surrounded. Well-aired, amoving, to peacock, cared-for, share dancing inner to be among aware. Peacock around, peacock to care for dancing, an air, fairing, will he become, to stare. Peacock around, rounded, to turn the wearer, turning in air, peacock and I declare, to wear for dancing, to be among, to have become preferred. Peacock, a feather, there, found together, grounded, to bearer share turned for dancing, among them peacock a feather feather, dancing and to declare for turning, turning a feather as it were for dancing, turning for dancing, dancing being begun turning together, together to become, barely a feather being, beware, being a peacock only on the stair, staring at, only a peacock to be coming, fairly becoming for a peacock, be fair together being around in air, peacock to be becoming lastly, peacock around to be become together, peacock a very peacock to be there. (*Collected Poems*, 10)

In this uncharacteristic aesthetic foray into *vers libre* and the modern prose poem, Empson's repetitive and riffing involutions of word play (reminiscent also of stream of consciousness) read like Stein's stylized development of modernist writing through verbal repetition and the riffing recirculation of central motifs. In addition, the poem's style adheres remarkably to the defining principles of Vorticism: constant dynamic movement and aggressive formal disruption via non-linear unconventional syntax.

Not surprisingly, Empson's note for the poem is a complete disavowal of its innovative formalism: "There is a case for hating this type of poetry and calling it meaningless; I had better explain, to protect myself, that no other poem in the book disregards meaning in the sense that this one does" (*Collected Poems*, 95). He then proceeds to explicate the multiple meanings of these supposedly "meaningless" lines: "The main idea is the clash between pride in the clothes etc. and moral contempt for it. *Air:* an atmosphere, a tune, a grand manner" (*Collected Poems*, 96). In the 1935 introductory remarks to the Notes for his poetry, Empson concedes that in cases like this "[i]t is impertinent to expect hard work from the reader merely because you failed to show what you were comparing to what, and though to write notes on such a point is a confession of failure it seems an inoffensive one" (*Collected Poems*, 93). This desire not to offend and to produce modern poetry that was challenging, yet still accessible, made Empson appear almost antimodernist in his dismissive attitudes about the state of contemporary poetry: "But it seems to me that there has been an unfortunate suggestion of writing for a clique about a good deal of recent poetry, and that very much of it might be avoided by a mere willingness to explain incidental difficulties" (*Collected Poems*, 93). For Empson, the very presence of explanatory notes—whether they actually aided in interpretation or not—signify that an "author wants to be intelligible" (*Complete Poems*, 113). They also signify a desire to distance one's poetry from the perceived elitist and unforgiving poetics of experimental modernist literature.

Indeed, Empson practiced a reserved modernism that often appears undecided in its aesthetic commitments. Defending the published notes for his poetry, he argues that "partly they are meant to be like answers to a crossword puzzle; a sort of puzzle interest is part of the pleasure that you are meant to get from the verse" (*Collected Poems*, 112).[7] All Joycean echoes of a commitment to aestheticized puzzling ("the only way of insuring one's immortality") are strongly qualified by this one important distinguishing feature that, unlike the "snob interest" in difficult modernist literature, the "puzzle interest" in Empson's poetry "is not offended by seeing the answers in notes" (*Complete Poems*, 113).

By his own admission, Empson knew his poetry was difficult, or as he claimed "too narrow" and "too specialized" (*Complete Poems*, 123) in its erudite use of scientific vocabularies and cultural allusions.[8] In the self-reflexive notes for "Your Teeth Are Ivory Towers," Empson claims that the poem is a defense of such difficult modernist poetics, but it is one he makes using strict *terza rima* verse forms. He orients his poetic defense specifically towards critics who "often say that modern poetry retires into an ivory tower, doesn't try to make contact with a reader, or escapes facing the problems of the time," but his concluding notes for the poem undermine both the poem's intent and his annotated defensive efforts: "I suppose the reason I tried to defend my clotted kind of poetry was that I felt it was going a bit far" (*Collected Poems*, 110, 111). In fact, within the poem itself, Empson's defense of evasive and escapist modern poetics gets tempered by an equivocal warning about excessive obscurity:

> But if its parts
> Into incommunicable spacetimes, few
> Will hint or ogle, when the stoutest heart's
> Best direct yell will not reach; though you
> Look through the very corners of your eyes
> Still you will find no star behind the blue. (*Collected Poems*, 47)

The conflicted nature of this poem's content (inaccessible difficult poetry), coupled with its use of a traditional verse form, exemplify the tensions surrounding Empson's ambiguous relationships with literary modernism.

The publication of *Ambiguity*, however, drastically recontextualized the reception of Empson's poetry (arguably placing it even more squarely within modernist poetic traditions): prior to 1930, Empson's poetry had only appeared occasionally in various Cambridge publications, often alongside the book and movie reviews he also wrote; with the publication of his 1935 *Poems*, in the wake of *Ambiguity*, Empson is again cast as an incarnation of Eliot's modernist critic-poet:

> Having shown the ambiguity of great poetry, he seems to wish to prove the worth of his own by making it ambiguous, and so ambiguity becomes an end in itself. This is particularly obvious in one or two of the later poems . . . where it is impossible to see the poems for the puns. (Cooke, 59)

To this particular reviewer, Empson's "tendency to use words, which bear not so much the meaning required, as the greatest number possible" was a "defect" that actually got in the way of his poetry. This actually sounds strikingly similar to Empson's own negative criticism of experimental modernist form; however, in the context of this 1935 review, Empson figures as a radical modernist poet: "The whole charge of 'obscurity' against modern verse is, of course, based on a lack of general knowledge of even the 'well educated' reader; Mr. Empson, in particular, will suffer for his familiarity with subjects that baffle even the minority" (59). In review after review of *Poems*, Empson's poetry is described using distinctively modernist vocabularies and situated in relation to other recognizable works of literary modernism: "Mr. Empson, more than any other contemporary poet of importance, seems to raise the question of obscurity in verse" (59). Another reviewer argues that Empson "is a great hand at words, his syntax arrests, and he can manage the significant pun," but that he writes "[i]nhuman poetry," which at best provides "parlour-game exercise" (MacNeice, 58).

However, even when other forms of modernist poetry are evoked to contrast with Empson's, the comparison effectively locates the contrasted poetic forms within a shared field of modernist cultural production. This occasionally became a complicated process as evidenced in a 1935 review that both praises Empson's poetry as "a long way ahead of the pseudo-Eliot-Pound school with their unrhythms, misallusions, and faked significance" and condemns it for not privileging "sparseness and clarity" (58). According to this review, Empson's poetry falls uncomfortably somewhere between the modernist poles of esoteric free verse and Imagistic simplicity. For most reviewers, his poetry has a decidedly modernist sensibility that is measured in terms of obscurity and elitism—this despite Empson's annotations. "His poetry is so self-enclosed, so perfectly and primly circular," writes one critic while reviewing *Some Versions of Pastoral*, "that for most readers it will probably always remain inaccessible—a distant island in the traffic" (Stonier, 62).

Even I. A. Richards, who was from the outset much more reserved and cautious about his student's contribution to modern poetry, configured Empson in relation to the main currents of literary modernism. In a 1936 review of *Poems,* he noted that "At the worst, Mr. Empson will allow [readers] to say that modern poetry is in an even more desperate state than [they] feared," and that the poems "[i]f they do not grow to full life, . . . will show, I think, that excessive demands are being made upon words—not that Mr. Empson's poetic powers are too slight, but that he has been there experimenting with impracticable modes" (Richards, 76, 77–78). For Richards, Empson is a misdirected modernist poet whose commitment to formal experimentation ("impractical modes") and defiant referential obscurity sometimes gets in the way of what is otherwise a "superlative book of riddles" (76).

With the 1940 publication of Empson's second book of poetry, *Gathering Storm,* Eliot's Faber and Faber continued rhetorically to market Empson's poetry as distinctively modernist. The collection's cover copy hails Empson as "the most brilliantly obscure of modern poets" (*Complete Poems*, xxvi).[9] In fact, it was Eliot's strong endorsement of Empson's poetry that—when it eventually came (after continued pressure from Empson)—led to the publication of *The Collected Poems of William Empson* in the United States. Writing to Allen Tate in 1948, Eliot stressed that "until I can get William Empson's poems published in New York I am not so much interested in anyone else," and he later makes another personally invested appeal for a British version of *The Collected Poems:* "I think it would be a great pity if Empson's poems ceased to be available" (*Collected Poems*, xxvii).

In the decades that followed the American (1948) and British (1955) publications of Empson's *Collected Poems,* his celebrated status as an early-twentieth-century critic-poet became even further invested with modernist credentials, even though other mid-century poets like Delmore Schwartz called Empson an "intelligent," but "boring" poet (qtd. in *Complete Poems,* lv; n. 42). Reviewers and literary critics alike somewhat (mis)leadingly figured Empson as a modernist poet on a par with Yeats, Pound, and Eliot. One of the strongest statements to this effect came from John Wain in 1949 when he published "Ambiguous Gifts: Notes on a Twentieth-Century Poet"—an article-length analysis of Empson's underappreciated poetic contribution to modern literature. He begins this essay lamenting that Empson's name has been recently listed in the *Sewanee Review*'s "Notes on Contributors" as "British critic," to which Wain responds, "but in Empson's case it would be a pity if he were known simply as the 'ambiguity' man, and not as a poet" (Wain, 169). His analysis of Empson's poems is remarkably balanced, finding both fault and value in selected pieces. That said, he evaluates the poetry in light of both its "advertised" obscurity and the poet's own claims that his verse contains "puzzles," only to conclude that Empson's "intellectual and elliptical poetry," once again, amounts to a modernist versioning of metaphysical poetics: "a kind of general modernity which leads poets to bring in current ideas and current language, and a strong, at times almost perverse, desire to follow the argument wherever it leads the poem" (178). Wain tests for literary modernism in Empson's poetry and not surprisingly finds it: where "a minor-verse form . . . exactly fits its content" in one poem, and where "a riot of subsidiary meanings" is grouped around a "hub of meanings" in another (176, 177). His critical privileging of Empson's literary modernism even finds its way into passing statements like his concluding observation that "[i]ndeed, [Empson's] two books of criticism are valuable chiefly as a very telling attack on the idea that we understand what we read" (175). Here Wain reads Empson's scholarly work in *Ambiguity* and *Pastoral* as implicit theoretical endorsements for modernist obscurity and semantic ambiguity. According to this view, Empson's critical search for submerged meaning via close verbal analysis not only legitimized modernist aesthetic practice, but, more importantly, it also legitimized the reception of such practice.

In another 1949 review of *The Collected Poems,* the reviewer for the *New Republic* does not simply situate Empson's poetry in relation to landmark figures and texts of literary modernism; he actually inflates Empson's verse into an aesthetic benchmark for modernist poetics: "If we were to work out a coherent view of modern poetry, if it were only to recognize and put a proper value on our various appetites and pleasures, we would have to keep the works of William Empson and William Carlos Williams simultaneously in mind" (Fitzgerald, 182).

The review effectively relocates Empson's modernism within an American context through the contrast with Williams; even though "they represent the extremes of formal difference in contemporary verse," they both share the modernist commitment to uncompromisingly difficult poetics: "the refusal . . . to adopt the formulae that come most easily to the mind, with the most specious comfort or the most fashionable portentousness" (183). For this reviewer, Empson's poems were already "famously difficult": "A few of them resemble quartzlike fusions that will resist analysis almost as long as they will decomposition. All there is to say on this point is that every one of them means more the more it is studied, and that the study is always worth making" (183). What is described here is the "difficult pleasure" of modernism—the promise of interpretive payoff after sustained critical analysis; it is this critical mapping of Empson's difficult poetry onto American versions of literary modernism, to reveal their shared attendant values, that qualitatively justifies Empson's aesthetic choices and marks them as conspicuously modernist.[10]

If the Empson hype sounds excessively repetitive and hyperbolic, that's because it was. At some level, it doesn't even matter whether or not Empson's poetry is as legitimately modernist as it was said to be; his poetry was rhetorically endorsed as literary modernism by a coterie of reviewers (many of them other modernist poet-critics), with the, by this point, institutionalized status of *Ambiguity* figuring as a central part of the evaluation. In similar hyperbolic fashion, A. Alvarez's book *The Shaping Spirit: Studies in Modern English and American Poets* (1958) participates in this public relations work of maintaining Empson's reputation as modernist critic-poet. His chapter devoted to Empson's poetry (subtitled "A Style from a Despair")[11] appears in his table of contents preceded by a chapter on Eliot and Yeats, and one on Pound; it is followed by four more chapters each focused on Auden, Crane, Stevens, and Lawrence, respectively. Sandwiched between these recognizable pillars of modernist literature, however, Empson appears retrospectively as the odd modernist out. Alvarez unwittingly acknowledges as much when he concludes that Empson is important as a "stylist of poetry and ideas" who "took over all Eliot's hints about what was most significant in the English tradition, and he put them into practice without any of the techniques Eliot had derived from the French and Italians" (86).

Indeed, Hugh Kenner noted this comparative disjunction as early as 1950 in a review of *Collected Poems* entitled "The Son of Spiders." His justification for reading Empson's work as inferior to known and established works of modernist literature is a result of "the late twenties . . . being superimposed on the new fifties"; Kenner argues that Empson's poems necessarily pale in comparison with other works of literary modernism currently being read:

> [I]t is because they are occurring in America after rather than before the impact of *Finnegans Wake, Four Quartets,* and *The Pisan Cantos,* three of the most considerable works of imagination of the century, that they exhibit themselves now in immediate rather than proscriptive relation to final causes. (212)

Measured against the *tour de force* modernist aesthetics found in the later works of Joyce, Eliot, and Pound, Empson's poems figure, according to Kenner, "as contrapuntal outriders commenting on certain features of 'period' sensibility accidental to Eliot's analogical drama [*The Waste Land*]" (214). Put differently, Empson's self-contained poetry has neither the "protuberances," nor the "excisions," needed to elevate his modernist practice to the level of Joyce, Eliot, and Pound, who necessarily "provide a context for assessing the limitations of the sensibility there at work" (216). Empson's poetry—far from exhibiting the paratactic poetic structures of formal fragmentation or the dense intertextual networks of elitist allusion exemplified by leading modernists—helped to fill in the modernist field of cultural production between the formally innovative experimental avant-garde and the blank mimicry of conventional forms and traditional literary content inherited from canonized predecessor poets. In this comparison, Empson appears as a procedural modernist, going through the motions of complexity and obscurity, always with reservations.

In a 1933 letter to John Hayward, Empson concludes a discussion about cultural production by pondering, "I suppose most of our Great Traditions are only histories of refusals to follow up opportunities" (*Letters,* 57). By his own admission "half drunk" at the time of writing, his statement resonates prophetically with his choice not to foreground literary modernism in his most influential critical works of verbal exegesis, most notably *Ambiguity.* Even his modern poetry evinces a strong discomfort with difficult modernist aesthetics in the perceived necessity for accompanying notes of explication. As a quick reading through his limited poetic output (seventy-seven published poems) will impart, he was a difficult modern poet because he chose complicated metaphorical subjects, not because experimental form complicated his poetic reception. With the critical long view of modernism afforded by the twenty-first century, it becomes clear that Empson's direct contribution to modernist literature as a poet was negligible. Without question, Empson's poetry participated in the field of modernist cultural production, but it did not define it. In fact, his idiosyncratic version of modernist poetics was developed largely in opposition to what he considered the elitist formal experimentation of foundational works of literary modernism. He practiced an equivocal modernism that, in a 1931 letter, he articulated through (dis)qualifying aesthetic commands: "a poet must not pander to a public, but he must be intelligible" (*Letters*, 30).

This essay has sought to offer a metacritical survey of the multiple intersections among William Empson's criticism, poetry, and literary modernism. Rather than only regarding Empson as one of literary modernism's critics of missed opportunity because he failed to engage representative works of modernist literature with the types of verbal analysis he helped to make so widespread, I have reconsidered him as an unexpected enabler of difficult modernist poetics. Indeed, Empson served to enable both literary modernism and modernist studies because he helped to create a reception environment (as well as helping to institutionalize close reading practices) that supplied the critical means of exploring experimental modernist forms of semantic uncertainty and open-endedness. The very terms the New Critics used to explicate (and domesticate) literary modernism are evidence of Empson's enabling ambiguities: irony, tension, paradox. Empson knew all too acutely that the power of ambiguity lies in its ability to open up critical space for things to be alternative and otherwise—this is why so many modernists exploited it and why *Ambiguity* still has, what one 1933 *Scrutiny* reviewer called "unusual fertilizing power" (Bradbrook, 53). As a methodological primer for close reading literary modernism—and as a modernist text in its own right—*Ambiguity*, one might say ironically, helped set the institutional stage for studying literary modernism by avoiding it.

Notes

1. John Crowe Ransom describes Empson's third and fourth types of ambiguity as "III. Where one locution simultaneously has two meanings, and only one of them has logical relevance. This type includes pun" and "IV. Where one locution has two or more meanings which do not agree very well" (*"The New Criticism,"* 112).

2. T. S. Eliot, Wyndham Lewis, and Virginia Woolf also make appearances in the book, but for their critical perspectives as readers of the texts under scrutiny.

3. According to both John Wain ("Ambiguous Gifts") and A. Alvarez (*The Shaping Spirit*), I. A. Richards also quoted Empson's poetry in his lectures at Cambridge.

4. In 1926, at Trinity College, Cambridge, Eliot entitled his Clark Lectures, "The Metaphysical Poets of the Seventeenth Century." Empson apparently did not attend any

of the lectures, but met with Eliot informally over breakfast to discuss literature and criticism.

5. Twice, Leavis somewhat misleadingly draws critical attention to what he calls Empson's poetic focus on "technique"; however, "technique" for Leavis does not mean "technique" in the Shklovskyan sense as strategically innovative formalism that creates experiences of modernist defamiliarization. Instead, it means Empson's penchant for elaborately artificial stanza forms with strict rhyme schemes and regulated meter.

6. Consider the following representative sampling from Empson's poetry: "nostrum-plastered" ("The Ants"); "glass-cautered," "blood-gorged," and "void-centered" ("Plenum and Vacuum"); "Earth-bound" and "Blue-sea-bound" ("Sea Voyage"); "wolf-chased" ("High Dive"); "Day-cycled," "iron-fruited," "sag-fruited," "sand-born," "mail-dark," and "grit-silted" ("Part of Mandevil's Travels"); "many-fingered" ("Letter II"); not to mention "gulf-sprung," "Snow-puppy," and "rose-solemn" ("The Scales").

7. Empson defends the comparison between modern poetry and crossword puzzles as historically contingent: "the fashion for obscure poetry, as a recent development, came in at about the same time as the fashion for crossword puzzles; and it seems to me that this revival of interest in poetry, an old and natural thing, has got a bad name merely by failing to know itself and refusing to publish the answers" (*Complete Poems*, 113).

8. The pool of allusions in his poetry ranges from classical to contemporary. Direct references to recognizably important figures of modern thought and literary modernism serve not only to self-reflexively legitimize Empson's status as modern poet, but also to signal his invested participation in and engagement with the ongoing cultural conversations of and about modernism. Darwin appears in "Invitation to Juno," Wittgenstein in "This Last Pain," Piaget and Leavis in "Your Teeth Are Ivory Towers," Dostoevsky in "Success," Freudians in "Ignorance of Death," Marx in "Just a Smack at Auden," and both Freud and Marx in "Autumn on Nan-Yueh," along with additional references to Yeats, Woolf, and Fraser's *The Golden Bough*.

9. In his introduction to Empson's *Complete Poems*, John Haffenden argues that the blurb on the jacket of *Gathering Storm*—although unattributed—is Eliot's: "there really can be no doubt that it is Eliot" (xxv–xxvi).

10. In a subsequent parenthetical observation, the legitimacy of such canonical positioning gets confirmed when Empson is compared to another foundational icon of American modernist poetry: "(He has, for example, taken over and extended E. E. Cummings' structural stunt of writing one poem in parenthesis inside another.)" (184).

11. Originally published as A. Alvarez, "A Style from Despair: William Empson," *The Twentieth Century* 161.962 (April 1957): 344–53.

Works Cited

Alvarez, A. *The Shaping Spirit: Studies in Modern English and American Poets*. London: Chatto & Windus, 1958.

Bradbrook, Muriel. "The Criticism of William Empson." 1933. In Constable, 53–57.

Constable, John, ed. *Critical Essays on William Empson*. Aldershot, England: Scolar, 1993.

Cooke, Fletcher. "Poems, by William Empson." 1935. In Constable, 59.

Eliot, T. S. "The Metaphysical Poets." 1921. In *Selected Prose of T. S. Eliot*, ed. Frank Kermode, 59–67. London: Faber, 1975.

Empson, William. *Argufying: Essays on Literature and Culture*. Ed. John Haffenden. London: Chatto & Windus, 1987.

———. *Collected Poems*. 1955. London: Hogarth, 1984,

———. *The Complete Poems of William Empson*. Ed. John Haffenden. London: Penguin, 2000.

———. *Selected Letters of William Empson*. Ed. John Haffenden. Oxford: Oxford University Press, 2006.

———. *Seven Types of Ambiguity*. 1930. 2nd ed. Edinburgh: Peregrine, 1961.

———. *Some Versions of Pastoral*. 1935. New York: New Directions, 1974.

———. *The Structure of Complex Words*. 1951. Ann Arbor: University of Michigan Press, 1967.

———. "The Theme of *Ulysses*." 1956. In *A James Joyce Miscellany*, ed. Marvin Magalaner, 127–54. 3rd series. Carbondale: Southern Illinois University Press, 1962.

———. *Using Biography*. London: Chatto & Windus, 1984.

———. "Virginia Woolf." 1931. In *Virginia Woolf: The Critical Heritage*, ed. Robin Majumbar, 301–8. London: Routledge, 1975.

Fitzgerald, Robert. "Bejeweled, the Great Sun." 1949. In Constable, 182–85.

Gardner, Philip, and Averil Gardner. *The God Approached: A Commentary on the Poems of William Empson*. London: Chatto & Windus, 1978.

Graves, Robert, and Laura Riding. *A Survey of Modernist Poetry*. London, W. Heinemann, 1927.

Haffenden, John. *William Empson, Volume I: Among the Mandarin*. Oxford: Oxford University Press, 2005.

———. *William Empson, Volume II: Against the Christians*. Oxford: Oxford University Press, 2005.

Hart, Clive. "Gaps and Cracks in *Ulysses*." *James Joyce Quarterly* 30.3 (Spring 1993): 427–37.

Kenner, Hugh. "The Son of Spiders." 1950. In Constable, 212–16.

Macneice, Louis. "Mr. Empson as Poet." 1935. In Constable, 58.

Ransom, John Crowe. "Mr. Empson's Muddles." 1938. In Constable, 91–108.

———. "The New Criticism." 1941. In Constable, 112–22.

Richards, I. A. "William Empson's Verse." 1935. In Constable, 76–78.

Stonier, G. W. "Complexity." 1935. In Constable, 60–63.

Wain, John. "Ambiguous Gifts." 1949. In Constable, 169–81.

Willis, J. H. *William Empson*. New York: Columbia University Press, 1969.

CHAPTER SIX

In Pursuit of Understanding

Louis Untermeyer, Brooks and Warren, and
"The Red Wheelbarrow"

CONNOR BYRNE

ALONG WITH the plural modernisms, we might well do these days to speak of New Criticisms. No longer regarding it as a monolithic (or malevolent) critical enterprise, scholars of the New Criticism now recognize the diverse array of nuanced theoretical positions held by its progenitors. But this is not a new development. Nearly thirty years ago, in his retrospective "The New Criticism: Pro and Contra," René Wellek addressed the misconceptions surrounding the so-called movement, just as key New Critics had themselves done nearly as many years before (Cleanth Brooks's 1951 essay "My Credo—The Formalist Critics" is a prime example).[1] If it bears repeating that the New Criticism has been and continues to be misunderstood, this is due to the institutionalization within the academy of only a limited range of its shared reading and pedagogical practices. As Gerald Graff has shown, the New Critics solidified their position with respect to the reigning scholarly approaches to literature of the time—philology and historical/biographical scholarship—by cultivating the serious study of literature as primarily an end in itself, isolating the text for analysis and bringing logical evidentiary argumentation to bear on it, thus at once illuminating the unappreciated richness and complexity of the literary work and gainsaying charges of impressionistic criticism.[2] The legacy of the New Criticism is the university English department as we know it. As Richard Ohmann puts it, the close reading advocated by the New Critics "taught us how to write papers as students, how to write articles later on, and what to say about a poem to our students in a fifty-minute hour" (79). The key text in this process—for both teachers and students—was Cleanth Brooks and Robert Penn Warren's *Understanding Poetry*. This textbook's status as a means by which New Critical reading strategy and pedagogy were proliferated in American universities is legendary. Part manifesto, part guide, part anthology, *Understanding Poetry* functioned on many levels to bring to the classroom a new way of looking at and discussing literature. Brooks and Warren took very seriously T. S. Eliot's imperative that "poets in our civilization . . . must be difficult" (65), and in adopting Eliot's perspective they staked out a secure, and ultimately stable, position within the academy against the established scholars.

Like Eliot's comment, however, this academic tussle was born out of a more general cultural debate over the function and value of literature, primarily poetry. The New Criticism rose to prominence on the heels of a general popularization of poetry and a rise in classroom study of modernist poetry in the United States. But as Craig S. Abbott explains, this popular modernism was of a decidedly different order than the Eliotic modernism espoused by Brooks and Warren, as well as others advocating serious academic criticism. This was the work of poets such as "Vachel Lindsay, Amy Lowell, Edgar Lee Masters, and Carl Sandburg—poets not thought especially difficult then or now" (Abbott, 209). Popular anthologies such as Louis Untermeyer's *Modern American Poetry* (1st ed., 1919) and *Modern British and American Poetry* (1st ed., 1920) were, at least initially, filled with the work of such figures. Espousing a poetic of simplicity and sincerity, Untermeyer—and others such as Harriet Monroe and Marguerite Wilkinson—felt poetry ought to speak to everyday experience, and made it a point to facilitate this process of democratization. Abbott points out, for example, that Untermeyer surveyed high school teachers to get a sense of which poets they wanted to see in textbooks. Abbott argues further that although Untermeyer would eventually include the more complex, difficult modernist poetry of Eliot and Ezra Pound (among others), the popular modernist aesthetic came to be well established, and thus the opponents of popular modernism had much ground to make up (213).

Enter *Understanding Poetry*. With its "Letter to the Teacher," its lengthy introduction, its structured division into sections concerned with specific aspects of poetic discourse (narrative, description, metrics and so on), and its selection of analytic mini-essays throughout (there are over forty in the first edition), Brooks and Warren's textbook provided an antidote to popular modernism—at least in the classroom—by developing both an analytic methodology and a canon with which to support it. Ultimately, however, with a successful professionalized praxis and secure place in schools came what Graff calls a "routinization" of the discipline (*Professing,* 227), as the new and sophisticated approach to literature cultivated by the New Critics was simplified and distorted with widespread use.[3] Hence the claim by opponents of the New Criticism that it "had trivialized literature and literary study by turning critical interpretation into an over-intellectualized game whose object was the solution of petty interpretive puzzles" (Graff, *Literature,* 129). Further, students of literature felt alienated by works of literature as presented to them by the new generation of English teachers. As Frank Lentricchia explains, the New Critics' expert ability to analyze and understand the text itself (especially the difficult text)—its complexities, ambiguities, and ironies—fostered perceptions of the movement as deeply elitist: the New Critic's work reflected a "priestly understanding," and as a result, "too many generations of students came out of New-Critical classrooms convinced that their teachers possessed knowledge of the hidden meanings of texts to which there was no systematic and disciplined access" (Lentricchia, 5).

The cultural tensions Abbott outlines between popular modernism and the burgeoning New Critical (read high) modernism resemble the academic tensions that would contribute to toppling the New Criticism after it had reached its peak in the 1950s and early 1960s.[4] Even well beyond the heyday of the New Criticism, figures outside the university remained vocal against the New Criticism and the damage it had apparently done to both the instruction of literature and literature itself. In his 1969 book *The Pursuit of Poetry,* for instance, Untermeyer is particularly disparaging of the New Critical analyst who in Untermeyer's view sucks the life right out of poetry. These critics treat poetry as "a mine of buried meanings, irresistibly tempting to anyone intent on digging the last nugget from seemingly inexhaustible lodes" (81). "Confounded by a complex of explanatory ambiguities," Untermeyer claims, "the reader, lost in a network of allusions, is too dismayed to enter, let alone find his way through, the labyrinth" (82). Untermeyer's frustration could only have been aggravated by the fact that such an approach—one so trying for students—had become so prolific. As Lentricchia's plural "generations" testifies, this was no fad but an entrenched practice.

Is Brooks and Warren's *Understanding Poetry* to blame for this situation? In some respects, yes. As Alan Golding illustrates, *Understanding Poetry,* along with Brooks and Warren's other important textbook, *An Approach to Literature,* circulated widely. In addition to identifying numbers of printings for each of the textbooks' editions over the years, Golding highlights the editors' selection of poems and poets in order to illustrate that Brooks and Warren's canon was—despite some idiosyncrasies (chiefly Robert Frost)—a high modernist canon (102–7). Certainly these famous New Critical text-books made space for difficult poetry that demanded analysis. But as for the ways in which these texts were analyzed—the ways, in other words, instructors across the United States put the textbooks to use; the ways in which they presented poetic analysis to students—this is not as easy a matter to evaluate. There is much that we will never know about how teachers actually delivered this material.

In other respects, then, *Understanding Poetry* cannot be held responsible for the brand of analysis attributed to the New Criticism by the likes of Untermeyer. For certainly close reading as practiced and promoted by Brooks and Warren was not about uncovering nuggets of meaning, nor was it about solving puzzles. Brooks argues as much in his 1962 essay, "Literary Criticism: Poet, Poem, and Reader." Such "symbol mongering"—as it had come to be known—was antithetical to a New Critical interest in articulating how a poem's form and content are inextricably related, such that to extract a simple meaning *from* a poem—such as the answer to a puzzle—is to do it the worst of injustices (95). If there is a puzzle here, then, it is that surprisingly, in certain important respects, these two opposing camps (for my purposes here, New Critical editors Brooks and Warren, and Louis Untermeyer, popular anthologist and amateur critic) share a similar approach to reading and understanding literature—one that treats poetry as poetry without losing sight of its propensity to excite the emotions as well as the intellect.

The seeming antipathy between these figures is thus deceptive. To illustrate the complications inherent in this ostensible conflict, this essay examines a small but significant area of ground shared by these opponents: William Carlos Williams's famous poem, "The Red Wheelbarrow." Both Brooks and Warren's textbooks and Untermeyer's anthologies and critical work address Williams's poem at length and, importantly, arrive at similar conclusions about it. By reading closely each of their responses to Williams's poem, I complicate the picture put forth by Abbott of the divide between popular and high modernism, and between the advocates thereof. "The Red Wheelbarrow" is an appropriate ground for comparison for a number of reasons. First, Untermeyer, along with other opponents of the New Criticism, turns to the poem in order to ground his critique of New Criticism, a curious situation given Williams's secure position today within the modernist canon—a canon that still bears the imprint of the New Criticism. Williams was never really a New Critical favorite, so it would be inaccurate to position his work squarely within the New Critical high modernist canon (Williams's well-known disgust at Eliot's *The Waste Land* suggests as much). But he was certainly "making it new," and his inclusion in *Understanding Poetry* and *An Approach* to *Literature* signals that Brooks and Warren recognized this. His presence in Untermeyer, moreover, attests to the fact that such seeming advocates of popular modernism were, like the New Critics, reshaping their own canon— and moreover, were doing so according to certain critical assumptions that accord to a degree with the more serious and professionalized aims of the New Criticism.

The similar ways in which Brooks and Warren and Untermeyer understand "The Red Wheelbarrow" illustrates both the flexibility of New Critical analysis and the critical acumen displayed by the extra-academic Untermeyer. Like more recent work by critics re-examining important distinctions among New Critics, and work considering the similarities between New Critics and their critical descendants and opponents,[5] my discussion advocates a reconsideration of the relationship between documents like *Understanding Poetry* and Untermeyer's anthologies, attending to the points at which they intersect, while also recognizing that both were subject to change over time. In order to counter the persistent typical perception of New Critical analysis—and, moreover, of literary criticism in general—as essentially elitist and excessively difficult, critics would do well to consider such meeting points between academic and popular discourse. Doing so can break down the barriers, both personal and cultural, that continue to limit the roles of literature and criticism according to an unfortunate cultural divide.

OUTSIDE *Spring and All,* which appeared in 1923, Williams's "The Red Wheelbarrow" first appeared in a collection compiled by William Rose Benét entitled *Fifty Poets: An American Auto-Anthology* (1933). Benét assembled the anthology to give voice to some of his favorite modern American poets: "I thought it would be especially interesting to write to those I conceived to be the best fifty poets in America and to see whether it were not possible for them to select from all their published work one of their shorter poems by which they would like to be remembered" (vii). Benét asked the poets, "what poem of yours would you choose to represent you?" (vii) and requested an explanation for their particular choice, expressing his interest in the events surrounding its inception (viii). Williams was forthcoming in his response:

> I am enclosing a favorite short poem of mine for your anthology with the paragraph to accompany it which you asked for. It's a nice idea. The wheelbarrow in question stood outside the window of an old negro's house on a back street in the suburb where I live. It was pouring rain and there were white chickens walking about in it. The sight impressed me somehow as

about the most important, the most integral that it had ever been my pleasure to gaze upon. And the meter though no more than a fragment succeeds in portraying this pleasure flawlessly, even it succeeds in denoting a certain unquenchable exaltation—in fact I find the poem quite perfect. (60)

By contrast, Williams's friend and fellow proponent of the "new" literature, Ezra Pound, responded much less agreeably to Benét's request. "I invited the vials of Mr. Ezra Pound's wrath," writes Benét, recounting Pound's convictions that the collection would "aid in further muddling the critical sense (if any) of the pore bloody ole public"; that Benét and his colleagues were "preserving mildew" and "falsifying critical standards"; and that their anthology would contain only the "'sobstuff' of the 'personal touch'" despised by Pound (qtd. in Benét, ix, x). Pound's typical nastiness springs from his distaste for anthologies, but it also falls in line with the sentiments of the new generation of critics in advocating a more sophisticated, critical approach to literature. Indeed, other notable figures also recoiled from such an apparently anticritical, antimodern anthology, if less violently. According to Benét, E. E. Cummings recommended not one of his own poems but one of Marianne Moore's; New Critical heavyweight-to-be, John Crowe Ransom, neglected to respond despite several attempts made by Benét to reach him; and, unsurprisingly, ruling literary patriarch T. S. Eliot also declined to participate: "I have no poem which I should care to have presented to the public as my favorite. I am very sorry, but I am afraid there is nothing to be done about it" (Eliot in Benét, viii).

"The Red Wheelbarrow," now one of modernism's most identifiable poems, thus begins its anthology career in a collection deemed inappropriate, even detrimental, by many of the figures whose work has come to constitute—and who had a hand, through their criticism, in constituting—the modernist canon. As noted above, Williams's place in this canon has been secured in recent years, but it was not a given then. The position he occupies within *Fifty Poets*—one in relative opposition to Pound and Eliot, who would not allow their work to appear in such a context—speaks to his liminal position within this cultural debate. On the one hand, for instance, Williams disliked Eliot's poetry, especially *The Waste Land*, which in Williams's estimate "gave the poem back to the academics" (*Autobiography,* 146); and Williams's critical work was far less important to him and far less systematic than both Eliot's and Pound's. On the other hand, however, much of Williams's work aligns with the Poundian imagism so important to the modernist break with tradition. Williams's placement in *Fifty Poets* thus points nicely to his status as a bridge, as it were, between these two rival factions; moreover,

it presages his ultimate position with respect to the New Critical and Untermeyerian anthologies.

Turning first to Untermeyer's Williams, note that "The Red Wheelbarrow" is used in fact to bolster the point made in *The Pursuit of Poetry* about
the "dismayed" reader in the New Critical labyrinth of literary analysis. For
Untermeyer, the poem has been subjected to "the academic wrecker who
tears into a poem and reduces it to a pile of literary rubble" (86):

> [It] has been subjected to interpretations that are as absurd as they are
> astonishing. Looking for the ineluctable meaning beyond the meaning,
> one searcher found that the solid utility of the wheelbarrow was a stand-
> ing reproof to the short-lived foolishness of the chickens, that the poem
> was a picture of contemporary life with its utilitarian values ignored by the
> younger generation, while another explicator discovered that Williams was
> making a veiled statement about sexuality, the hard male impulse (red) being
> pitted against a flutteringly female (white) virginity. (85–86)

Such readings, anathema to Untermeyer, are the same kind of "absurd" interpretations he describes the "young offshoots of New Criticism" giving in
response to his showing them Lewis Carroll's "The Walrus and the Carpen-
ter," of which they were of course, as modern critics, unaware:

> One of the students maintained that the poem was an allegory of the world
> today, its speed, its cruelty, its apathy, its loss of security—"the fate of the
> oysters shows that we rush too fast, that we cannot trust anyone, and that
> no one cares." Another found that the meaning of the poem was in the lines
> about the quantity of sand:
>
> > *"If this were only cleared away,"*
> > *They said, "it would be grand."*
>
> "That is a symbol of the poverty that surrounds us," declared the young
> critic, "and it is an appeal for us to clear up the mess."
>
> A more startling interpretation was presented by a student who was
> specializing in political economy. He saw the figure of the Carpenter as the
> image of Soviet Russia, the Walrus as its weak willing ally, and the Oysters
> as the gullible satellites who were bound to be gobbled up. (84)

To Untermeyer's pleasure and relief, however, there is a student in the class
yet uncorrupted by the critical disease: "Only one student—a fifteen-year-old

girl who had not been sufficiently exposed to the New Criticism—ventured a bald opinion. 'I may be wrong,' she said timidly, 'but I thought it was funny'" (84). Not needing to belabor the obvious, from here Untermeyer's discussion moves coolly to something new. This last student's response to Carroll's poem is clearly the proper one, and for Untermeyer responses to Williams's poem ought naturally to display the same degree of honesty, without searching reductively for a single—and comically elaborate—meaning and thus reducing the pleasure afforded by the poem.

Untermeyer first includes "The Red Wheelbarrow" in one of his anthologies in the 1950 edition of *Modern American Poetry*. Because these collections are not explicitly instructive, however, a better place to look to see his thoughts on the poem is *The Pursuit of Poetry*. The semi-anthological, semi-instructional work announces itself as "a guide to [poetry's] understanding and appreciation with an explanation of its forms and a dictionary of poetic terms." Its aversion to the criticism of the academy is clear, as in his foreword Untermeyer asserts that "The book is not addressed to the advanced scholar or to the trained analyst" (11). It need not be, for as Untermeyer maintains (admittedly somewhat naively), "Poetry presented no problems either to the ancients or to those who, until the industrial revolution, lived on the land. Its comprehension was there from the beginning; the poetic impulse and its reception were taken for granted. Poems were not difficult to understand" (36). Published well after the advent and rise to prominence of New Criticism, Untermeyer's text looks back to a foregone age of poetic simplicity, lamenting its loss. *The Pursuit of Poetry*'s prologue— seventeenth-century poet Edmund Waller's "Of English Verse"—multiplies this sense of nostalgia, as Untermeyer harks back to a poet himself harking back:

> But who can hope his lines should long
> Last in a daily changing tongue?
> [. . . . .]
> Chaucer his sense can only boast
> The glory of his numbers lost!
> Years have defaced his matchless strain,
> And yet he did not sing in vain. (9)

Untermeyer's choice of Waller's poem may also very well reflect his suspicion of the modern turn from traditional form, in which case his taste for Williams is, again, curious (albeit telling of his taste for certain forms of difficulty, despite his assertions to the contrary).

The Pursuit of Poetry is full of jabs at the "advanced scholar" and the "trained critic," one of the most amusing of which is a lengthy digression on the subject of gardening. Untermeyer could hardly be more heavy-handed in his critique of the analytic language used by critics to treat poetry, selecting as he does the well-worn metaphor of flower picking to deliver it:

> [F]eeling for poetry is found in countless ways, in none more charming than in the field of flowers. . . . Contrast, for example, the language used by the botanist and the wildflower gatherer. In every instance the common country name is not only more charming than the botanist's appellation but also far more poetic. The object, a flower or a fern, is even more accurately described because it has been more lovingly observed. (37)

In Untermeyer's view, this is the emotion which difficult modern poets neglect but which is essential to the poetic experience. And where else does Untermeyer see proof of this but in Williams's "The Red Wheelbarrow"?

> For Williams nothing was without beauty and a significance waiting to be perceived. An emotion may be stripped to a single sensory image, but bare though the image may be, it does not lose emotional impact. Williams proved it in the verbal economy of "The Red Wheelbarrow." [Untermeyer quotes the poem] The precision, the final effect—the red of the wheelbarrow heightened by the glaze of rainwater and the contrasted whiteness of the chickens—suggests and even intensifies the emotions "that come from everywhere" and emanate from the very thinginess of things [Untermeyer here refers back to a quotation he takes from a discussion of Picasso's notion of artistic receptivity]. (25)

Despite Untermeyer's obvious anticritical stance, however, he has still offered what is essentially a close reading of Williams's poem, attending to Williams's juxtapositions and linguistic concision and thus treating the poem critically as poem even as he stresses its "emotional impact" upon the reader. Indeed, notwithstanding his attacks on the "trained critic," his book is a critical text, with its "dictionary of poetic terms" and measured discussions of poems such as Williams's, which do much more than simply paraphrase—unlike the simplistic allegorical equations and summations offered by the "searching" "young offshoots of the New Criticism."

Of course, the ridiculous overreadings at which Untermeyer scoffs could hardly be classified as strictly New Critical, and so we cannot conclude with Untermeyer that Williams's poem functions as a condemnation of New Critical reading strategies. Quite the opposite: ultimately (and likely unbeknownst to Untermeyer) both he and the New Critics demonstrate serious concern over "the academic wrecker" born of the routinization of New Critical close reading strategies. In fact, amateur status, such as Untermeyer's, is one key element offered up by New Critics as a way to avoid and respond to professionalist routinization. Golding underscores the New Critics' loyalties to writers like Eliot, I. A. Richards and William Empson, who were not entrenched in the university environment and who were poets as well as critics. The goal was "to establish a professional criticism while maintaining a sense of its non-academic, amateur, or maverick origins" (82–83). Ironically, then—and quite tellingly—while New Critic Allen Tate contrasted Brooks and Warren's *Understanding Poetry* with the likes of Untermeyer's and Wilkinson's anthologies in an effort to promote the New Critical textbook, he would later call for a dose of just that brand of Untermeyerian criticism conveyed by Untermeyer's anthologies and, later, his work in *The Pursuit of Poetry* (Golding, 83).

Moreover, as the twentieth century unfolded, anthologies like Untermeyer's would play a major role in shaping conceptions of modernism. Untermeyer's concerns were not, like those of the New Critics, related to the goals of the academy (professionalization, pedagogy, and the like), but still they betray his critical faculty, in this case his awareness of poetry as cultural analysis. So, despite Abbott's claim that popular modernism "was not characterized by intellectual complexity or informed by any sense of cultural crisis" (210), by 1930 Untermeyer proclaimed in the preface to his *Modern American Poetry* that "The poets of the [modern] period answered the demands put upon them by a rapidly changing civilization. They reflected the paradoxical energy of the age and its sterility, its contradictory appetite for realism and fantasy, its skepticism and the faith submerged beneath doubtful searching" (32). Untermeyer makes clear his aim to promote the enjoyment of poetry—as opposed to, we can assume, the lifeless, academic, analytic study of poetry. But the province of this enjoyment includes poems that Untermeyer studiously recognizes are marked by these crises; poetry, furthermore, that generates such crises, such that readers are challenged to re-examine and reform worn-out reading practices. If this is enjoyment, it is certainly not of a simple kind:

> the best of [these contentious poets], oppressed by the dead hand of the past, were effective in their revolt; they destroyed that semi-comatose condition which so often attends the reading of poetry and (being a criticism of bad poetry as well as of the reader) revealed new wit, new vitality, new signals of beauty beneath the surface oddities. (29)

Clearly responding to the new poetic forms emerging in the early decades of the twentieth century—and, even more, highlighting them as exemplary—Untermeyer's anthologies move beyond the gentility widely associated with popular modernism, casting a critical eye on what constitutes valuable modern verse (he even calls his collection a "critical anthology") and promoting an engaged reading practice sensitive to the complexities of the modern age and aesthetic.

Untermeyer's work clearly accords with the modern poetry anthologies that, according to Leonard Diepeveen, give shape to a concept of modernism by framing a narrative of rupture in which modern poetry breaks from a fictitious singular Victorianism characterized by stifling conventionality.[6] Diepeveen's work illuminates the crucial role such simplifying narratives play within literary history, as proponents of burgeoning modes of literary and critical discourse aim to establish firm, and thus necessarily oppositional, positions with respect to their forebears or opponents. Certainly the many New Criticisms were also guilty of such strategic critical positioning with respect to the literary past. More important to my purposes here, however, is the similar distortive narrative about the relationship that obtains between Untermeyer and Brooks and Warren—a narrative that can be destabilized by tracing the affinities between these apparent adversaries, taking account of the ambiguities within their projects.

Such affinities are evident in Untermeyer's and Brooks and Warren's treatment of Williams's "The Red Wheelbarrow," as there are significant similarities between Brooks and Warren's account of the poem in both *Understanding Poetry* and *An Approach to Literature* and Untermeyer's treatment of it in *The Pursuit of Poetry*. The poem first appears in the third edition of *Understanding Poetry*, within the section on "Metrics." The editors discuss the poem in terms of its use of free verse and highlight what they perceive to be the "arbitrariness" of Williams's line divisions:

[T]he very arbitrariness is the point. We are forced to focus our attention upon words, and details, in a very special way, a puzzling way. Now the poem itself is about that puzzling portentousness that an object, even the simplest, like a red wheelbarrow, assumes when we fix our attention exclusively upon it. Reading the poem is like peering at some ordinary object through a pin prick in a piece of cardboard. The fact that the pin prick frames it arbitrarily endows it with a puzzling, and exciting, freshness that seems to hover on the verge of revelation. And that is what the poem is actually about: "So much depends"—but what, we do not know. (*UP*, 3rd. ed., 173–74)

I will consider more fully Brooks and Warren's discussion of the poem's structural arbitrariness in a moment, but first let me emphasize that like Untermeyer—for whom the "precision" of the poem's focus "intensifies" the emotional experience it provides—Brooks and Warren are stimulated by Williams's sharp "pin prick" focus and the sense that the object under consideration is somehow associated with something significant beyond itself. For Untermeyer these are the "emotions 'that come from everywhere'"; for Brooks and Warren, this is the ineffable "so much" of Williams's poem.

Subsequent editions of *Understanding Poetry* and *An Approach to Literature* reveal subtle but key changes in Brooks and Warren's approach to their subject matter, "The Red Wheelbarrow" included. The editors themselves do not comment on the poem in its first appearance in *An Approach to Literature*'s fourth edition (1964), but they do offer a quotation from Philip Wheelwright and ask students if they agree with his take on Williams's poem. Wheelwright argues that the poem's attempt to convey the import of the moment fails because the reader, who can only look to the poem itself, cannot connect to the poet's "personal associations" which lie outside the poem (qtd. in *Approach*, 4th ed., 304). Given its hallmark New Critical attitude, we might anticipate that Brooks and Warren would agree with Wheelwright's assessment, but this is uncertain here; they leave it up to the reader to decide. In the next edition of *An Approach* (1975), however, the editors directly address Wheelwright in an expanded discussion of the poem, arguing that while his criticism cannot be dismissed outright, it is nevertheless worthwhile to consider what Williams means by "so much depends." "Is he not saying," Brooks and Warren ask, "that life is grounded in the world and that we must not lose ourselves in abstractions and intellectual bemusement?" (364). As a basis for their interpretation, Brooks and Warren refer to Williams's aphorism "No ideas but in things" and note that as "a physician with the scientific training of that profession, [he] could have intended that slogan only in a special context; as a reminder of the fundamental concreteness of poetry" (364). I must admit I do not quite follow this last assertion—the suggestion that Williams's medical training leads him to hold that the Aristotelian notion that ideas inhere in things must apply to poetry alone. More important, though, than debating Williams's ontology and its relation to his poetry, is that in terms of typical understandings of the New Criticism, Brooks and Warren's discussion of "The Red Wheelbarrow" makes some apparently very un-New Critical moves. First, they offer a paraphrase of the poem ("life is grounded . . . ")—contra Brooks's own admonition against this "heresy" in "The Heresy of Paraphrase"; and, ironically enough, one that sounds a lot like what opponents of the New Criticism would say of the movement ("we must not lose ourselves in abstractions and intellectual bemusement"). Second, they appeal to the author's intentions—contra Wimsatt and Beardsley's infamous intentional fallacy.

This discussion (and the near identical one found in the fourth and concurrent edition of *Understanding Poetry* [1976]) may mark a response to general critiques of New Criticism—of the movement's notions of the antipropositional nature of poetry, for example, or of its bracketing of the text. But even if the editors do make some concessions, they hardly expose any critical inconsistencies and ultimately still give voice to the position they articulated at the outset of their critical endeavor. After all, *Understanding Poetry*'s first "Letter to the Teacher" addresses the issues of paraphrase, intentionality, and historicity, recognizing their significance, but arguing for a better understanding the specific functions unique to poetic language and structure:

> Of course, paraphrase may be necessary as a preliminary step in the reading of a poem, and a study of the biographical and historical background may do much to clarify interpretation; but these things should be considered as means and not as ends. And though one may consider a poem as an instance of historical or ethical documentation, the poem in itself, if literature is to be studied as literature, remains finally the object for study. Moreover, even if the interest is in the poem as a historical or ethical document, there is a prior consideration: one must grasp the poem as a literary construct before it can offer any real illumination as a document. (*UP*, 1st. ed., iv)

To level criticism at Brooks and Warren's discussions of "The Red Wheelbarrow," as I have done, is thus not to disparage the textbooks' analyses, but rather to highlight their divergence from the stereotyped form of New Critical discourse which Untermeyer sketches, and which ultimately distorts the relatively balanced reading strategies promoted in Brooks and Warren's anthologies.

If Brooks and Warren's analysis of Williams's poem in *Understanding Poetry* is strikingly in line with Untermeyer's, it is even closer in *An Approach to Literature*. While Brooks and Warren place equal emphasis in *An Approach* on the arbitrariness of the poem's lineation, they conclude further that this aspect of the poem's structure turns one's attention—to use Untermeyer's words—towards "the very thinginess of things":

> by refusing to consider syntax, phrase structure, or idea as related to the line division, Williams asserts the minimal, sharply focused "things" and aspects of things so that they stand forth clearly in their own right, whatever their own right may be. Even the word upon—which is certainly not a "thing"—

is isolated in its own special "thing-y" significance. We focus upon "upon-ness" as it were; for this is what Williams uses as the key to his poem. (365)

Thus, faced with "The Red Wheelbarrow," what are supposedly two diametrically opposed reading strategies yield highly similar interpretations: "The Red Wheelbarrow" stresses the significance of experience in itself and underscores the crucial role played by the relations between the objects that constitute experience. Both, moreover, are attuned to the poem's emotional charge, to what Williams himself described (perhaps a touch hyperbolically) as an "unquenchable exaltation."

There is a further irony to this comparison: not only do Untermeyer and Brooks and Warren react similarly to Williams's now-famous poem; while Untermeyer turns it into an anti-New Critical advertisement, Brooks and Warren may well have turned it into an exemplary model highlighting their key poetic theories. After all, the call of the "The Red Wheelbarrow" to experience the poignancy of an isolated moment with its significant related components is almost a perfect analog of the ideal New Critical poetic experience of a single, self-contained poem. If this looks like "overreading," certainly Brooks and Warren could have extended their examination of the poem's particular form-content relationship. Building upon their analysis—considering the relation between the poem's formal structure and its ideas—reveals the continued relevance and effectiveness of their close reading strategies. Brooks and Warren emphasize the arbitrariness of the poem's structure. But by their very own analysis, one would think they could arrive at the opposite conclusion—that Williams is hardly being arbitrary in his treatment of these elements. Consider that Brooks and Warren emphasize both the sharp focus on things in themselves and the concern over the relation between those things—their dependence "upon" something else, that ineffable "what." Given this, they point out that Williams underscores that sense of dependence—that "upon-ness"—by isolating "upon." The next logical step would be to conclude that Williams underlines what Untermeyer terms "thinginess"—what Brooks and Warren term as "'thing-y' significance"—precisely by isolating "barrow," "water," and "chickens," each of which has its own line in the poem, like the isolated "upon." But Brooks and Warren fail to make this explicit and insist upon Williams's arbitrary use of line.[7] Moreover, by separating each of the three compound "things" presented in the poem (wheelbarrow, rainwater, and white chickens), Williams focuses our attention on discrete components of these entities—not on the "wheelbarrow" as thing but on both "wheel" and "barrow" as thing—and furthermore leads us to consider again the sense of "upon-ness," as each of these—"barrow," "water," and "chickens"—depends respectively upon "wheel," "rain," and "white" to fulfill its compound nature. The lineation and syntax are thus crucial to the ideas raised by the poem; Williams clearly employs them with purpose. Even the stanza form suggests the notion that "so much depends / upon," as each group of three words that composes the first line of each stanza is positioned above each of the four isolated words that composes the second line of each stanza. In each case, the three words resting above the single, isolated word are supported by it; they "depend / upon" it.

By offering a closer reading than the close readers themselves, I aim less to highlight the limitations of Brooks and Warren's understanding of Williams's poem than to illuminate the continued relevance of their legacy.[8] Importantly, though, I would not want this attention to specifics to overshadow the famous anthologists' awareness of the affective impact of "The Red Wheelbarrow," for to do so would be to lose sight of key intersections between Brooks and Warren's academic discourse and Untermeyer's amateur criticism—intersections that reveal, on the one hand, the openness of New Critical literary criticism and pedagogy, in contrast to charges of elitism and hyperdifficulty; and on the other hand, the relatively critical eye of this balanced popular modernist reading strategy.

To find something of Untermeyer in Brooks and Warren is thus to make more accessible the oft-conceived fortress of New Criticism, as well as the works which support it. Equally, to find something of Brooks and Warren in Untermeyer is to validate widespread unintimidated critical attention to an area supposedly reserved for specialists. If there is a place to make such ironies clear, it is in the classroom, where students' guards come up in the face of the ostensibly insurmountable difficulty of literature, particularly poetry, and literary analysis. For in the classroom, there is a sense that analyzing literature is inevitably about a new form of symbol mongering, such that the skepticism about over-reading that Untermeyer values in certain of his students has, depending on how you look at it, either faded away entirely, or become so distorted as to turn into an outright rejection of certain poetic modes as poetry.

For instance, upon encountering Williams's "The Red Wheelbarrow" in my introductory poetry class, one of my students stood firm in her conviction that it was not a poem at all, admitting that she had been forced previously to write on it and had "given in," producing what she felt was the required analogical reading (in this case one involving political tension in communist Russia). That for her there were only two possibilities—that such an artifact could not possibly be a poem, or that it was simply a puzzle needing to be solved in order to fulfill a course requirement—is a sign of the obvious gap still remaining between a more hospitable, though not simplistic, approach to literature (one similar to that of popular modernism) and the "default aesthetic" of difficulty (Diepeveen, *Difficulties*, 223) initiated by New Criticism and then distorted by a routinization of its practices. Witness my student who, while continuing to participate in the process of reading with and for difficulty, had given in, or given up, disenchanted by the extreme lengths to which this activity had led her. The irony, of course, is that here the student is unable to identify with the work not necessarily because of the poem's inherent difficulty but because of the cultural assumptions governing her response.

Leonard Diepeveen's assessment in *The Difficulties of Modernism* of the vexing legacy of the New Criticism accords with my analysis of the confluence between the work of Untermeyer and Brooks and Warren. Routinized analysis predicated upon difficulty is, as Diepeveen notes, a "mind-numbing exercise" (243); but importantly, it is one in which neither Untermeyer nor Brooks and Warren engage. And although Untermeyer fails to see past the prevalence of this routine to recognize the nuances of his supposed critical adversaries, the two groups' similarities allow us to recognize such subtleties and correct misconceptions and misrepresentations surrounding both Untermeyer's critical work and Brooks and Warren's New Critical pedagogy. As for "The Red Wheelbarrow," if it continues to puzzle students and generate outlandish readings, we can be thankful that its visible position within a tradition of "difficult" works allows us to shed light on this tradition, so as to understand the formative conditions of its reading practices and unsettle authorized modes of analysis made inflexible by routine.

Notes

1. Both essays are reprinted in the very useful Spurlin and Fischer.

2. See Graff, *Professing Literature*, especially 121–82.

3. Graff , *Professing Literature*, 226–43.

4. Lentricchia's *After the New Criticism* investigates this changing critical and theoretical landscape, taking up the criticism of Northrop Frye, Paul de Man, and Harold Bloom, among others.

5. See Spurlin and Fischer's collection, especially sections II and III: "Reflections since the New Criticism" and "New Approaches to the New Criticism and Contemporary Theory."

6. See Diepeveen, "When Did Modernism Begin?"

7. As Alan Golding helpfully pointed out to me in response to an earlier version of this paper, Brooks and Warren's insistence in this regard may spring from their inability or perhaps unwillingness—given a New Critical organicism—to recognize Williams's use of syllabics. See Robert Duncan's perceptive reading of the poem in "Ideas of the Meaning of Form," in Duncan, *A Selected Prose,* ed. Robert J. Bertholf (New York: New Directions,

1995), 26–29. My sincere thanks also go to Erik Bachman for his most insightful comments on an earlier draft of this paper.

8. Many critics have already established this fact, for example, by tracing the connections between the New Criticism and its theoretical successors in the academy. See, for example, in Spurlin and Fischer, eds., *The New Criticism and Contemporary Theory*, Paul A. Bové's "Variations on Authority: Some Deconstructive Transformations of the New Criticism," 161–84, and Michael Fischer's "The New Criticism in the New Historicism: The Recent Work of Jerome J. McGann," 321–32.

Bibliography

Abbott, Craig S. "Modern American Poetry: Anthologies, Classrooms, and Canons." *College Literature* 17 (1990): 209–21.

Benét, William Rose, ed. *Fifty Poets: An American Auto-Anthology*. New York: Dodd, Mead, and Co., 1933.

Brooks, Cleanth. "Literary Criticism: Poet, Poem, and Reader." In *Varieties of Literary Experience: Eighteen Essays in World Literature*, ed. Stanley Burnshaw, 95–114. New York: New York University Press, 1962.

Brooks, Cleanth, and Robert Penn Warren, eds. *Understanding Poetry*. New York: Holt, 1938.

———. *Understanding Poetry*. 3rd ed. Toronto: Holt, 1960.

Brooks, Cleanth, John Thibaut Purser, and Robert Penn Warren, eds. *An Approach to Literature*. 4th ed. New York: Appleton-Century-Crofts, 1964.

———. *An Approach to Literature*. 5th ed. Englewood Cliffs, New Jersey: Prentice-Hall, 1975.

Diepeveen, Leonard. *The Difficulties of Modernism*. New York: Routledge, 2003.

———. "When Did Modernism Begin? Formulating Boundaries in the Modern Anthology." *English Studies in Canada* 30.1 (2004): 137–56.

Eliot, T. S. "The Metaphysical Poets." In *Selected Prose of T. S. Eliot*, ed. Frank Kermode, 59–67. New York: Farrar, Strauss and Giroux, 1975.

Golding, Alan. *From Outlaw to Classic: Canons in American Poetry*. Madison: University of Wisconsin Press, 1995.

Graff, Gerald. *Literature against Itself: Literary Ideas in Modern Society*. Chicago: University of Chicago Press, 1979.

———. *Professing Literature: An Institutional History*. Chicago: University of Chicago Press, 1987.

Lentricchia, Frank. *After the New Criticism*. London: Athlone, 1980.

Ohmann, Richard. "Teaching and Studying Literature at the End of Ideology." In Spurlin and Fisher, 75–100.

Spurlin, William J., and Michael Fischer, eds. *The New Criticism and Contemporary Theory: Connections and Continuities*. New York: Garland, 1995.

Untermeyer, Louis, ed. "Preface." In *Modern American Poetry: A Critical Anthology*, 3–34. 4th ed. New York: Harcourt, Brace, 1930.

———. *The Pursuit of Poetry*. New York: Simon and Schuster, 1969.

Williams, William Carlos. *Autobiography*. New York: Random House, 1951.

CHAPTER SEVEN

Through Fields of Cacophonous Modern Masters

James Baldwin and New Critical Modernism

ADAM HAMMOND

IN A WORK that predated even his own proto-modernist poetry, Charles Baudelaire, whom T. S. Eliot called "the greatest exemplar in *modern* poetry of any language" (426), produced in his *Salon de 1846* a pre-emptive prescription for a productive and positive engagement between modern art and the city. "La vie parisienne," he declared, "est féconde en sujets poétiques et merveilleux. Le merveilleux nous enveloppe et nous abreuve comme l'atmosphère; mais nous ne le voyons pas" (*Œuvres*, 496).[1] The role that Baudelaire saw for the modern artist, as he had argued in the *Salon de 1845*, lay in discovering the forms by which the shock and disruption of urban life could be redeemed for art: "Celui-là sera le *peintre*," he wrote, "qui saura arracher à la vie actuelle son côté épique, et nous faire voir et comprendre, avec de la couleur ou du dessin, combien nous sommes grands et poétiques dans nos cravates et nos bottes vernies" (407).[2] While Baudelaire's subsequent poetry, however, and many strains of twentieth-century modernism embraced the life of the city, modernism has often been caricatured as an art of despair and disillusionment especially remarkable for its laments about the horrors of urban life. As Desmond Harding notes in *Writing the City: Urban Visions & Literary Modernism*, "a consensus emerged" in the early twentieth century "of the city as a menacing force beyond the capacity of human experience to control or even sometimes comprehend" (13). The text that would become the paradigm of English modernism—"T. S. Eliot's excoriation of the cultural and spiritual topos of London in *The Waste Land*—*the* 'unreal city' of modernity" (13)—enshrined, Harding argues, this modernist antipathy for the urban.

While Harding's work—which considers writers such as Joyce and Dos Passos in order to recover a positive strain of modernist urban thought, or the "possibilities [the city] provides as a site of liberation from the very forces that would seem to crush the individual" (13)—is representative of a new strain in modernist scholarship, it does little to address the role that previous scholarship played in enforcing the increasingly discredited conception of modernism as a city-loathing art form. Indeed, as modernism's origins in a redemptive Baudelairean poetics suggest—and as the very fact that Harding is able to carry out his analysis supports—the "consensus" of which Harding speaks emerged largely from the institutions which arose in the modernist period to account for and interpret contemporary art, rather than from that art itself. This is a view strongly supported by James Baldwin's peculiarly and periodically modernist 1962 novel *Another Country.* Indeed it is a text whose denunciations of modernism's anti-urban bias demand a parallel investigation of its author's ambivalent relationship with the New Criticism, that unabashedly city-phobic and conspicuously Eliot-centered school of criticism that popularized not only the conception of modernism as a form directed against the urban, but also popularized modernism itself. In *Another Country,* Baldwin both vehemently attacks and helplessly reproduces the New Critical conception of modernism, one that attracted him as an aesthetic means of countering the effects of industrialization and urbanization, but also one which, for this very reason, failed to develop a redemptive discourse on the city.

After nearly four hundred pages in a naturalist mode, *Another Country* switches abruptly in Book Three into an idiom that recognizably and polemically engages with modernism. It is a switch signalled initially by its portentous title—"Toward Bethlehem," an allusion to the slouching figure in Yeats's "The Second Coming"—but perhaps most obviously and most self-consciously by the visit paid by Eric and Cass to the Museum of Modern Art. Though it remains unclear whether he does so in his own voice or through those of his characters, Baldwin presents in this MoMA scene the specific grounds for his denunciation of modernist art. As Cass and Eric meet to commiserate over Richard's discovery of their affair, the scene is described as follows:

> They reached the first of a labyrinthine series of rooms, shifting and crack-
> ling with groups of people, with bright paintings above and around them,

and stretching into the far distance, like tombstones with unreadable inscriptions. The people moved in waves, like tourists in a foreign graveyard. Occasionally, a single mourner, dreaming of some vanished relationship, stood alone in adoration or revery before a massive memorial. (402)

At the level of the aesthetic, modern art is dismissed here as garish ("bright paintings"), lifeless ("tombstones"), and—though the critique of the container (the MoMA) and its contents becomes somewhat confused—as monolithic and alienating ("labyrinthine"; "stretching into the far distance"). It is not merely the quality of the signifier itself that comes under attack in this passage, however, but also the absence of its relationship to any signified. Inscrutable, confusing, and "unreadable," the modernist paintings described in this scene are pure, unreferential surface. As such, the paintings are not merely *symbols* of death—"tombstones"—but are themselves *dead symbols:* tombstones whose markings can't be made out. Analogous to Walter's Benjamin's analysis in the *Trauerspiel* of allegory as "in the realm of thoughts, what ruins are in the realm of things" (178), works of modern art become in this scene "ruins": not merely gazed upon by mourners, they are mourning in their very mode of representation. Signposts of unsuccessful representations pointing in vain at their putative signifieds—mere sites of "vanished relationships"—they become utterly detached from the real, purely abstract, and thus merely (and paradoxically for such a "garish" style) aesthetic.

While presenting a similar critique, a passage further on in the MoMA scene reveals also *Another Country*'s complicity with the modernist mode it is so intent on denouncing. Following Cass's initial description of her conversation with Richard, the scene is described thus:

They passed not far from a weary guard, who looked blinded and dazzled, as though he had never been able to escape the light. Before them was a large and violent canvas in greens and reds and blacks, in blocks and circles, in daggerlike exclamations; it took a flying leap, as it were, from the wall, poised for the spectator's eyeballs; and at the same time it seemed to stretch endlessly and adoringly in on itself, reaching back into an unspeakable chaos. It was aggressively and superbly uncharming and unreadable, and might have been painted by a lonely and bloodthirsty tyrant, who had been cheated of his victims. (405)

Here, in amplified form, are the scene's principal arguments against modernism. An ugly, abstract, brashly colored, violent and "daggerlike" art form, it succeeds neither in pleasing its audience aesthetically nor in awakening their critical intelligence; instead it leaves them—like the hapless guard who spends his days in its baffling proximity—"blinded and dazzled." Failing to establish any representational connections with the world beyond the museum, moreover, it becomes involuted, self-referential, and also self-satisfied, stretching "endlessly and adoringly in on itself." This very critique, however, could just as easily be applied to Book Three of *Another Country* itself. While it is possible to read this passage as the free-indirect discourse musings of Cass rather than as the direct pronouncement of the Baldwinian narrator, its analysis of modernist aesthetics cannot be entirely detached from a book that begins in a representational mode just as violent, garish, and disorienting as the painting on the wall. Indeed, this denunciation of modernist self-referentiality is at same time paradoxically a reference to the book's own recognizably modernist aesthetic. That it is unclear who is speaking in this passage only heightens, in ways that further disorient its reader, the passage's hints of self-parody.

Much like the MoMA paintings that attract the narrator's ire further in, Book Three begins decisively detached from the real in a disorienting, garishly rendered dream-space filled with jarring symbols in need of decoding. The content of Vivaldo's dream reads as a clumsily rendered allegory: he is running in the rain towards a high wall topped with broken glass which, once ascended, is revealed as dividing a cold, nightmarish landscape from a pastoral space. On one side is Rufus; on the other is Ida. If the final meaning of the dream-allegory is ultimately irresolvable, its general sense is quite clear. The passage serves to introduce the novel's most conspicuous scene of male homosexuality: that between Vivaldo and Eric. And though a first reading—unaware of the impending context—might not reveal the depth of the imagery, a second shows the scene to be a sort of proleptic phallic dystopia: Vivaldo is torn by "thorns and nettles"; the broken glass takes the form of "sharp points standing straight up, like spears"; the rain falls in "long, cruel, gleaming shafts." Observing the interplay of rain and glass, Vivaldo feels "an answering rearing in his own body . . . such as he might have felt for a moment had there been the movement and power of a horse beneath him" (381); when he falls onto "the rearing, uplifting glass," he "[feels] again the random, voluptuous tug" (382). Even to the dreamer, however, this homosexual content remains hidden behind a frustrating veil of modernist figuration. Vivaldo, much like the reader, is "blinded by the rain beating down" (381) and troubled by his failing comprehension ("He had forgotten—what? how to escape or how to defeat his enemy" [382]). More specifically, he complains—much like the reader seeking to recover from the insistently bleak *Another Country* some positive commentary on the liberatory character of homosexual love—that whatever redemptive kernel might exist in the dream remains obscure to him: he is "made sick by the certainty that he had forgotten—forgotten—what? some secret, some duty that would save him" (381).

While this dream-sequence arguably functions as an implicit critique of modernism, then—exposing how its difficult symbolism, disorientations of narrative, and garish style blunt its political content—it is also a viable target of its own objections. Indeed, while realism struggles to reassert itself within the ensuing detailed and explicit account of the lovemaking of Vivaldo and Eric (384), the narrative seems to reduce homosexuality itself to a parodic symbol of its own modernist representations. As he and Eric lie with "the hand of each on the sex of the other," for example, Vivaldo offers a description of homosexuality-as-tautology: "It was strangely and insistently double-edged, it was like making love in the midst of mirrors, or it was like death by drowning. But it was also like music, the highest, sweetest, loneliest reeds, and it was like the rain" (385). Like the modernist monstrosities that "stretch endlessly and adoringly in on themselves," homosexuality itself becomes in this description a death-like closed loop: a figure of involution and disengagement. And if the "But" clause seems to offer a positive counterpoint, the closing reference to the "rain"—a dominant motif in Book Three— deflates it forcefully. For as in Vivaldo's dream, the rain that falls throughout the chapter serves as yet another self-reflexive figure of the distorting, obfuscating, ontologically confusing nature of modernist form. Describing Eric's preparations to meet Cass at the MoMA, Baldwin notes, "He forgot about going to the store, and merely watched the rain, comforted by the anonymity and the violence—this violence was also peace. [. . . T]he speeding rain distorted, blurred, blunted, all the familiar outlines of the walls, windows, doors, parked cars, lamp posts, hydrants, trees" (393). A violent, abstract, and anonymous veil that obscures the meaning and the urban setting of Baldwin's novel, the rain presents a further manifestation of *Another Country*'s self-loathing modernism.

Though it is centered on notions of self-containment, the pointed ambivalence of *Another Country*'s engagement with modernism is one with a history. It is a history dating back, in fact, to Baldwin's earliest publication, his 1949 essay "Everybody's Protest Novel," where he champions modernism as a political aesthetic preferable to the target of his polemic, Wrightian naturalist protest fiction. According to Baldwin's essay, the problem with protest novels is that rather than offering a credible challenge to a racist, homophobic society, they play into its hands by tacitly accepting its assumptions. In his analysis of *Uncle Tom's Cabin*, for instance, he argues that in attempting to counter the stereotype of black men as savage, angry, and hyper-sexual,

Stowe simply inverts it. Beholden to a racist society for the terms of her rebuttal, she produces a picture of black men as false and one-dimensional as that of her rivals: "She must cover their intimidating nakedness," Baldwin argues, and "robe them in white, the garments of salvation . . . Tom, therefore, her only black man, has been robbed of his humanity and divested of his sex" (14). Baldwin argues that this situation is internalized in the character of Bigger Thomas from Richard Wright's *Native Son*. Bigger too has accepted the racist simplification of his character, and through his efforts to disprove it succeeds only in reinforcing it. "Bigger's tragedy," Baldwin says, "is not that he is cold or black or hungry, not even that he is American, black; but that he has accepted a theology that denies him life, that he admits the possibility of his being sub-human and feels constrained, therefore, to battle for his humanity according to those brutal criteria bequeathed him at his birth" (18). Protest novels, in other words, fight caricatures with caricatures: they resort to the same simplifications of black/white, straight/gay, human/subhuman against which they purport to "protest."

Baldwin's essay sees such simplifying modes of thought as the master-cause of racism, and attributes them to industrialized, urban modernity. If, as Baldwin argues, "It must be remembered that the oppressed and the oppressor are bound together within the same society; that they accept the same criteria, they share the same beliefs, they both alike depend on the same reality" (17), he is quite specific in identifying which society and which beliefs they share. It is, he argues, "our glittering, mechanical, inescapable civilization which has put to death our freedom" (15):

> We have, as it seems to me, in this most mechanical and interlocking of civilizations, attempted to lop this creature [the Human] down to the status of a time-saving invention. He is not, after all, already a member of a Society or a Group or a deplorable conundrum to be explained by Science. He is—and how old-fashioned the words sound!—something more than that, something resolutely indefinable, unpredictable. In overlooking, denying, evading his complexity—which is nothing more than the disquieting complexity of ourselves—we are diminished and we perish; only within this web of ambiguity, paradox, this hunger, danger, darkness, can we find at once ourselves and the power that will free us from ourselves. (12–13)

The impetus to reduce a complex and ambiguous creature to a finite set of traits is one that is not only shared by the racist, the homophobe, and the protest novelist, but one which is at the root of a mechanized, positivist, industrial economy. As a result, the naturalist, realist protest novel is generically anathema to the project of true protest. "What is today parroted as [the novelist's] Responsibility," Baldwin observes,

> which seems to me to mean that he must make the formal declaration that he is involved in, and affected by, the lives of other people and to say something improving about this somewhat self-evident fact—is, when he believes it, his corruption and our loss; moreover, it is rooted in, interlocked with, and intensifies this same mechanization. (13)

Baldwin's decidedly political solution to the problem of the naturalist protest novel, then, is one of form rather than of content. As he argues later in the essay,

> One is told to put first things first, the good of society coming before nice-ties of style or characterization. Even if this were incontestable—for what exactly is the "good" of society?—it argues an insuperable confusion, since literature and sociology are not one and the same; it is impossible to discuss them as if they were. (15)

To reject the oppressor's mechanistic reality—"his terror of the human being" and "determination to cut him down to size" (13)—means for Baldwin to draw upon what is unique to literary language and to exploit its resources of paradox, ambiguity, and obscurity in order to challenge that reality's most fundamental assumptions. In other words, it means to write in the difficult, inscrutable mode so strongly critiqued in Book Three of *Another Country:* modernism.

To endorse an aesthetic of "ambiguity" and "paradox" in the year 1949 was not, of course, to go out on a very precarious limb, nor was it to endorse a peculiar conception of modernism. Indeed, coming at the end of the decade in which critics such as John Crowe Ransom, Robert Penn Warren, and Allen Tate carried out a somewhat hostile takeover of Ameri-can English departments, Baldwin's prescriptions read almost as doctrinaire New Criticism. But while the New Criticism—whose methods are most often seen as deliberately apolitical, ahistorical, and conservative—would seem to make strange bedfellows with a black gay writer who, despite his rejection of the naturalist protest novel, nevertheless did so from genuine political motivation, there is nonetheless much commonality of purpose between them. Though it is often forgotten, the New Criticism in fact began as a political movement. All three of these New Critics—Ransom, Warren, and Tate—were committed Southern Agrarians, and each had published an

article in the 1930 manifesto *I'll Take My Stand.* As that collection's introduction states, the book's purpose was to "support a Southern way of life
against what may be called the American or prevailing way," and its argument was predicated on the simple opposition "Agrarian *versus* Industrial"
(ix). Believing, as Baldwin did, that scientific rationalism and industrial capitalism were to blame for an increasingly mechanized and dehumanizing
modern society, the Agrarians argued for a return to a pre-capitalist, farm-
based economy. As the introduction to *I'll Take My Stand* makes clear, their
appeal was directly political: "If a community, or a section, or a race, or an
age, is groaning under industrialism, and well aware that it is an evil dispen-
sation, it must find a way to throw it off. To think that this cannot be done
is pusillanimous" (xx). Not succeeding in their efforts to elect agrarian sena-
tors and representatives, however—and reluctant to be charged with pusilla-
nimity—Ransom, Warren, and Tate decided upon a different strategy rooted
in literary criticism.

The three-point hermeneutic program laid out in the prefatory "Letter to
the Teacher" from the New Critics' 1938 polemical textbook *Understanding
Poetry* stands as an unlikely call to arms:

1. Emphasis should be kept on the poem as a poem.
2. The treatment should always be concrete and inductive.
3. A poem should always be treated as an organic system of relationships,
   and the poetic quality should never be understood as inhering in one or
   more factors taken in isolation. (Brooks and Warren, ix)

While precepts such as these have generally been taken—and indeed have
functioned in practice—as conservative, apolitical, and ahistorical, recent
criticism such as Mark Jancovich's *The Cultural Politics of New Criticism*
has worked to recover the genuinely subversive intentions behind them. For
readers like Jancovich, the insistence of the New Critical methodology that
attention be focused on the language of a poem could be seen as "radical"
because the New Critics believed that poetic language—ironic, paradoxical, ambiguous, not resolvable to any scientific or mechanical "truth," and
thus "organic"—presented an implicit challenge to the rationalistic bases of
the capitalist economy. As Allen Tate argued in his 1940 essay "The Present
Function of Criticism," literary criticism as it was being practiced—in his
arguably reductive account, historical scholarship and source-hunting which
paid little attention to the language of poetry itself—was complicit in the
industrial economy:

These attitudes of scholarship are the attitudes of the *haute bourgeoisie* that support it in the great universities; it is now commonplace to observe that the uncreative money culture of modern times tolerates the historical routine of the scholars. The routine is "safe," and it shares with the predatory social process at large a naturalistic basis. (201–2)

The New Critics were thus drawn to the difficult, fragmentary, arguably anti-rational work of the modernists, which in their reading of it became deliberately and radically anti-bourgeois, anti-capitalist, and thus paradoxically *anti-modern*. As Tate argued in another essay, "Modern Poetry," such work "resisted the strong political pressures which ask the poet to 'communicate' to passively conditioned persons what a servile society expects them to feel"; and by expressing itself in "rhythms and insights that one has not already heard and known" (217), it promoted an ambiguity- and paradox-attuned "mode of perception" in the reader that served as prophylactic against the mechanistic, black-and-white world view of capitalism. To a writer like Baldwin interested in challenging the epistemological underpinnings of racism and homophobia, New Critical modernism thus represented a surprisingly coherent political strategy.

Of course, there were a number of serious problems with Baldwin's espousal of a New Critical aesthetic. For all their shared opposition to industrial capitalism, the interests of a black gay city-dweller and a group of Southern Agrarians were bound to diverge. A particularly salient point of departure was that the pre-capitalist society to which the New Critics hoped to return America was substantially identical with the slave-based economy of the Old South. *I'll Take My Stand* indeed included a defense of racial segregation, Robert Penn Warren's "The Briar Patch," and laments such as Frank Lawrence Owsley's that abolition and the attendant "loss of nearly $2,000,000,000 invested in slaves" turned the South ruinously over to "the three millions of former slaves, some of whom could still remember the taste of human flesh" (62).[3] As might be expected, then, there was vigorous opposition to New Critical modernism as a politically viable black aesthetic during the Civil Rights era, and this opposition was based heavily on its perceived racism. In his 1963 "Black Boys and Native Sons," for example, Irving Howe cast Baldwin's rejection of naturalism as both premature and immature. In the context of arguing that *Another Country* represented a return to naturalism, he argued that between 1949 and 1962 "Baldwin [had lived] through some of the experiences that had goaded Richard Wright into rage and driven him into exile" (100). This maturation process, Howe argued, produced a realization that "to write simply about 'Negro experience' with the aesthetic distance urged by the critics of the fifties, [was] a psychological impossibility, for plight and protest [were] inseparable from that experience" (114). It was not Baldwin himself but Ralph Ellison, however, who received the harshest attacks for his perceived complicity with New Criticism. Howe, for example, called Ellison "'literary' to a fault" (112). In a 1970 article in *Black World,* Ernest Kaiser, noting the Southern and racist origins of Ellison's adoptive movement and characterizing its practitioners as "art for art's sakers in the extreme" (1), said "the creative writing called for by the New Critics" was "unemotional, uncommitted and uninvolved in the people's problems" (1). It thus failed utterly, he argued, in its putative anti-capitalist program: "It is the antithesis," he said, "of progressive writing and art committed to and concerned with the people's problems and struggles" (1). Written in this cold, apolitical mode, *Invisible Man* stood for Kaiser as a "nightmarish, escapist; surreal, non-social protest, existential novel" (2). As Addison Gayle, Jr., noted in the introduction to his 1971 collection *The Black Aesthetic,* "A critical methodology has no relevance to the black community unless it aids men in becoming better than they are": "such an element," he concluded, "has been sorely lacking in the critical canons handed down from the academies by the Aristotelian Critics, the Practical Critics and Formalist Critics, and the New Critics." By the time of his 1975 *The Way of the New World,* Gayle called the formalism of New Criticism a strategy for eviscerating the subversive content of black art. "To evaluate the life and culture of black people," he wrote,

> it is necessary that one live the black experience in a world where substance is more important than form, where the social takes precedence over the aesthetic, where each act, gesture, and movement is political, and where continual rebellion separates the robot from the revolutionary. (Qtd. in Gates, 65)

Gayle's statement stands as evidence of the vanished credibility by the mid-seventies of Baldwin's 1949 belief in the inseparability of aesthetics, form, and social change.

Baldwin's own rejection of New Critical modernism in Book Three of *Another Country,* however, is based upon a different element. It is neither the racism of the New Criticism nor the perceived conflict between formalism and black emancipation that he attacks in the MoMA scene, but rather the New Criticism's anti-urban bias. The Southern Agrarian opposition to industrialism, to science, to machines, and to "progress" itself, was, one must remember, also an opposition to the spatial locus of these modern ills: the city. As John Crowe Ransom made clear in his contribution to *I'll Take My Stand*, "Reconstructed but Unregenerate," that volume's "Agrarian *versus* Industrial" opposition could also be written as "Rural *versus* Urban." Looking to the South itself, he charged its cities with complicity with "American," as opposed to "Southern," values and located defiance in the countryside: "The urban South, with its heavy importation of regular American ways and regular American citizens, has nearly capitulated to [industrial] novelties. It is the village South and the rural South which supply the resistance" (20). Calling his fellow Southerners to armed violent conflict against Northern forces, he maintained that "it will be well to seize upon and advertise certain Northern industrial communities as horrible examples of life we detest—not failing to point out the human catastrophe which occurs when a Southern village or rural community becomes the cheap labor of a miserable factory system" (23).

As he formulated it in his appeal to conservatives all across the nation to rise up against the encroaching catastrophe of industrialism, "The unifying effective bond between these geographically diverse elements of public opinion will be the clean-cut policy that the rural life of America must be defended, and the world made safe for the farmers" (25). As Ransom made emphatically clear in these passages, the New Critical critique of industrial capitalism exhibited and reflected a spatial as well as racial bias. It could dismiss modernity and its metropolitan centre because its analysis was carried out from the putatively pure, pastoral, agrarian South. But while the New Critics had a distinct space from which to launch their attacks on New York, Baldwin, as a black Northern urban writer, was not only unlikely to see the Old South in the same nostalgic light as they were, but also actually lived in the city against which they railed.

Given the spatial problematic of the New Criticism, it is significant that Baldwin stages his rejection of modernism in the distinctive space of the museum. First, this is important because the institution which mediates between art and the public is denounced as forcefully as the art itself. Indeed, much as the New Critical appropriation of modernist art as anti-urban and anti-industrial became inseparable from the concept of "modernism" itself, so too in Baldwin's rendering does the institutional container become indistinguishable from the artwork it contains. Like the art that "blinds and dazzles" visitors to the museum, the museum itself is described as a "cold, dazzling place" (402); where the art "[stretches] endlessly and adoringly in on itself"; the museum exhibits a similar spatial *mise-en-abîme*, consisting of "a labyrinthine series of rooms" (402). In one of his most characteristically muscular examples of modernist prose, Baldwin writes that Cass and Eric continued their frightening promenade though the icy and angular jungle. The colors on the walls blared at them—like frozen music; he had the feeling that these rooms would never cease folding in on each other, that this labyrinth was eternal. And a sorrow entered him for Cass stronger than any love he had ever felt for her. She stood as erect as a soldier, moving straight ahead, and no bigger, as they said in the South, than a minute. (404)

As abstract, unreadable, violent, and inescapable as the art on the walls, the museum also becomes here a figure of political disinterest and stagnation. Converting all movement and rhythm into stasis—both the "frozen music" of the exhibited artwork and the spatializing clichés of Eric's language ("no bigger than a minute")—the only action the museum permits is that of the vortex, slowly spiraling and folding in on itself.

Forming this synecdochial relationship with the art it contains, the MoMA is significant secondly because it provides an entry into the twentieth-century debate about the proper role of the museum in relation to the industrial city. In *Museums and American Cultural Life,* Stephen Conn reads the "extraordinary institution building" that characterized the period 1876–1926 as responding to the same twin impetuses as those of the New Criticism: "Americans erected imposing edifices of many kinds," he writes, "At one level a part of," and "at another a reaction to the dislocation brought about by rapid industrialization and urbanization" (9). In his analysis of the art museum in particular, Conn reads Philadelphia's Pennsylvania Museum against New York's Metropolitan Museum of Art as embodying a struggle between notably different visions of the museum's role in reacting to urbanization. The Pennsylvania Museum, he argues, took after London's South Kensington Museum and oriented itself as a school and a force for managing the rise of industry. Taking an active role in the city's economy as both a laboratory for the improvement of industrial design and "a place where all city residents . . . might learn lessons to be put later to productive use" (203), the museum was for Philadelphians "an indirect way to increase the value of industrial production in the city's factories" (200). The Met, on the other hand, was modeled on the Louvre, and was characterized by its paradoxical rejection of industry and the urban. Though linked to the industrial economy by the vast fortunes of its founders and donors, and though complicit in promoting a "culture of acquisitiveness" through its department-store-like displays of treasured objects, Conn argues that the Met positioned itself as a "place of ritual" set apart from the forces of mechanical reproduction: "the objects inside continued to retain their 'aura'" (194). The Met-style rejection of modernity, Conn argues, won out over the Pennsylvania Museum's efforts to deal positively with it: "The 'losers' . . . were those who envisioned a different kind of art museum, one . . . which would be not merely a cultural antidote to the vulgar materialism of the late-nineteenth-century world, but an uplifting part of that world" (193). Like the New Criticism that voiced its polemic against industrial capitalism from the perspective of the South, the art museum in New York construed itself as a space detached from and opposing the life of the city.

In this context, the MoMA presents an interesting case, initially envisioning its role as one of involvement with the industrial economy but transforming over time from a laboratory into an archive. Founded in November of 1929—by no means a bright time for the modern economy—the MoMA nevertheless took its roles as those of "establishing and maintaining in the City of New York, a museum of modern art, encouraging and developing the study of modern arts and the application of said arts to manufacture and practical life, and furnishing popular instruction" (qtd. in Alexander, 69). For Hilton Kramer, this South Kensington–style mandate was best carried out by Alfred Hamilton Barr, first director of the MoMA. Under Barr's influence, Kramer argues, "what governed the museum's outlook from its earliest days was a vision that attempted to effect a kind of grand synthesis of modernist aestheticism and the technology of industrialism" (422). Influenced by the rejection of aesthetic hierarchies at the Bauhaus, where "a poster might be equal to a painting, a factory or a housing project as much to be esteemed as a great work of sculpture," Barr nonetheless divorced this Bauhaus perspective from its radical politics. The "great success" of the Barr-directed MoMA, Kramer argues, was that "the aesthetic that originated at the Bauhaus and other avant-garde groups [was] stripped of its social ideology and turned into the reigning taste of the cultural marketplace" (422). For critics like Carol Duncan and Alan Wallach, this deliberate depoliticization made the MoMA complicit with "the ideology of late capitalism." While such a policy engaged the museum in a relationship with the city and with industry, they argue, it was a relationship of simple submission, and the MoMA became "a monument to individualism, understood as subjective freedom" (485). As the "modern" art within its walls ceased to be "contemporary," however, and came increasingly to represent an art-historical period, Kramer argues that the MoMA's role was forced to change entirely. In 1984, the year in which Kramer wrote, the choice was between "MoMA as historical archive and MoMA as a living artistic force" (424). The MoMA's only choice, Kramer argued, was to sever its direct productive engagement with the city and to adopt an outlook "of art-historical formalism"—effectively to sever the tie of its paintings to the contemporary world surrounding them, to detach the signifier from the signified, to turn modernism into a historical and aesthetic phenomenon: to accept modernism, in the most pessimistic formulation, as a ruin.

In Baldwin's 1962 text, this severance of city from artwork is already well underway, though his presentation is somewhat contradictory. On the one hand, the space of the museum—cold, labyrinthine, self-enfolded—is criticized as the apolitical and aloof, "sacred and sterile" (401), preserve of polite society. When Eric first steps into the MoMA, "The museum was crowded, full of the stale, Sunday museum stink, aggravated, now, by the damp. He came through the doors behind a great cloud of windy, rainy, broad-beamed ladies; and they formed, before him, a large, loud, rocking wall, as they shook their umbrellas and themselves and repeated to each other, in their triumphant voices, how awful the weather was" (401).

Employing once again the imagery established in Book Three's opening dream sequence, in this passage Eric runs up against the barrier of triviality that separates the MoMA from its urban context. The lone force of transit between inside and out is the paradoxically "windy" wall of the "broad-beamed ladies": the undifferentiated mass of unthinking politeness which comes and goes, to pun on a favorite poem of the New Critics, talking of Picasso. On the other hand, Baldwin seems also to dismiss the MoMA as an institution too beholden to the mass public. The scene of the denunciation is set, after all, on a Sunday: the one day of the week that a factory worker would be able to visit an art gallery, and a day on which the Met agreed to open only after what came to be known as the "overalls controversy" (Conn, 204). There is a distinct narratorial distaste, moreover, not only for the small crowd of the ladies, but also for the public at large, who "[move] in waves, like tourists in a foreign graveyard" with what Baldwin describes sarcastically as a "democratic gaiety" (402). When Eric finally manages to pass into the museum, it is paradoxically through the sinister interaction of these two competing forces: "People now came crushing in through the doors behind him, and their greater pressure spat him past the ladies" (401).

Baldwin's frustration, however, is not with the presence of the public in the MoMA—not with the fact that they're looking at the art—but with the fact that it can mean nothing for them in this context. His concern is with the urban public's blind acceptance of an aesthetic antipathetic to their interests:

Three young men and two young girls, scrubbed and milky, gleaming with their passion for improvement and the ease with which they moved among abstractions, were surrendering their tickets and passing through the barriers.

Others were on the steps, going down, coming up, stationary, peering at
each other like half-blinded birds and setting up a hideous whirr, as of flying
feathers and boastful wings. (401)

If the "improvement" they seek is more substantive than the "status" that
draws the ladies to the MoMA, these young people have come to the wrong
place. Already comfortable with the "abstractions" of modernist form, no
longer faced with the shock of a contemporary phenomenon but rather in
the presence of Kramer's canonized "art-historical formalism," the MoMA's
guests are reduced to the sort of mechanized slavery from which Baldwin in
1949 believed modernism would save its audience: once inside the museum,
they too become mindless puppets, following whatever pre-determined paths
the MoMA's hallways offer. If they sought an aesthetic capable of reaching
beyond the museum's walls and effecting positive change in the city, they
get instead the despair of a modernism paradoxically displayed only to
mourn and reject the urban. Showing herself an adept New Critical reader
of modernism, Cass looks at the aforementioned "large and violent canvas
in greens and reds and blacks" and tells Eric almost immediately, "I'm beginning to think . . . that growing just means learning more and more about
anguish. That poison becomes your diet" (405). In a passage that cannot
escape the tint of meta-commentary, Cass responds wearily to Eric's question,
"You think that there isn't any hope for us?": "'Hope?' The word seemed to
bang from wall to wall. 'Hope? No, I don't think there's any hope. We're too
empty here'—her eyes took in the Sunday crowd—'too empty—here'" (406).
"Here," amidst the claustrophobic echoes of the Museum of Modern Art,
and "here," in Baldwin's modernism-denouncing-yet-modernist Book Three,
modernism stages its own defeat.

Again evincing complicity with the aesthetic it attacks, *Another Country*
ends by enacting exactly that which it criticizes, producing a bitterly ironic
New Critical modernist representation of the city. The final chapter of Book
Three and of *Another Country* begins with Yves's airplane approaching New
York:

The sun struck, on steel, on bronze, on stone, on glass, on the gray water
far beneath them, on the turret tops and flashing windshields of crawling
cars, on the incredible highways, stretching and snarling and turning for mile
upon mile upon mile, on the houses, square and high, low and gabled, and
on their howling antennae, on the sparse, weak trees, and on those towers,
in the distance, of the city of New York. (432)

The insistent alliterations on harsh "s" and "z" sounds ("sun," "struck," "steel," "bronze," "stone," "glass") combined with the passage's hard, cold, and sharp imagery of "steel," "turret tops," "flashing windshields," and "howling antennae," produce a tableau as verbally violent and alienating as the most garish abstract canvas. The city's "incredible highways," which stretch vortex-like "snarling and turning for mile upon mile upon mile," baffle the comprehension. From the air, the city is an abstraction, populated not by people but by anthropomorphized metonyms: "crawling cars." Fittingly, then, *Another Country,* a book that succeeds in identifying the problem with its own aesthetic mode but remains powerless to address it, concludes on a note of resigned and indignant sarcasm: "and he," the innocent and unknowing foreigner Yves, "strode through the barriers, more high-hearted than he had even been as a child, into that city which the people from heaven had made their home" (436).

Notes

1. "The life of our city is rich in poetic and marvellous subjects. We are enveloped and steeped as though in an atmosphere of the marvellous; but we do not notice it" (*The Mirror of Art,* 129).

2. "The painter, the true painter for whom we are looking, will be he who can snatch its epic quality from the life of today and make us see and understand, with brush or with pencil, how great and poetic we are in our cravats and our patent-leather boots" (*The Mirror of Art,* 38).

3. David A. Davis in "Climbing Out of 'The Briar Patch': Robert Penn Warren and the Divided Conscience of Segregation" places the article in relation to Warren's later repudiation of his support for segregation and active involvement in civil rights activism. He offers the somewhat pat conclusion, "As a young man, Warren fell victim to misplaced values, but he eventually found the vision and the courage to face his heritage and the public and to overcome the split in his own conscience" (120).

Bibliography

Alexander, Edward P. *The Museum in America: Innovators and Pioneers.* Walnut Creek, CA: Altamira, 1997.

Baldwin, James. *Another Country.* 1962. New York: Vintage, 1993.

———. "Everybody's Protest Novel." 1949. In *Collected Essays,* 11–18. New York: Library of America, 1998.

Baudelaire, Charles. *The Mirror of Art: Critical Studies by Charles Baudelaire.* Trans. and ed. Jonathan Mayne. London: Phaidon, 1955.

———. *Œuvres complètes.* Ed. Claude Pichois. 2 vols. Paris: Gallimard, 1976.

Benjamin, Walter. *The Origin of German Tragic Drama.* Trans. John Osborne. London: NLB, 1977.

Brooks, Cleanth, Jr., and Robert Penn Warren, eds. *Understanding Poetry: An Anthology for College Students.* New York: Henry Holt, 1938.

Conn, Steven. *Museums and American Intellectual Life, 1876–1926.* Chicago: University of Chicago Press, 1998.

Davis, David A. "Climbing out of 'The Briar Patch': Robert Penn Warren and the Divided Conscience of Segregation." *Southern Quarterly* 40.1 (Fall 2001): 109–120.

Duncan, Carol, and Alan Wallach. "The Museum of Modern Art as Late Capitalist Ritual: An Iconographic Analysis." 1978. In *Grasping the World: the Idea of the Museum*, ed. Donald Preziosi and Claire Farago, 483–500. Aldershot: Ashgate, 2004.

Eliot, T. S. "Baudelaire." 1930. In *Selected Essays,* 419–30. London: Faber and Faber, 1951.

Gates, Henry Louis, Jr. "Preface to Blackness: Text and Pretext." In *Afro-American Literature: The Reconstruction of Instruction*, ed. Dexter Fisher and Robert B. Stepto, 44–70. New York: MLA, 1979.

Gayle, Addison, Jr. "Introduction." In *The Black Aesthetic*, ed. Addison Gayle Jr., xv–xxiv. New York: Doubleday, 1971.

Harding, Desmond. *Writing the City: Urban Visions and Literary Modernism.* New York: Routledge, 2003.

Howe, Irving. "Black Boys and Native Sons." In *A World More Attractive*, 98–122. New York: Orizon, 1963.

Jancovich, Mark. *The Cultural Politics of the New Criticism.* Cambridge: Cambridge University Press, 1993.

Kaiser, Ernest. Excerpts from "A Critical Look at Ellison's Fiction & at Social & Literary Criticism by and about the Author." *Black World.* 1970. In *Literature and Culture of the American 1950s* (website). 31 May 2007 <http://www.writing.upenn.edu/~afilreis/50s/kaiser-on-ellison.html>.

Kramer, Hilton. "MoMA Reopened: The Museum of Modern Art in the Postmodern Era." In *The Revenge of the Philistines: Art and Culture, 1972–1984*, 394–426. New York: The Free Press, 1985.

Owsley, Frank Lawrence. "The Irrepressible Conflict." 1930. In *I'll Take My Stand: The South and the Agrarian Tradition*, 61–91. New York: Peter Smith, 1951.

Ransom, John Crowe. "Reconstructed but Unregenerate." 1930. In *I'll Take My Stand: The South and the Agrarian Tradition*, 1–27. New York: Peter Smith, 1951.

Tate, Allen. "Modern Poetry." 1955. In *Essays of Four Decades*, 211–21. Chicago: Swallow, 1968.

———. "The Present Function of Criticism." 1940. In *Essays of Four Decades*, 197–210. Chicago: Swallow, 1968.

Twelve Southerners. "Introduction: A Statement of Principles." 1930. In *I'll Take My Stand: The South and the Agrarian Tradition*, ix–xx. New York: Peter Smith, 1951.

Warren, Robert Penn. "The Briar Patch." 1930. In *I'll Take My Stand: The South and the Agrarian Tradition*, 246–64. New York: Peter Smith, 1951.

PART III

Legacy and Future Directions

PREFACE

THIS SECTION of the volume features essays that, together with the Epilogue, meditate on how we might draw upon the New Criticism with the benefit of hindsight—as body of theory, repertoire of critical practices, and cultural development—toward future work in literary studies and neighboring fields. As Cecily Devereux's essay underscores, "close reading" is now widely invoked by diverse commentators from different sectors of literary studies as what we need to revive toward a strengthening of disciplinary identity, health, rigor, value, and continuation. Many advocating renewed emphasis on close reading concomitantly espouse a renaissance of attention to literary form. Others urging a return to close reading, such as Jane Gallop, choose not to accent "formalism" per se. According to Gallop, what we read when we close read is "what the text actually says," whether we attend to form or otherwise. In this volume, Tara Lockhart's essay addresses how careful historical engagement with how the New Critics themselves developed pedagogical methods for teaching close reading can enrich current approaches for the classroom.

A second related legacy of the New Critics is the theoretical attention they devoted to defining the specifically "literary" dimension of texts, critical engagement with which required, in their view, a disciplinary-specific critical lexicon and range of techniques. As Devereux notes, we need to reflect again on how to distinguish "literary studies" from such adjoining fields as history, sociology, and philosophy—much as Ransom and his compatriots did in the 1930s.

Alexander MacLeod's extensive rereading of the evolving careers of several prominent New Critics models yet another way of considering the legacy of the New Criticism. MacLeod addresses how the New Critics, before they were established as such, theorized regionalism with a subtlety and sophistication that anticipates the work of contemporary geographers such as Edward Soja, and from which theorists today might learn. MacLeod's example gestures toward the possibility of recovering little-acknowledged dimensions of the work of New Critics such as Ransom and Warren, apart from their literary criticism and theory per se, and finding in them ways to speak to contemporary theory, both within and beyond literary studies.

While stressing the importance of not discarding valuable legacies of the New Criticism, Devereux also emphasizes the importance of remaining mindful of the question of how to uncouple New Critical techniques and theories from the suspect political projects and institutional practices with which they came to be associated—which subsequent generations of literary academics have rightly challenged. The essays of this volume aim to provide readings of the New Criticism that can contribute to this effort to parse the phenomenon of the New Criticism into its various dimensions, understand different vectors of its cultural politics, and make decisions about what to preserve, leave behind, or adapt for contemporary practice.

CHAPTER EIGHT

"Disagreeable Intellectual Distance"

Theory and Politics in the Old Regionalism of the New Critics

ALEXANDER MacLEOD

Transition and the Individual Talent

In May of 1939, Allen Tate sent an awkward letter to his long-time friend and colleague, Donald Davidson. "Alas, it is not a rumour," Tate opens, "I have accepted the Princeton offer" (Fain and Young, 319). As he delivers this difficult message, Tate struggles throughout his letter to convince Davidson that his reasons for taking the new, higher-profile job have nothing to do with Princeton's prestige, its northeastern location, or the more generous salary he will be earning. Instead, he focuses on the working conditions available at the Ivy League institution. The Princeton job will be in the creative arts program, rather than the regular English department, and the position has been specifically designed for "the writer as writer" (320). It is an opportunity Tate cannot refuse. He tells Davidson that he has always seen himself as a "special man in the academic system" and that at Princeton he will, at last, be "*used* in (his) special capacity" (320).

Although, then as now, most academics would likely consider Tate's move to Princeton as a step up the professional ladder from his former teaching position at the Women's College of North Carolina in Greensboro, Tate knows the timing of his decision will trigger a political firestorm in the tightly knit community of Southern arts and letters that he and his friends helped to establish and expand in the 1920s. He tells Davidson that he can already "hear the gossip" accusing him of "selling out" to "Yankee Money" and that he is well aware that his individual choice to leave the South will be seen as part of a much larger, more troubling pattern of intellectual outmigration, a 1930s Southern brain-drain, during which many of the leading literary artists and scholars left the region behind to further their careers in other places (320). Robert Penn Warren, the youngest key contributor to Vanderbilt's celebrated literary journal *The Fugitive*, left Nashville immediately after his graduation and followed his studies from Berkeley to Yale before accepting a Rhodes scholarship to Oxford in 1930. He returned to Nashville in 1931 for a brief but disastrous limited-term teaching appointment in the Vanderbilt English Department, then left the city for good in 1934. More dramatically, John Crowe Ransom (Tate and Warren's creative mentor and their most influential professor at Vanderbilt) terminated his twenty-three year tenure at the school in 1937 and made his infamous move to Kenyon College in Gambier, Ohio. Just months before Tate delivered his news, Lyle Lanier, another of the important contributors to the Agrarian manifesto, *I'll Take My Stand* (1930), announced that he too was leaving Vanderbilt to take a better paying job as the chair of the Department of Psychology at Vassar College in Poughkeepsie, New York. Although Tate is certainly aware of all these departures, and of his own shifting status within his home region, he feels compelled to restate his passionate support for the South even as he leaves it behind. "I would rather be at Chapel Hill than Princeton," he tells Davidson, and "[i]f a southern institution ever makes me a similar proposition, even with less money, I will take the first train South" (320).

As this letter demonstrates, there is an obvious tension developing during this phase of Tate's career between his desire to project and protect a "special" status for his literary work and his complex, often confused feelings of loyalty toward Davidson, the Fugitive-Agrarian movement, and the South as a whole. Like his friends, Ransom and Warren, Tate struggled throughout his writing life to reconcile his divergent intellectual commitments, and all three men wrestled with a range of often contradictory personal, political, and aesthetic concerns. Caught between the history of their home region and the future of literary criticism, Ransom, Warren, and Tate were forced continually to weigh and rebalance their regionalist convictions and their theoretical ambitions. As their reputations expanded through local, national, and international circles, they faced many of the same challenging questions that continue to circulate in regionalist literary criticism today: Was it possible, or preferable, to be a thoughtful literary scholar while simultaneously maintaining an authentic regional identity? How (or where) did cultural geography and literary theory intersect? Could any worthwhile critic ever be fully committed to "literary" and "regional" values at the same time? Where did these two terms meet? How did they come together? What would a true "Southern Intellectual" look like or do?

These familiar but conflicted classifications—the literary and the regional—have provided generations of scholars with a useful shorthand to describe two different historical phases in the theoretical development of Ransom, Warren and Tate, as well as two very large, but very different bibliographies of critical work that have developed in response to the group's contributions in each of these areas. For one set of scholars, Ransom, Warren, and Tate are read as canonical figures of mid-twentieth-century literary theory and criticism, best known for the widely influential and often controversial aesthetic arguments they advanced primarily in the years after they moved away from Nashville. When most experts address the relative strengths or weaknesses of "The New Critics" and evaluate the signature pedagogical methodologies of this school, they are usually referring, at least in part, to this trio of thinkers and to works they published after 1941, the year that Ransom's volume, *The New Criticism,* officially gave the movement its name.[1]

At the other extreme, a second collection of scholars, interested in Southern regionalism and the historical development of the Southern literary canon, interpret Ransom, Warren, and Tate in a different way. Although this group is smaller than the former group, its members have been more prolific, and, revealingly, the essays, reviews, and critical volumes they have produced mention the New Criticism only tangentially and rarely devote significant attention to works Ransom, Warren, and Tate published after 1941. Instead, they expand the famed trio into a quartet and normally include Davidson in discussion of the work the group produced between 1922 and 1939.[2] For them, The New Critics are not nearly as interesting as "The Fugitives," or "The Southern Agrarians," and though all three groups—The Fugitives, The Agrarians, and The New Critics—were dominated by the same key members, for those committed to regionalist analyses, Ransom, Warren, Tate, and Davidson are celebrated more for the roles they played in ushering in "The Southern Renaissance" than for the national and international revolution in literary criticism they effected in their later lives.[3]

In this essay, I bring these two streams of critical dialogue into closer contact with each other. Specifically, I focus on the key period before the Agrarian movement ended and the New Criticism began—when the opposing intellectual commitments of Ransom, Warren, Tate, and Davidson were held in a temporary interdependence and the group actively dedicated itself to the production of a new model for regionalist literary theory that might somehow blend the core strengths of these two traditionally separate discursive positions. Although several commentators have already paid considerable attention to this shift from Agrarianism to the New Criticism, the reasons and motivations behind the transition remain difficult to identify, and we continue to lack a satisfying critical narrative that might explain exactly how and why Ransom, Warren, and Tate moved so quickly from the messy, overtly political, social, and cultural arguments they endorsed in *I'll Take My Stand* in 1930 to become, only ten years later, the key members of a literary movement which, according to some scholars, "eschewed sociology and politics altogether" in an effort to isolate the literary work from any contaminating contact with the real world (Spikes, 7).[4] This drastic swing from one form of extreme social and political engagement to another equally extreme form of separation certainly re-charted the course of literary theory in mid-twentieth-century North American literature—and it unquestionably contributed to the dominant misreadings of the New Criticism which continue to circulate in the academy today. As I hope to demonstrate, however, the pure literary ambitions of the New Critics and the messy political regionalist loyalties of the Agrarians were never quite so easy to separate.

The Fugitive-Agrarians' quest for an alternative version of regionalist discourse—a new, more theoretically advanced model that might better understand, interrogate, and articulate the complex relationship between a literary work and the real-world social spaces it both creates and represents—pushed this group of friends to their social and intellectual limits. The search opened bitter divisions which would never completely close between Davidson and his former colleagues, and it ignited several long-burning personal feuds within the group. Although the death of Agrarianism may not have led directly to the near simultaneous birth of the New Criticism, the end of one movement and the beginning of the other were not unrelated; and the transition from aggressive political action to contemplative literary criticism can be traced back to the group's passionate and seemingly irresolvable debates over the true nature, purpose, and possibilities of regionalist theory. In the 1920s and 1930s, Ransom, Warren, Tate, and Davidson wrestled with the same questions that continue to haunt regionalist criticism today: Was literary regionalism simply a form of patriotism in disguise? Did it demand and require a blind loyalty to the home place? Were Southern critics expected or forced to appreciate Southern writing simply because both came from the same place? Or could regionalism be theorized in different ways? Rather than simply replicating a stable social reality and mimetically representing a fixed geographical place, was it possible that regionalist discourse might be powered by a different kind of motivation and that, instead of reproducing particular places, it might actively explore the broader social, political, and cultural forces that combined to produce any type of social space?

If we follow the key exchanges of this debate through selected essays, letters and reviews produced by Ransom, Warren, Tate, and Davidson during this period, we can begin to appreciate how advanced their version of regionalist discourse actually was and thus better understand the daunting challenge it presented within the group. The subtlety of the New Critics' old regionalism has never received the attention it merits because the group's brief commitment in this area is sandwiched between the more fervently patriotic work of their collective Agrarian pasts and the fame of their New Critical futures. Caught in a destabilized cultural geography where different politically charged readings of literature, history, economics and sociology were all actively competing to redefine the South, Ransom, Warren and Tate grappled with difficult arguments relating to the discursive flexibility of social space that were far ahead of their time, and they anticipated some of the key insights that currently enliven cutting-edge, twenty-first-century debates on the spatialization of critical theory. Though they seem like strange bedfellows and improbable allies, it turns out that the conservative, anti-industrial arguments Ransom and his colleagues developed as Agrarians in the 1930s share much with some of today's most widely read analyses of North America's postindustrial (and even postmodern) cultural geography.

Patriots vs. Theorists:
The Struggle for a Philosophical Regionalism

Anyone familiar with the early careers of Ransom, Warren, Tate, and Davidson will know that this group never felt completely comfortable locating their work within the restrictive confines of traditional Southern culture. It was, in fact, a collective hostility toward the Romantic stereotypes of Southern identity that had brought them together in the first place, initially for their informal discussion soirées at Sidney Mittron Hirsch's apartment and later for their more formalized work as the editors and recurring contributors to *The Fugitive* from 1922 to 1925. The early anti-regionalist sentiments of the group were easy to identify, not only from the escapist title they chose for their journal, but also in the aggressive editorial foreword which ran in the first issue in April 1922. Readers coming to *The Fugitive* for the first time quickly learned that this was a magazine on the run from "the high-caste

Brahmins of the Old South" and that its contributors strongly believed that "the literary phase known rather euphemistically as Southern literature (had) expired" (Cowan, 48).

The Fugitive's highly stylized flight from the old South was, of course, also a journey toward an alternative set of modern European influences, and it is important to note that the literary inspiration which helped usher in the Southern Renaissance originated not in the South itself, but in literary sources far beyond the rather narrow borders of the region. Even at those earliest stages—Warren and Tate were only undergraduate teenagers during their first *Fugitive* years—it was clear that the relationship between the region they inhabited and the type of literature the Fugitives produced and promoted could never be adequately explained by the mechanistic sociology of environmental determinism and its axiom that "the place makes the poet." As the very public squabbles between Ransom and Tate clearly demonstrated, the Fugitives of the mid 1920s were anything but traditional regionalists: these scholars were more interested in passionately debating the merits and weaknesses of T. S. Eliot's newly published poem, *The Waste Land,* than they were in mimetically capturing an image of the "real" South (O'Gorman, 289).

During the key years of *The Fugitive,* Ransom, Warren, Tate, and Davidson were so focused on their literary activities that it took the infamous 1925 Scopes Monkey Trial in Dayton, Tennessee—and the controversy that swirled around that courtroom—to drag them away from their elevated aesthetic pursuits and back down to the earthy, blood-feud battles of sectionalist politics. With newspapers across the country and around the world running stories about the intellectually backwards South, its crippled civilization, corrupt history, inescapable racism and blinkered, anti-evolutionary Christian fundamentalism, the Fugitives felt an acute need to strike back against this portrayal and promote their own alternative reading of their home place. Years earlier, H. L Mencken's widely read 1917 New York *Evening Mail* essay, "The Sahara of the Bozart" had mocked even the South's capacity to pronounce the words "Beaux Arts" and described the former confederacy as a "stupendous region of worn-out farms, shoddy cities and paralyzed cerebrums" (157). Mencken even comically suggested that in the early twentieth century, a true Southern poet would be as hard to find as "an oboe player, a dry-point etcher or a metaphysician" and proposed that contemplating the vast intellectual "vacuity" of the South forced one to think of "interstellar spaces" and the "colossal reaches of the now mythical ether" (157). For the Fugitives, a group that so openly prided themselves on their refined tastes and their elite appreciations, such insults were particularly irritating and demanded some kind of response.

In a letter to Davidson, written in March of 1927, Tate formally cast off the disinterested persona of the literary critic and initiated the group's regionalist resurgence: "I've attacked the South for the last time," he declared (Fain and Young, 191). Davidson enthusiastically encouraged Tate's rising patriotic passion, and both felt the need to re-contextualize their intellectual work and rededicate themselves to the Southern cause. Davidson had always been the most vitriolic partisan and the most conservative traditionalist in the group, and in later years the dangerous racist and paternalistic underpinnings of his thought would emerge and eventually come to dominate his readings of regionalist discourse. His arguments, some of them collected in his 1957 volume, *Still Rebels, Still Yankees,* re-entrenched the most essentialist patriotic readings of regionalism and served almost as the unavoidable antithesis of the more nuanced theoretical work that Ransom, Warren, and Tate were trying to produce. Throughout his career, Davidson was undoubtedly the most polarizing figure in the group; and in some ways, Ransom, Warren, and Tate's migrations away from Nashville in the 1930s can be interpreted as symptomatic of their more fundamental intellectual movement away from Davidson's way of thinking about regionalist discourse.

In 1927, however, before the gaping divisions within the group became impossible to ignore, there was still enough common ground for the friends to share, and though they bickered continuously amongst themselves, it was easy enough for the Fugitives to direct passionate anger outward against a common foe. In responding to Tate in May of 1927, Davidson fumed that the "progressive" politics of journals like *The New South* made him "sick with black vomit and malignant agues," and that he was "too mad to die just yet, and ichin' for a fight" (Fain and Young, 201). Even the normally more reserved Ransom, the self-appointed philosopher of the group and the most theoretically focused member of both the Fugitive and the Agrarian movements, was caught up in this wave of patriotic fervor and openly wondered how his introductory "Statement of Principles" for *I'll Take My Stand* might "properly indoctrinate" enough writers to make the Agrarian project a success (Young and Core, 189). In less than one year, the group quickly disavowed their once passionate attacks on the old-fashioned romantic values of the South and distanced themselves from their former roles as moderately avant-garde Fugitive poet/critics. The newly minted Agrarians emerged as a militantly conservative group of pseudo-social theorists committed to a defense of the South's traditional plantation economy, a critique of Yankee arrogance and influence, and, most importantly, an all-out assault on modern America's infatuation with scientific positivism and industrial progress. As Agrarians, the Fugitives abandoned their former aversion to Southern

stereotypes and instead took full rhetorical advantage of the regionalist clichés they once mocked. The Agrarians' first symposium took its controversial
title from the lyrics of "Dixie," the near-national anthem of the confederacy,
and when *I'll Take My Stand: The South and the Agrarian Tradition* appeared
in 1930, its contributors identified themselves not as individual authors but
rather as a solid patriotic collective of "Twelve Southerners."

Though the quality of writing in *I'll Take My Stand* wavers dramatically,
and the longed-for Agrarian revolution ended ultimately in failure, the symposium itself has been recognized as one of the most important texts in the
cultural and political history of the South (Grammer, 127). As John Shelton
Reed observes, "whatever else it may be, *I'll Take My Stand* is a very *southern* book" (43). Freely intermingling aesthetic, sociological, religious, historical, and economic concerns, the Agrarians argued that a clear, regional
distinction could be drawn between "a Southern way of life" and the scientific abstraction that characterized the "American or prevailing way" of life
(xxxvii). In almost every essay, the Twelve Southerners criticized the abstracting tendencies of positivist philosophy and they stormed against the "Cult of
Science" and the "uncritical" dominance of "industrial logic" in American
life (xxxix–xl). Rather than endorsing the bland nationalist generalizations
that promised a single coherent but conformist American identity stretching
from sea to sea, the Agrarians, explicitly locating their claims always in the
Southern context, argued for a more diverse understanding of the country's
cultural geography and suggested that such a diversity needed to be protected
from the homogenizing forces of the "American industrial ideal" (xxxviii).

Despite its perceptive critique of industrialism, *I'll Take My Stand* is still a
product of its time and should be interpreted as a deeply flawed text, scarred
by the divisive politics and the systemic prejudice of a troubled period in
the history of the South. For Warren in particular, the symposium—dominated by its conservative "backward" look, racism, paternalistic antebellum
nostalgia, and near mystical embrace of the Southern landscape—was problematic from its very inception and, as the book moved toward completion,
he became increasingly aware of the chasm that was opening up between
his Southern loyalties and his broader literary consciousness. He detested
the title "I'll Take My Stand" and tried to suppress it, and he struggled to
produce his contribution for the symposium, a controversial segregationist
essay entitled "The Briar Patch" (Blotner, 113). When Davidson (the true, but
often unacknowledged editor of the symposium) first read Warren's essay, he
was so angry he almost refused to publish the piece because he felt that the
"'progressive' implications" of Warren's work might "irritate and dismay the
very Southern people to whom we are appealing" (Fain and Young, 251). In

later decades, as *I'll Take My Stand's* influence expanded and generations of Southern scholars organized special anniversary events to commemorate the volume's publication, Warren, who later became a strong advocate for desegregation and the Civil Rights movement, insisted that he be recognized only as a contributor to the symposium rather than as a true member of the Agrarian movement (Blotner, 301–2, 344).

Though *I'll Take My Stand* raises many undeniable challenges and most contemporary critics would likely want to avoid any direct association with the symposium's social or political arguments, the text should still be read as an essential document in North American literary history, especially for scholars interested in literary regionalism, socio-spatial theory and cultural geography. The volume's introductory "Statement of Principles" is particularly significant because even as the essay seems to officially initiate the Agrárian movement, it also provides a fascinating glimpse into Ransom's thinking during this key interval and reveals the latent irresolvable theoretical tensions in his work that would eventually overwhelm his Agrarian politics and make his migration into the New Criticism almost unavoidable. At the time of its original publication, the "Statement of Principles" appeared as an anonymous text designed by Ransom to function as a manifesto for the Agrarian movement, "a test of faith" that would demand each of the Twelve Southerners be "committed equally to the cause" (Young and Core, 189). Today, however, with the benefit of hindsight, it seems obvious that even in 1929 and 1930, Ransom's broader theoretical ambitions were already making themselves felt in his political writings, making it difficult for him to endorse one-dimensionally patriotic readings of the South (189).

The "Statement of Principles"—like so much of the regionalist criticism Ransom produced later and like so much of the regionalist work that continues to be produced today—struggles to reconcile the most brutal materialist conventions of traditional environmental determinist doctrines with a more fluid idealist reading of Southern cultural discourse. Ransom seems unsure if the "South" he is defending should be considered as a thing or an idea: an inert and objective "natural" geography that can be mimetically reproduced; or a discursively active ensemble of historical, political and sociological forces. Even as he ploughs through his Agrarian call to arms, Ransom can never settle the issue and never comfortably rely on the stable naturalized option on which so much traditional regionalism is based. Though the "Statement" is designed as a political defense of Southern culture and though such a defense would normally require an appeal to nature and an argument in favor of a direct connection between that Southern culture, its Agrarian economy and its natural environment, Ransom never once suggests that such a linkage even exists. Instead his version of Agrarianism is framed very clearly as a set of principles, a discursive construction that actually has very little to do with the natural environment. His defense of the South's right to live its own kind of life is based not on environmental determinism, but on his long-held belief in the ontological specificity of this particular social space and the clear ontological differences he sees between different types of American cultural geography. The "Statement" is essentially comparative and, at its most fundamental level, its defense of Agrarianism is also an explicit critique of Industrialism. For Ransom, this is a clear question of choice: Agrarianism and Industrialism are read as two different discursive models of American cultural geography that create two dramatically different ontological experiences of social space. Because *I'll Take My Stand* is designed as an antagonistic document, these two positions are never far from each other, and Ransom's passionate argument in favor of Agrarianism functions simultaneously as one of the most explicit and aggressive anti-industrial statements ever recorded in early-twentieth-century American literature.

In his influential chapter devoted to Ransom's transition from his Fugitive past to his New Critical future, "The Critical Theory of Defensive Reaction," John Fekete argues that the rise of the New Criticism should be interpreted as a kind of scholarly surrender or capitulation to the forces of industrial capitalism which forced the marginalized Southern critics to shed their former regional commitments before they could move into "a new social location as part of the new professional (academic) intelligentsia" (46). Fekete suggests that Ransom eventually reconciled his "escapist" Fugitive tendencies and his failed "Agrarian protest" into the "cultural apology" of the New Criticism (47). In a dense but fascinating analysis of Ransom's intellectual migration through these three phases, Fekete observes:

> The important point is that through his concerns with a traditional ontology slipping away from him in the social economic, cultural and religious spheres, and through his search for a new ontology, Ransom is able to develop out of the internal dialectic of his own historical position outside and somewhat distanced from the society as a whole, the adequate cultural ideology for a social formation itself in transition of social ontology, of the basic forms of its life, of the production, reproduction, and communication of its world. (47)

Although many critics have suggested, following Fekete's example, that Ransom's regionalist writings (as well as his later New Critical formulations) were essentially and even primarily concerned with this conservative idea of preserving a lost tradition that was "slipping away," the essays he actually produced during this period suggest instead that Ransom's version of regionalist theory shared very little with traditional models of the discourse—as well as that his emphasis on shifting socio-spatial ontologies was actually far ahead of its time. In contemporary scholarship, for example, many influential voices associated with the "spatial turn" in critical theory—including thinkers as diverse as Edward Soja, David Harvey, Derek Gregory, Gillian Rose, and Doreen Massey—have argued that most of the readings of place on which we rely today need radically to reconsider exactly the type of "spatialized ontology" Ransom first recognized in the 1920s and 1930s (Soja, *Postmodern Geographies,* 118).[5] Soja, in particular, drawing much of his inspiration from Henri Lefebvre, has argued convincingly that the simultaneously "real-and-imagined" qualities of cultural geography have never been adequately theorized and that scholars in all fields of humanities research need to re-examine carefully their most basic assumptions about "the ontological priority" of social space and the "essential connection between spatiality and being" (*Postmodern Geographies,* 119).

In the late 1920s and early 1930s, Ransom's essays on regionalism were consistently focused on these kinds of questions; and his work continually drew connections between social space and ontology and interpreted the South as a discursive, intellectual construction. Throughout "Statement of Principles," Ransom argues that if the South wishes to lay claim to its own unique experience of place, then the same, equally unique linkages between human cultures and the physical geographies they produce and inhabit must exist elsewhere throughout the country and around the world. Ransom routinely equates "The South" with other "minority communities opposed to industrialism" and argues that since the "proper living" Agrarianism endorses "does not depend on the local climate or geography" and is "capable of a definition that is general and not Southern at all," the Southern Agrarian movement must "seek alliances with sympathetic communities everywhere" (xxxix). As far as Ransom is concerned, if Agrarian economic principles are to be endorsed as the potential savior of a unique Southern culture, those principles must be intellectually defensible on a broader scale, and any patriotic defense of the home place must rest on a solid theoretical foundation.

From Place to Poem: Regional and Textual Ontologies

The challenging relationship between Ransom's theory and his politics which was only beginning to emerge in "Statement of Principles" becomes the primary focus and later an irreconcilable conflict as his work progresses. Although his early commitment to the Agrarian cause had been strong and sincere, by the mid-1930s the signs of strain were evident, and it is clear that Ransom's writing was moving away from a defense of the South and toward a broader engagement with aesthetic theory. In one very important year, 1934, Ransom produced his two most explicit statements on regionalist discourse— "The Aesthetic of Regionalism" and "Regionalism in the South"—as well as his most explicit statement thus far on New Critical doctrine—"Poetry: A Note on Ontology." In retrospect, this twelve-month period seems a critical crossroads in his intellectual development. Both regionalist essays are directed by wider theoretical ambitions, and by 1938—a year after Ransom made his move to Kenyon and formally disassociated himself from the cause of regionalism—the true significance of "Poetry: A Note on Ontology" would be confirmed by its republication as the concluding chapter of *The World's Body*.

Although these three texts seem to be speaking to very different constituencies and addressing very different topics, there are startling structural similarities among them. Both regionalist texts were produced after a summer trip Ransom made to an academic conference in New Mexico in 1933, and in both essays Ransom's reflections on regionalism seem very different from his 1929 work. In "The Aesthetic of Regionalism" and "Regionalism in the South," Ransom's vision expands; he reflects on general principles of regionalist thought and continually portrays himself as a "philosophical regionalist" trying to elevate the discourse out of its marginalized and paralyzing local status ("Aesthetic," 45). Despite its title, there is nothing patriotic about "Regionalism in the South," and the text does not even offer a particularly positive analysis of Southern writing. Throughout the essay, Ransom struggles with his own terms and strains for clarity. In one revealing moment of frustration, he even mocks the entire critical category of Southern Regionalism. He notes:

> It is just as difficult in the South as it is elsewhere to tell precisely in what the regionalism consists. We hear it said here that the South has some characteristic arts, or a characteristic culture, or an economy, or a philosophy, or a "way of life," that sets the region apart from other regions, and we hear it asserted that pains must be taken to make this differentiation persist. But how shall it be defined? (108)

Traces of Ransom's earlier Fugitive-era skepticism toward romanticist stereotypes resurface in "Regionalism in the South," and he resists the easy temptation to ally his new model of regionalist discourse with its traditionally naturalized predecessors. The question, "But how shall it be defined?" is an obstacle he cannot easily overcome; he returns to it again and again. "What shall the Southern apologist name as the sacred essence?" he asks:

> Is it the magnolias, the banjoes, and pickaninnies? I cannot but sympathize with the gentlemen of the *New Republic* in detesting these pretty properties as the way of salvation. Is it the drawl of the Southern speech, and the ritardato of labor? Or is it fundamentalism, agrarianism, classicism, the Democratic party, or some other variety of abstract doctrine? It is probably a great many things at once. (108)

The tone is important here. Ransom, in an essay ostensibly devoted to regionalism in the South, openly criticizes the most basic (and often the most beloved) tenets of environmental and/or cultural determinism. In his new formulation, it obviously cannot be the magnolias, banjoes or "pickaninnies," nor the accents, the fundamentalism nor, very interestingly, not even the Agrarianism, which make or unmake the regionalism of the South. Instead, Ransom's argument moves away from such one-dimensional essentialisms and embraces a more textured model which recognizes the simultaneous and continual re-combination of all these physical and imaginary elements; he argues that "there cannot be a regionalism at one place without there being a general philosophy of regionalism, and a number of distinct examples" ("Regionalism in the South," 109).

Just as Ransom struggled to articulate the core insights of his general philosophy of regionalism, contemporary scholars descend into a similarly tongue-tied state whenever they attempt to explain the relationship between a located subjectivity and the seemingly objective conditions of social space. The same seventy-five-year-old question ("How shall it be defined?") remains a common refrain in most scholarship today: for nearly a century, regionalist criticism has been at a loss for words, unable to locate, define, or precisely identify even its own object of study. As Michael Kowalewski observes, regionalism has been "condescended to by critics or simply ignored as a category because many of them simply lack a vocabulary with which to ask engaging philosophical, psychological, or aesthetic questions about what it means to dwell in a place whether actually or imaginatively" (174). David Jordan outlines the problem in a similar way when he observes that scholars who rely on terms such as the "'the mystery of place'" or the "'indefinable air'" of regionalism only "hint at the limitations of empirical observation, but they do little to clarify exactly what it is that the regionalist author is trying to represent" ("Representing Regionalism," 105). As Ransom discovered decades earlier, the lack of a sufficiently sophisticated critical vocabulary has been the single most influential factor in regionalism's arrested development.

In "The Aesthetic of Regionalism," Ransom embarks on his most ambitious and sustained effort to test his localized philosophy of regionalism against a foreign cultural landscape and establish a new working critical vocabulary for regionalist criticism.[6] Though the climate, the history, the economy and the landscape change as Ransom moves across the continental United States into New Mexico, the formal structure of his argument remains consistent, and he sees many analogous socio-spatial forces at work in both the South and the Southwest. In "The Aesthetic," he returns to his high religious rhetoric—the essay was originally presented as a public lecture in Baton Rouge—and the document captures perhaps the last gasp of his near fanatical faith in the discourse. Rather than view region as an intellectual construct that comments only on where people live—their physical location against an inert and stable objective reality—Ransom uses the term to describe how people live, how they interrelate with the economic, aesthetic cultural and historical processes that both produce and are produced by any particular place. He argues that "regionalism is as reasonable as non-regionalism" and that "cosmopolitanism, progressivism, industrialism, free trade, interregionalism, eclecticism, liberal education, the federation of the world, or simple rootlessness" should be considered only as equivalent alternatives, rather than superior theoretical models to describe the relationship between the self and social space (47). For Ransom, regionalism produces a better local economy and a better local society, as well as a better local art, because it encourages an understanding of social space that is more intimately materialized and "less abstract" than the economic logic of "big business" (48). He believes that regionalism encourages an aesthetic potential that is unavailable in an over-rationalized industrial system and that "the machine economy, carried to the limit with the object of 'maximum efficiency,' is the enemy of regionalism" (54). In his formulation, the whole history of capitalism in the United States is seen as an unrelenting attack on regionalist values. Ransom claims that Americans suffer from a "mortal infatuation" with progressive philosophy and are consciously or unconsciously destroying the various regional identities that once made up the country (54). With obvious envy, he points to the ecological balanced existence of aboriginal communities of New Mexico and argues that, unlike the rest of "white America"—for whom regionalism "is so little an experience that it is often obliged to be a theory"—the cultural lives of the natives are so completely interwoven with their physical landscape that they "do not have to formulate the philosophy of regionalism" (48). As one of the few American cultures that continue to exist outside the industrial economy, the "noble" aboriginal community of 1933, at least as Ransom imagines it from his seat in a passing railway car, seems able to isolate and insulate itself from the homogenizing effects of the mass market (55).

The spiritual component of Ransom's argument here cannot be denied. In his rapturous appreciation for the aboriginal community and the nearly impossible to articulate linkages it forges between subjects and the social space they inhabit and create, he characterizes the interdependence of this relationship as "the birth of a natural piety: a transformation which may be ascribed to man's intuitive philosophy" and "to the operation of a transcendental spirit which is God ("Aesthetic," 49). For Ransom, at this stage of his development, a true region with a true regionalist culture is interpreted as a sacred site where a miraculous transubstantiation perfectly counterbalances the strict geographical materialism of nature with the more fluid cultural idealism of the local custom. "(R)egionalism is a compound effect with two causes," he writes; it is a discursive construct, formed by the dialectical engagement which results when "the physical nature of the region" interacts with "genius of human 'culture'" (49). Ransom sees this carefully balanced relationship between nature and culture, materialism and idealism, things and ideas, as the true achievement of any regionalist art and calls it "the best gift that is bestowed on the human species" (49). This is the core assertion that dominated his engagement with regionalist discourse from the very beginning. In his mind, regionalism captures a completely different type of social space, a different order of ontological being in comparison with the positivist options promised by the abstracting idealism of industrialism. Just as his embrace of Agrarianism was essentially defensive, Ransom sees the fragile ontological specificity of the distinct cultural geographies of America as the only alternatives to the mindless positivist aggression of industrialism.

In Mark Jancovich's seminal rereading of this phase in Ransom's career, he rightly identifies the shift from Agrarianism to the New Criticism as an "active tactical manoeuvre" that allowed Ransom, Warren and Tate to adapt and extend their economic and political criticisms into the aesthetic realm (12). According to Jancovich, "[t]he appeal of this cultural criticism was not that it failed to challenge capitalist relations or that it submitted to capitalist rationality"—as Fekete and many others have argued—"but that it argued for the need to reorganize aspects of society and culture" (13–14). For Jancovich, Ransom's regionalist and New Critical projects are directly linked by their common hostility toward the intellectual abstractions of positivism and their common defense of complex cultural ontologies. "Poetry: A Note on

Ontology" (1934) changes the object of study from the region to the poem, but in many ways Ransom's oft-cited literary essay replays and reapplies the arguments from his almost forgotten regionalist work. Much as "The Aesthetic" argued that regionalism was a compound effect with two causes, created by the dialectical tension which results when the physical nature of the region interacts with the genius of human culture, the "Note on Ontology" rejects both the overly materialist tendencies of Physical poetry ("too realistic") as well as the rarefied abstractions of Platonic poetry ("too idealistic") to argue in favor of the dialectical tension which exists in an integrated metaphysical poetry (92). Both essays map out ontological differences between types of regions and types of texts, and both essays defend the fragile metaphysically balanced sites they prefer against what Ransom sees as the homogenizing effects of positivist discourse. In the regionalist debate, positivism is represented obviously by an industrializing economy that sweeps across the landscape leveling all difference into one blandly conformist cultural geography; and in the literary debate, the same kind of positivism is represented by an equally bland and one-dimensionally utilitarian type of writing or sociohistorical scholarship that cannot or purposely does not recognize the unique ontological status and possibilities of the literary text. Much as a region cannot be defined entirely by a materialist analysis of its physical landscape, nor by a completely idealist analysis of its cultural discourse, the literary text, in Ransom's infamous formulation, is more than just a thing or an idea.

With so many common methodological parallels between the two arguments, it shouldn't be surprising that the same religious rhetoric Ransom employed when describing the compound effect in "The Aesthetic of Regionalism" returns in "Poetry: A Note on Ontology," and we see the unique recombination of materialist and idealist components in metaphysical poetry described as a kind of supernatural "miraculism" (87). For Ransom, the metaphysical literary text, like an authentic regionalism, possesses a different, and clearly sacred, ontological status. He claims that the "little secular enterprises of poetry" have a similar ontological status to religions and that, in an interesting interdependence, "[r]eligion depends for its ontological validity upon a literary understanding" (91). At the close of the essay, the metaphor of transubstantiation returns, and Ransom suggests that the type of poetry he favors functions very much like religion and crosses over that materialist/idealist divide to provide readers with "a God who has his being in the physical world as well as in the world of principles and abstractions" (92).

Most of the structures, metaphors, and methodologies that Ransom references in these three 1934 essays on regionalism and poetry can be traced back to the mysterious, failed critical manuscript he abandoned and eventually burned in 1927. Provisionally titled *The Third Moment,* this book would have been Ransom's first real contribution to criticism; and though no copy of the text exists, the core of its argument can be reconstructed from a letter Ransom wrote to Tate in 1926. Here, Ransom once again moves through his three phases or "moments" of literary experience, and he breaks these up into a first moment of purely materialist perception, a second moment of purely intellectual conception and a third moment of reconciliation, "a mixed world" and a "very advanced state" where art can be "conscious of the scene as we might have conceptualized it, and at the same time of the scene as we actually do persist in intuiting it" (Young and Core, 156). Although Ransom abandoned *The Third Moment* before even the Agrarian cause demanded his attention, it is clear that this structural and methodological template remained almost as a kind of default intellectual framing device for much of his subsequent work.

Although I do not wish to overstate this point, the tripartite structuring of Ransom's literary and regionalist analysis anticipates almost exactly the kind of "Thirding-as-Othering" advocated by Soja in his landmark 1995 text, *Thirdspace* (60). Ransom's early regionalist discourse and Soja's contemporary readings of spatialized cultural geography are not identical, but the similarities between Ransom's Third Moment and Soja's Thirdspace are nevertheless quite remarkable. As Ransom called for a passage through his First and Second moments, before the "advanced" possibilities of his "mixed world" could be achieved, Soja's contemporary analysis of social space rejects both the materialist assumptions of Firstspace analyses and the idealist assumptions of Secondspace analyses and calls instead for a similar "ontological restructuring" of the way we read and understand cultural geography (*Thirdspace,* 81). Like Ransom's Third Moment, Soja's Thirdspace "draws upon the material and mental spaces of the traditional dualism" but also "extends well beyond them in scope, substance and meaning" (*Thirdspace,* 11). A detailed comparison of these two arguments would extend well beyond the scope of this paper, but it is clear that in their shared rejection of exclusively materialist or exclusively idealist readings of social space, as well as their shared endorsement of "mixed," "ontologically restructured" interpretations of place, Ransom and Soja's work suggest that a conservative, anti-positivist, anti-industrial regionalist critic from the Agrarian South of the 1930s and a Marxist, postmodern, postindustrial critic from the L.A. School of contemporary cultural geography might actually have more in common than we might assume or anticipate.

"We are too far apart on these matters": Regionalist Resignation

History tells us that Ransom's efforts to redefine regionalist discourse and to extend the theoretical foundations for Agrarianism beyond the immediate confines of the South were ultimately unsuccessful. *I'll Take My Stand* never attracted the national audience its leading contributors sought to address and in the end, the fragile, more fluid and complex model of regionalism Ransom advocated in his later essays could never escape the overpowering influence of Southern politics. The challenges of regionalist theory were more daunting than the Agrarians first realized; and eventually, Ransom, Warren and Tate grew more and more frustrated with the patriotic demands of the discourse. In a letter to Tate in 1936, Ransom announced his formal shift away from regionalist questions and his new desire to pursue the New Critical possibility of "an objective literary standard" (Young and Core, 217). As he sets out to establish his *American Academy of Letters*—even going so far as to include a rough canonical list of twenty-five poets who be welcomed into his elite institution—Ransom stresses that his quest for a new, more standardized evaluation of literary work will share nothing with the fool's errand of his regionalist past. He tells Tate that this purer form of literary criticism will be strategically free from political influence and that it will "counteract the Agrarian-Distributionist Movement in (their) minds" (217). It is clear that Ransom is leaving regionalism behind because the social implications of defending the South have had negative effects on his national reputation and his literary work. "*Patriotism* has nearly eaten me up," he writes, "and I've got to get out of it" (217). Though he admits that it will be "hard to reject the brethren and sistren," Ransom is fully committed to the break and wants Tate to understand that his new Academy will never be "confused with a Fugitive or Agrarian organization" (219).

As we have seen, many different personal, professional, and theoretical influences combined to trigger the end of Fugitive-Agrarian movement and the beginning of the New Criticism. By 1940, one year after Tate's controversial move to Princeton and still one year before the publication of Ransom's famous text, Davidson was the only one of the key Agarians still living in Nashville and still committed to his traditional definitions of the old regionalist cause. He had been intellectually abandoned by his friends; and in a letter written to Tate in February, Davidson churns through an emotional mix of sadness and scholarly outrage. Although the letter overflows with self-pity and anger, Davidson's diagnosis of his own position within the group is correct, and his descriptions capture the unique tensions of regionalist criticism and map out the exact point at which the literary ambitions of the New Critics finally overwhelmed their patriotic loyalties to their old friends and their home region. "We are too far apart on these matters," Davidson tells Tate: "[w]e have not understood each other" (Fain and Young, 322). In one particularly revealing moment, he admits:

> I am decidedly grieved by being isolated from my friends. I don't mean physical isolation, deplorable though that is. I mean that I find myself suddenly at a disagreeable intellectual distance for reasons that I do not in the least understand. . . . It is this intellectual isolation, this lack of communion, which I feel the most. And it began before any of you left these parts. Why, is a mystery I can't solve. What fault was I guilty of? Did I just fail to keep up with the pattern of your thinking, and, though once worthy, thus become unworthy? I felt, more than once, that there was a cloud between me on one side and you, J. C. R., and perhaps more on the other side. We were all apparently as good friends as ever, yet there was this cloud. I am not speaking, of course, of mere differences of personal opinion, about this or that, at any given time, but of something more impalpable. . . . I have been almost *forced* into isolation by my own friends. (323–24)

It is difficult not to feel sympathy for Davidson during this period of loss. But apart from his frustration and his isolation from the group, his overview of the Agrarian movement's last days is accurate, and it provides contemporary scholars with an insightful analysis of both how and why the New Critics left their old regionalism behind. Although Davidson does not want to admit it, it is simply true that he did not "keep up with" his friends' thinking: while they persistently tried to steer regionalist thought away from Southern politics and the objectifying pretensions of pure mimetic representation, he stubbornly refused to dilute his most troubling and offensive political commitments. The "cloud" that descended over the group was one of mutual frustration. Ransom, Warren, and Tate could not accept the limitations of a regionalism exclusively tied to the South, and Davidson was unwilling to support a more theoretical model of the discourse that explicitly abandoned its connection with these cultural and political indices.

Though this position will run counter to much critical opinion, I would maintain that many North American scholars have ignored regionalism's continuing relevance in twenty-first-century criticism not because the discourse is simplistic, too conservative, or old-fashioned, but because it represents too much of a theoretical challenge. The highly charged personal and public arguments which tore the Agrarian movement apart in the late 1930s continue to be replayed in contemporary regionalist debates; and the same disagreeable intellectual distance between patriots and theorists that once separated Davidson from his friends remains "in place," as it were, today. Even the briefest survey of recent regionalist criticism will show that in the twenty-first century most of the criticism written about Southern, Western, Midwestern, Eastern, Prairie, or Maritime literature of North America continues to be published by journals or university presses from within these same geographical areas and that broader, general examinations of regionalist theory are still very rare and difficult to find. Rather than returning to Ransom's failed quest and re-attempting the important but arduous work of constructing an entirely new critical vocabulary for regionalist discourse, and rather than rethinking the many fertile connections that might exist between literary regionalism and the expanding fields of contemporary spatial theory, most contemporary scholars have gone back to Davidson's methodology and relied too heavily on the problematic critical inheritance of most traditional nineteenth-century versions of the regionalist discourse. Before we can even begin to evaluate regionalism's role in a contemporary postindustrial North America that is so obviously dominated by shifting social spaces and by a cultural geography that is at least as imaginary as it is real, scholars first have to find a way to talk about regionalism's function, and to explain exactly what it is that the regionalist text is exploring. The experience of the Fugitive-Agrarians in the 1920s and 1930s reveals this as a difficult task. But as Kowalewski accurately observes, "not knowing what kind of link can be established between self and environment is clearly not the same as denying that there is nothing to be known"; and moreover that "[h]aving doubts about the possibility of adequately defining regional identity is not the same as asserting that it does not exist" (175).

Notes

1. Every undergraduate textbook on literary theory contains a reference to the New Criticism and a historical description of the role it played in helping to define the study of literature within the North American academy in the postwar period. For the most influential contemporary scholarly characterizations of the movement, see Lentricchia, Fekete, Eagleton, and Selden and Widdowson.

2. Southern literary scholarship is a broad and multifaceted field that cannot be quickly defined or summarized. Working from a wide variety of different positions, Southern academics have moved through many of the most challenging and controversial regionalist debates in North American literary criticism. See Gray, Beck, Bradbury, Conkin, Cowan, Kreyling, and O'Gorman.

3. Though they were closely related and shared their four most famous members, the Fugitives and the Agrarians were two separate groups. Beyond Ransom, Warren, Tate, and Davidson, the Fugitive group included Merrill Moore, Laura Riding, Jesse Wils, Alec B. Stevenson, Walter Clyde Curry, Stanley Johnson, Sidney Hirsch, James Frank, William Yandell Elliot, William Frierson, Ridley Wills, and Alfred Starr. The eight others of the titular Twelve Southerners who contributed essays to *I'll Take My Stand* were Andrew Lytle, Stark Young, John Gould Fletcher, Frank Lawrence Owsley, Lyle Lanier, Herman Nixon, John Donald Wade, and Henry Blue Kline. For more on the founding of *The Fugitive* and its membership, see Cowan. For biographies on the Agrarians, see Virginia Rock's "The Twelve Southerners: Biographical Essays," an appendix to the 1962 edition of *I'll Take My Stand*. For a more detailed account of the relationship between the two groups, see John L. Stewart's *The Burden of Time: The Fugitives and Agrarians*.

4. The best analyses of this transition are found in Fekete, Jancovich, O'Kane, Gray, and O'Gorman.

5. For a good overview of the spatialization of contemporary critical theory, see the essay collections edited by Keith and Pile and Dear and Flusty.

6. For a contemporary reappraisal of "The Aesthetic of Regionalism," see Wyile.

Bibliography

Beck, Charlotte H. *The Fugitive Legacy: A Critical History.* Baton Rouge, LA: Louisiana State University Press, 2001.

Blotner, Joseph. *Robert Penn Warren: A Biography.* New York: Random House, 1977.

Bradbury, John M. *The Fugitives: A Critical Account.* Chapel Hill, NC: University of North Carolina Press, 1958.

Conkin, Paul K. *The Southern Agrarians.* Knoxville, TN: University of Tennessee Press, 1988.

Cowan, Louise. *The Fugitive Group: A Literary History.* Baton Rouge: Louisiana State University Press, 1959.

Dear, Michael J., and Steven Flusty, eds. *The Spaces of Postmodernity: Readings in Human Geography.* Malden, MA: Blackwell, 2002.

Eagleton, Terry. *Literary Theory: An Introduction.* Minneapolis: University of Minnesota Press, 1983.

Fain, John Tyree, and Thomas Daniel Young, eds. *The Literary Correspondence of Donald Davidson and Allen Tate.* Athens, GA: University of Georgia Press, 1974.

Fekete, John. *The Critical Twilight: Explorations in the Ideology of Anglo-American Literary Theory from Eliot to McLuhan.* London: Routledge, 1977.

Grammer, John M. "Reconstructing Southern Literature." *American Literary History* (2001): 126–41.

Gray, Richard. *Southern Aberrations: Writers of the American South and the Problems of Regionalism.* Baton Rouge: Louisiana State University Press, 2000.

Jancovich, Mark. *The Cultural Politics of the New Criticism.* Cambridge: Cambridge University Press, 1993.

Jordan, David. "Representing Regionalism." *Canadian Review of American Studies* 23.2 (1993): 101–114.

Keith, Michael, and Steven Pile, eds. *Place and the Politics of Identity.* London: Routledge, 1994.

Kowalewski, Michael. "Writing in Place: The New American Regionalism." *American Literary History* 6 (1994): 171–83.

Kreyling, Michael. *Inventing Southern Literature.* Jackson: University of Mississippi Press, 1998.

Lentricchia, Frank. *After the New Criticism.* Chicago: University of Chicago Press, 1980.

Mencken, H. L. "The Sahara of the Bozart." In *The American Scene: A Reader,* 157–68. New York: Knopf, 1977.

O'Gorman, Farrell. "The Fugitive-Agrarians and the Twentieth-Century Southern Canon." In *A Companion to the Regional Literatures of America,* ed. Charles Crow, 286-305. Malden, MA: Blackwell, 2003.

O'Kane, Karen. "Before the New Criticism: Modernism and the Nashville Group." *The Mississippi Quarterly* 51 (1998): 683–97.

Ransom, John Crowe. "The Aesthetic of Regionalism." In *Selected Essays of John Crowe Ransom,* ed. Thomas Daniel Young and John Hindle, 45–58. Baton Rouge, LA: Louisiana State University Press, 1984.

———. "Poetry: A Note on Ontology." In *Selected Essays of John Crowe Ransom,* ed. Thomas Daniel Young and John Hindle, 74–92. Baton Rouge, LA: Louisiana State University Press, 1984.

———. "Regionalism in the South." *New Mexico Quarterly* 4 (1934): 109–113.

Selden, Raman, and Peter Widdowson. *A Reader's Guide to Contemporary Literary Theory.* 3rd ed. Lexington: University of Kentucky Press, 1993.

Soja, Edward. *Postmodern Geographies: The Reassertion of Space in Critical Social Theory.* New York: Verso, 1989.

———. *Thirdspace: Journeys to Los Angeles and Other Real and Imagined Places.* Oxford: Blackwell, 1996.

Spikes, Michael. *Understanding Contemporary American Literary Theory.* Columbia, SC: University of South Carolina Press, 1997.

Twelve Southerners. *I'll Take My Stand: The South and the Agrarian Tradition.* 1930. Baton Rouge, LA: Louisiana State University Press, 1977.

Wyile, Herb. "Ransom Revisited: The Aesthetic of Regionalism in a Globalized Age." *Canadian Review of American Studies* 28.2 (1998): 99–117.

Young, Thomas Daniel, and George Core, eds. *Selected Letters of John Crowe Ransom.* Baton Rouge, LA: Louisiana State University Press, 1985.

CHAPTER NINE

Teaching with Style

Brooks and Warren's Literary Pedagogy

TARA LOCKHART

> If your educational experience in any way resembled mine, you have been uncertain about what style is. Style was a familiar enough word for you, but your concept of style was probably vague . . . because our own teachers spent little or no time talking about style. . . . If we listed ourselves as members of that post–World War II generation of students who regularly practiced the Brooks-and-Warren method of close analysis, we could talk about the linguistic features of a poem with great specificity. Yet we may well have been stymied when we wanted to talk about the linguistic features of a prose text.
>
> —Edward P. J. Corbett, "Teaching Style"

IN A 1954 article for *The Journal of Higher Education*, Clarence Kulisheck assessed the influential and "widely used . . . storm center" of *Understanding Poetry*—the most famous textbook by Robert Penn Warren and Cleanth Brooks—and the consequent entry of New Criticism into the "hurly-burly of the sprawling undergraduate world" (174). Positioning Brooks and Warren's collections as the primary texts which "herald[ed] the entrance of the New Criticism into the textbook field," Kulisheck maintained that works such as *Understanding Poetry* were "so conceived and so constructed as to change radically conventional conceptions of how literature should be taught . . . and what literature should be taught" (174–75). Arguing that such textbooks "recognize and emphasize the prime importance of a critical apparatus designed to acquaint the student (and the teacher, too . . .) with the exacting techniques of close reading," Kulisheck identified several "radical" features of these textbooks: an "introductory essay on applied aesthetics as it relates to the particular type of literature under consideration"; "detailed editorial analysis" following the excerpts of literature; "questions and exercises designed to stimulate further analysis along the same lines" of the criticism provided; and a glossary highlighting critical, often specialized, terminology (175). Kulishek concluded that the "elaborate apparatus was perhaps the most controversial feature of the original Brooks and Warren text" (176).

In 1953, a year before Kulisheck's article, the field had already felt the need to evaluate the mark made by the New Criticism, as evidenced by Randall Stewart's article in *College English*, which summarized the results of a questionnaire administered to thirty-four "New Critics" and "old scholars" alike. In nearly all the replies, professors noted re-animated attention to both literature and the teaching of literature, asserting that New Criticism prompted a productive move away from locating the "sources" of literary influence or inspiration, shifted graduate study toward critical subjects, and "tended to encourage the Socratic method in teaching and to discourage straightaway lecturing" (106–9).

In this article, I consider the specific pedagogical innovations Brooks and Warren introduced across editions of their first textbook, *An Approach to Literature*. I have deliberately chosen to investigate a New Critical textbook which has not received nearly as much critical attention as the *Understanding Poetry* series. Moreover, I focus on what I read as the most challenging literary genre the textbook duo tackled—the essay. In addition to surfacing the pedagogies involved in addressing a less central area of New Critical interest—nonfiction prose as opposed to the poetry typically venerated by the New Criticism—*An Approach to Literature* provides an especially useful site for considering the wider pedagogical practices that Brooks and Warren encouraged, practices which continue to be used not only in introductory English courses, but in literary studies and the humanities more widely.

What is most interesting and instructive about Brooks and Warren's theory and pedagogy on the essay emerges through small changes from one edition to the next, as the team encounters difficulty describing the essay's slippery, semi-literary form. The challenges of this task are registered through discussion of the essay's "style" and the necessary evolution of the textbook's pedagogical apparatus (the questions, exercises, definitions, explications, and structure that implicitly and explicitly "teach"). Brooks and Warren thus use the undertheorized genre and style of the essay as ground on which to build an increasingly useful apparatus.

The section that follows first provides a brief sketch of Brooks and Warren's relationship and the exigency for developing New Critical practices, as well as a consideration of the critiques the broader movement received. It then turns to the historical reception of *An Approach to Literature* and my analysis of its evolution across editions. By providing a genealogy of the changes made across editions, the final sections illuminate the texture of a particular form of New Critical pedagogy in order to demonstrate how close attention to texts read *qua* literature—in the manner Brooks and Warren advocated through their work with the essay—remains useful today.

Pedagogical Beginnings and the Growth of New Criticism

The story of the Brooks and Warren textbooks begins at Louisiana State University, where the two men were reunited as colleagues and as teachers. Although they had worked together previously as friends and fellow students—at both Vanderbilt and Oxford—it was at LSU that, faced with teaching four classes each semester in addition to producing scholarship and editing the journal *The Southern Review,* they developed a pedagogy of close reading for the classroom. The aim of such a pedagogy was democratic: to provide students a method and the necessary tools to interpret texts on their own, especially at large state universities such as LSU. Brooks later recalled the beginning of four decades of collaboration with Warren:

> Robert Penn Warren and I found ourselves in the mid 1930's teaching at the Louisiana State University. . . . Among other things, each of us was teaching a section of the department's course in literary forms and types. Granted that Warren and I were young men excited by the new trends in literature—Warren was already a published poet—and granted that our heads were full of literary theory—drawn from the poetry and critical essays of T. S. Eliot and from the then sensational books on theory and practical criticism written by I. A. Richards—nevertheless, our dominant motive was not to implant new fangled ideas in the innocent Louisiana sophomores we faced three times a week. Our motive was to try to solve a serious practical problem.
>
> Our students, many of them bright enough and certainly amiable and charming enough, had no notion of how to read a literary text. ("Forty Years of 'Understanding Poetry,'" 167–68)

As Jewel Spears Brooker notes, Brooks was clearly "stimulated in part by pedagogical earnestness" in his drive to move beyond early-twentieth-century textbooks whose "theories of mimesis, of genesis, and of reception seemed to have exhausted themselves" (131). According to Brooker, Brooks did not exclude these approaches as entirely unproductive, but read them as often ineffective in pedagogic isolation, instead favoring "an approach that stimulated readers to focus with intelligence on the text" (131).

Brooks and Warren began working on this "serious practical problem" by collaborating on *Sophomore Poetry Manual,* a pamphlet which expanded upon notes that Warren had developed for teaching an LSU poetry class. This initial foray into pedagogy was then expanded to include a range of genres; Brooks and Warren (along with John Thibaut Pursur) entitled this reader *An Approach to Literature,* which was printed by LSU in 1936. Thus began a sustained collaborative endeavor on textbooks. A few years later, as Brooks and Warren began revising a second edition of *An Approach to Literature* (1939), their next textbook, *Understanding Poetry,* had already hit the stands in 1938. This frenetic pace of textbook publishing continued for the next four decades, with new textbooks such as *Understanding Fiction* (1943) and *Modern Rhetoric* (1949) rounding out the mix. In addition to their creative and scholarly work, Brooks and Warren released or revised a new textbook every few years.

Understanding Poetry undoubtedly came to be the best known of their textbook series. First used at LSU and soon taught across the United States, notably at Yale where Brooks and Warren would later teach (Brooks arrived 1947; Warren in 1950), this popular volume was regarded as instituting the "New Critical approach." Each textbook aimed to establish links across several spheres of academe in order to allow critics authoring textbooks, teachers using them, and students studying from them to work together on problems of interpretation. The introduction to *Understanding Poetry* indicates the broad goals of the textbooks: to "dispose of a few . . . basic misconceptions . . . and therefore to prepare the student to enter upon an unprejudiced study of the actual poems" (xviii). These "misconceptions" are pithily named as "message hunting," "pure realization," and "beautiful statement of some high truth" (10–18), statements which still capture prevalent ideas about the interpretation of literature today. This opening statement in *Understanding Poetry* also makes evident New Critical assumptions broadly present across the textbooks: that students are intelligent yet prejudiced, and that students will easily relinquish their prejudices and misconceptions through exposure to the methodology of the volume.

This excerpt also assumes and addresses an implied teacher.[1] Faced with an enormous influx of students after the Second World War, many teachers were both overworked and undertrained. Accordingly, the editors seek to cleanse them of unwanted prejudices as well, to create the kind of level playing field that would be assumed by the New Critical methodology. Such an approach is democratic, then, not only because of the range of readers toward which the text directs itself, but also because of the ways that it discounts prior knowledge and experience, so that all readers may proceed in the same manner. Indeed, democratization of literary study, and of reading practices more broadly, was among the most prominent goals of the Brooks and Warren textbooks. To allow all readers equal access to textual interpretation, the textbooks focused on what was theorized as "the text itself," establishing as the object of study the words in front of the reader, whose accessibility did not depend on esoteric bibliographical knowledge that some students might possess and others might not.

From the outset, Brooks and Warren advanced their New Critical strategies as a corrective to approaches associated with other "popular" or current textbooks, which in their view often substituted for the primary object of study—the poem itself—other foci: paraphrase, biography, "historical materials," and/or "inspirational and didactic interpretation" (iv). The authors aimed to defend students from these practices by encouraging them to strive for precision, ground their analyses and interpretations in the primary texts, attend to all aspects of the text instead of isolating out particularities, and proceed through a series of questions toward articulation of the "grounds" for certain interpretations. The apparatus accompanying each primary text established, and implicitly theorized, a new pedagogical method which would persist for many decades.

A key implication of the textbook apparatus was that students could be liberated via the New Critical method, through both their increased knowledge and their increasing engagement with the particulars of literary work. This liberatory aspiration dovetailed with Brooks and Warren's effort to rescue literary theory from the limited interpretive frameworks of philology and literary biography that had marked pedagogy well into the twentieth century. Regarding these approaches as elitist and dilettantish, they sought to combat these with a democratic, reasoned, and incisive method.

Even now, though the field of "English" perceives itself as beyond the New Criticism, commentators such as Gerald Graff and Frank Lentricchia agree that the specters of the New Critical perspective continue to haunt contemporary theory and practice. Lentricchia notes that the New Criticism lives on not only as an "imposing and repressive father-figure" but also in the ways that contemporary theory is connected to, rather than discontinuous from, New Criticism (xiii). Graff further suggests that even opponents of the New Criticism often use the very methods and tenets of New Criticism in order to critique it.[2]

From our contemporary vantage, the tenets of New Criticism—and their attendant dangers—ring familiar in English departments across North America. The roster of charges usually runs somewhat like this: that the New Critics treated literature as a sacred text cordoned off from the world and from history, regarding it as art for art's sake; that the "Intentional" and "Affective Fallacies" theorized by the New Critics assisted in this exclusion, thus constricting the range of fruitful reading practices; that the focus on organic unity in texts, combined with a drive for recognizing universal systems of humanistic understanding applied in a scientific manner, flattened the dialectic between reader and text and among conflicting ideas; that these practices implicitly sought to establish a limited canon out of highly privileged, arbitrary and elitist values; and that New Critical tenets resulted in a hierarchy of proper reading practices (and thus "proper" readers), often elevating academic critics to its apex. These portraits of de-historicized, exclusive, mechanized practice persist in representations of the New Criticism. And there is truth to many of these charges.

Yet, as Gerald Graff suggests, such representations always risk oversimplification and caricature, and often fail to distinguish between what the New Critics initially advocated and how their methods later came to be "routinized" and broadly applied. Accordingly, Graff's discussion of New Criticism is crucial for understanding the original impetus of New Critical methodology, as well as why it ultimately faded from dominance—and, some would say, failed. Some of the reasons for this failure can be gleaned from the list of charges listed above: as Graff puts it, "the necessity to fight battles on so great a variety of fronts forced the New Criticism to stretch its concepts till they became ambiguous," and moreover, muddled and contradictory (141). To ward off the "hedonistic impressionism and genteel moralism" residual from earlier periods, the New Critics advocated an interpretive practice that did not linger in rapturous pleasure or didactic lessons (140). To guard against the popular practices advocated by biographers and philologists, the New Critics recommended concentrating on the text itself. And in order to defend literature from scientific positivism, the New Critics argued for literature's connection, as Cleanth Brooks put it, to the "facts of experience," a realm which could be objectively recognized as its own mode of knowledge (*The Well Wrought Urn*, qtd. in Graff, *Literature against Itself*, 142).

Literary works in this view were thus both objective and self-sufficient, while still somehow connected to the larger world and worldly experience.[3]

From this New Critical perspective, focusing on the text in isolation was (also paradoxically) a way to restore literature's place and value against the mechanistic, industrial, positivistic forces of society—a way to train students, as Mark Jancovich puts it, to be aware of "the paradoxes and contradictions repressed by capitalist rationality" (88). The method designed to fulfill these contradictory goals was, of course, close textual analysis. Graff summarizes the range of critiques this method was intended to dispel:

> The method of close textual analysis was a response on one side to those who dismissed literature as a frivolity and on the other side to those who defended it in terms which rendered it frivolous. Close textual analysis, producing evidence of the richness and complexity of literary works, simultaneously answered the impressionist, who viewed the work as a mere occasion for pleasurable excitement, the message-hunter or political propagandist, who reduced the work to mere uplifting propositions, and the positivist, who denied any significance to the work at all. And close analysis of meaning could also demonstrate to the historians and biographers that a literary work was more than a datum in the history of ideas or the life of the author. (141)

The New Critical method of textual analysis, though often perceived in retrospect as isolationist, was intended to result in precisely the opposite phenomenon: it sought to restore to literature a central place in the culture at large. Moreover, the New Critics sought to extend the values associated with literature to all, employing a democratic method of criticism to allow readers of all kinds to cultivate humanistic endeavors.

Given the number of challenges this method set out to correct, it comes as no surprise that it ultimately fell from disciplinary dominance. Part of the problem was the New Critics' oversimplification of the foes they set out to attack. As Graff suggests, for instance, the New Critics mistakenly equated rational thought with the mechanized societal forces they sought to disrupt, which prompted them to "oppose rational objectivity to experience and doom themselves to the polarizations they aimed to heal" (149).[4] And in attempting to save literature from its host of differently antagonistic opponents, the New Criticism was not only pulled in too many directions to sustain itself, but also experienced a fundamental dislocation of its body of theory from its methods of textual interpretation.

However, from a pedagogical point of view, the effects of this dislocation are minimal, particularly in the *Approach to Literature* series. Indeed, the pedagogical apparatus analyzed below reads as an important site from which theoretical nuances can emerge: I argue for this analysis as a new avenue into the theory associated with the New Criticism. In the sections that follow, I am particularly interested in the theorization of style as a literary feature, a way to reveal and access what is specifically "literary" about a text. As Brooks and Warren develop their handling of style via the pedagogical apparatus across editions, they also explore and refine their theoretical commitments. This is evidenced most clearly when style as a topic vanishes from the theoretical discussion of the essay, only to be pursued in the pedagogical apparatus. The apparatus thus becomes the central site for finding language to describe the workings of style and "literariness," so that students might learn to recognize, discern, and describe stylistic effects as part of their interpretive repertoire.

Barely Literary: *An Approach to Literature*

Although *Understanding Poetry* is popularly understood as the textbook which institutionalized the New Critical approach, *An Approach to Literature*—Brooks and Warren's first textbook—also importantly disseminated the New Criticism beyond LSU. As James Grimshaw, Jr., notes, as early as 1939, *An Approach to Literature* was being taught at institutions as geographically diverse as Auburn, Tufts, Cornell, Colgate, and North Dakota (27). As the textbooks swept the nation and as theoretical scholarship related to New Criticism continued to grow, the reception of Brooks and Warren's textbooks grew as well.[5] The textbooks ushered in new pedagogies that quickly gained ground. Josephine Miles describes the influence of the textbooks in a 1947 review:

> I do not think that any younger writer growing up in the 1930s and reading one or two years of the *Southern Review* and later the Brooks and Warren textbook could have failed to absorb some of the patience . . . some of their straight attention to every complex structure and every simple whole. . . . Every poem makes the more sense by such treatment. (185–86)

Generally positive, reviews of the literature-based textbooks note their wide influence on the field and the productive pedagogies they fostered.

Indeed the only critique the literature textbooks typically received considered the extent to which the text should offer a pedagogical apparatus. Geoffrey Wagner, for instance, reviewing in 1956, writes that

The Brooks and Warren readers . . . consist of admirably selected passages of literature—poetry, prose and drama—with pertinent and often profound comments. They are challenged as being too pedantically the fruit of the American school of New Criticism, of which Professor Brooks is allegedly the Dean. However, I personally feel that this is one place [the undergraduate classroom, especially in the first two years] where the New Criticism—close textual analysis keeping historical and biographical data to the background—is vitally to the point. My only criticism of the Brooks and Warren textbook is that it tends to do too much for the teacher: the numerous questions appended after each selection exhaust the topic and tend to rob the teacher of opportunities for exercising his own gifts. (227)

The problem that Wagner notes is certainly always an issue in textbooks; they walk a fine line between pedantry and providing a range of materials useful to both teacher and student. As Brooks and Warren often note in their introductions, volumes are rarely used from cover to cover, exercise by exercise; accordingly, their aim is to present more material than necessary from which the teacher may choose.[6]

Given the impact of the Brooks and Warren textbooks, as well as the ways that *An Approach to Literature* preceded and influenced the approaches later featured in the ubiquitous *Understanding Poetry,* this understudied volume merits enhanced critical attention. As the textbook where Brooks and Warren specifically considered differences between genres as well as differences between poetic and prosaic form, *An Approach to Literature* provides a valuable site for assessing the evolution over forty years of both New Critical pedagogical and theoretical approaches to the essay, as well as their theoretical premises and allegiances more broadly. I first sketch the editors' efforts to describe the relationship between the essay's content and its form, attempts which initially read as somewhat muddled. The section that follows illuminates how Brooks and Warren develop richer and more productive attention to the form of essays—and to their "style"—across revised editions of the textbook via the pedagogical apparatus.

An Approach to Literature addresses not only the essay, but several literary genres, seeking to "bring into the classroom some of the insights that had been provided by criticism since Coleridge and to set these insights, especially when dealing with more mature students, in some context of literary and social history" (v). The textbook devotes a section to each featured genre—fiction, poetry, biography, the essay, and drama—accompanying most selections with exercises. The preface details primarily the fiction and poetry sections, devoting less attention to the other three generic divisions, which mainly serve as connective devices between earlier selections.[7]

By the time we reach the introduction to the section on the essay—framed as one of the "most flexible of forms" and one which has suffered with the rise of the modern short story—we have already learned much about the authors' understanding of form and style as they operate within literary texts. Here, however, the authors do not spend as much time with how essays "are made" as they do when addressing fiction; nor do they fully elucidate topics such as "style," "movement," or "exposition" as they do in the section on fiction. Instead, the introductory section on the essay seems more intent on differentiating the essay from other prose forms through defining what exactly makes an essay an essay. They begin by addressing content:

> Of all the various forms of literature, the essay comes closest to having as its purpose merely the presentation of facts—for the sake of the facts. The essay lies therefore in a sort of borderland which touches on the one side the realm of "pure" literature and on the other the realm of practical and scientific writings, the realm of chemistry texts and medical prescriptions and cook books. In the essay the writer is concerned primarily with the explanation of a set of facts or perhaps with convincing the reader of the truth of a particular set of ideas. (113)

In this first nebulous attempt at defining the essay, the authors situate it broadly within the vast "borderland" between strict exposition and what they demark as "pure literature." Crucial, they point out, is the essay's purpose of relaying information that is chiefly factual. As the editors develop this basic definition, they elaborate the purpose of the essay as employing a story or incident as the means by which to illustrate or explore a general idea or position. This "separates the essay as a form rather sharply from the other literary forms we have mentioned," in that the "particular" is used in service of exploring the more "general" (509). This definition reads as both purposely broad and unnecessarily vague: the authors have a feel for what qualifies as essays—not magazine articles, for example—yet they can only begin to articulate the boundaries of the essay, primarily via taxonomies.

The introduction's discussion of the role of style in the essay highlights Brooks and Warren's tendency toward both categorization and broad description, as well as underlines the characteristics that, in their reading, qualify a text as "literature." Arguing that the essay may be "heavily burdened by the weight of facts," they note that the essay "can become literature," although the assumption remains that it must aspire more than other literary forms to do so (113). Despite the implication that the essay is more burdened by its content and accordingly less literary, however, the authors are at pains to point out that *"form* and *style* have an important and necessary place even when the main interest of the author may be in convincing his reader of the truth of some practical proposal" (113; original emphasis). Thus they emphasize what qualifies as a "literary" dimension of the essay: since the essay uses language, and language is interpretative and expressive (words are not, as the editors put it, "exact"), the way in which ideas are presented is constitutive of the essay's meaning. Thus, "form and style"—what they read as "literary" characteristics—are important to consider even when analyzing more factually driven pieces of writing. "Colored by the writer's own special and personal conception of them, and colored by his attitude toward them," the facts that the essayist presents always have—as even a cook book does, the editors remark—"the possibility of going off into poetry" through style and form (113).

Brooks and Warren provide several different ways of considering the content the essay details—the facts, as it were–and the form through which these facts are presented. Variously, the editors refer to "not statements of fact," but *"comments* on the facts and *opinions* about the meaning of the facts"; "an arrangement of facts"; "an interpretation of facts"; and finally, facts which are "shaped by his [an essayist's] writing to win the reader to his own interpretation" (509–10; original emphasis). Here the editors begin to move from content to the style of the piece—the ways in which the author shapes the content so as to persuade and engage. Brooks and Warren name this rhetorical impetus "emotional coloring": "The essay, then, may attempt to stir the emotions as well as offer facts to the intellect; and, therefore, it may be one of the works of the imagination, and as such, a form of literature" (510). The process leading up to the possibility that the essay might operate as a form of literature reads as arduous indeed, as the logic moves from content, to how content is shaped and presented, to the effects of this presentation, and finally, via imagination, to the possibility that some essays *may* therefore be understood as literature. Hence the essay is in some respects not literary— due to its factual content—while in other ways it is crucially literary, particularly by dint of the artistic arrangement of its parts which combine to create a "style" perceivable by the reader.

In an attempt to clarify the matter, the editors take pains to discuss the style of the essay as it both relates to and differs from those associated with other forms of literature (115). They note, for example, that the structure–in addition to the tone and atmosphere—may have a more "informal quality" (115). The structure of what they name the "informal essay" proves particularly difficult to pin down. The structure "at its best . . . is not a haphazard one":

> Ordinarily, the logic of exposition or the logic of the argument determines the arrangement of the essay. But since in the informal essay this matter does not bulk very large, the arrangement of the material often follows the apparent whim and impulse of the author himself or the apparently casual association of ideas. . . . (115)

However, the editors are careful to point out, twice, that this impression of random or chaotic "arrangement" of the essay's structure is only "apparent," and is most likely constructed purposefully to give that impression. After this round of vague clarifications, Brooks and Warren arrive at the final paragraph, where they most clearly attempt to define essayistic "style":

> It is this fact that sometimes causes us to think of the informal essay as having preeminently style and the other types of essays as lacking it. But the proposition is true, of course, only in a very special sense. It is impossible to have style in a vacuum. The *style*, in its broadest sense, is the arrangement of the writer's materials, the adaptation of his means to his ends in the use of language. If style is an arrangement, there can never be just style—there must be an arrangement of something. But the statement is true in this sense: namely, that in the familiar essay the material is not so much objective fact as it is the sort of fact which one finds in a poem or short story. Consequently, the form is prominent in the familiar essay for the same reason that it is prominent in the poem or short story. (115; original emphasis)

Despite its somewhat circular reasoning, this argument makes common sense: informal/personal essays "seem" as though they have more "style" in part because they have less "fact"; thus their material bears greater similarity to that of a poem or short story, and likewise, they are more literary than those essays the authors have deemed formal or factual.

Definitional slippages here mark the authors' attempts to acknowledge the more literary dimensions of the essay. They begin with the term "structure," which is related to the tone and the atmosphere of the piece and which comes to be synonymous with the essay's "logic" and its "arrangement." Yet the "arrangement of the writer's materials" is also the way that the editors broadly define "style." To add a layer of complication, the term "form" is introduced at the end of this exposition: "Consequently, the form is prominent in the familiar essay." Although not clearly defined, "form" is understood here to be associated with the style and arrangement of the essay; and form, like style, becomes more visible in the informal/personal essay than those essays more driven by factual content. Despite the overlap in these definitions, the goal remains the same: to acknowledge, pinpoint, and describe the essay as a literary genre.

These attempts at defining the essay, its style, and accordingly how it functions as a form of literature remain fraught for Brooks and Warren throughout the four editions of *An Approach to Literature*. The relationship of form to content within the essay reads as at the heart of these difficulties. The editors consider content to be the driving force of factual, personal, and speculative essays; and this, their maneuvering implies, threatens the ability of the essay to operate as literary text. Although the editors aim to narrow the gulf between "fine literature" and the essay's "practical exposition of facts," ultimately they present the essay as a genre that is barely literary, bound and determined by its content and the attendant presumptions of truth, fact, and the author's direct and sincere presence on the page (509). Over the course of the four editions, however, and despite their struggles to describe and deal with the literary aspects of the essay, Brooks and Warren eventually develop more effective ways to guide students' work with essays. For all of its murkiness, the struggle to elucidate how the essay works gives rise to a considerable enhancement and refinement of their pedagogical apparatus. In turn, the apparatus acts as a whetting stone which further sharpens the articulation of the textbook's theoretical assumptions—for students, teachers and for the editors themselves.

Pedagogy in Action:
Defining Essays and Student Reading Practices

The organization of the first edition of *An Approach to Literature* provides a point of departure from which Brooks and Warren then adjust and diversify the pedagogical points they wish to emphasize. In the first edition, selections are organized thematically, and most of the questions which follow each selection focus on content. The editors do encourage dialogue between the readings, often asking students to compare two essays or points of view. But by and large, the apparatus in this first edition remains (like the authors' definition of the essay) focused on the facts. Typical questions address what Author X says about Subject Y or how a student would define the essay's key words or concepts. The handful of questions that encourage attention to style—and the relationships among author, text, style, and reader—focus almost exclusively on discerning the author's "real attitude" toward his subject or his reader.

There are two notable exceptions to the first edition's pedagogical focus on "what" based questions. The first is a question about Montaigne's "Of the Resemblance of Children to Their Fathers": "Does this essay have any formal structure or is it merely haphazard? If it has a structure, what determines that structure?" (195). Attentive students will remember similar language from the Introduction to the Essay and thus assume that the question leads them away from the "haphazard" and toward finding a meaningful logic for the essay's organization. The second exception to the apparatus's focus on content also raises the question of style specifically, here in response to Arnold Bennett's piece "Literary Taste: How to Form It" (one of the few initial essays that disappears from the textbook in the revised edition). The authors ask, "What does Bennett say is the relation of style to content?" (206). Although this question might get students thinking about this relationship, the question itself guides students to report what Bennett "says" without obliging them to engage the connection Bennett makes. Other than the question regarding Montaigne's formal structure then, the pedagogical principles of this first edition steer students toward identification, comprehension, classification, and straightforward questions about the soundness or fairness of particular arguments—what Brooks and Warren read as the essay's "non-literary" dimensions.

Revised Edition, 1944

Although the revised edition's Introduction to the Essay remains exactly the same as the original edition's text, significant changes emerge in the pedagogical apparatus which indicate Brooks and Warren's attempt to supplement their theories of the essay and the ways they ask students to read and interact with essays. A key new feature is a series of several paragraph-long discussions that follow new essay selections. In these responses which precede the set of questions, the authors highlight specific features of the essays, draw connections between essays, and discuss the more challenging essays which do not fit neatly into the paradigm of a "closely knit, logical development" (133). In addition to the authors' discussion of the essay, each selection is followed by five to eight questions (rather than the two or three in the first edition) which are much more thorough in their efforts to engage students in the work of textual analysis. Many of these questions enact similar work as that described above, although in this edition the student is called upon more frequently to explain differences among authors' arguments and lend their own views to the discussion.

Despite the fact the revised edition constantly raises style—such as in the exposition following Emerson's essay—it often retreats to the "examination of ideas" as the best way to explain the essay's work. Such a move is likewise reinforced in the final question about Emerson's piece which reads, in part, "Even an evaluation of Emerson's style—if style is functionally related to the author's purpose—will be impossible, finally, without a broad basis of comparison. In general, this statement applies to all the essays; we can evaluate the style only in terms of the general intention" (133). It's difficult to discern how to interpret this statement, just as it's difficult to tell what action students are supposed to take in response. Such confusing directives co-mingle in this edition's apparatus with questions which ask students to grapple with the rhetorical and stylistic features of the text, such as "How does Pater make his answer to the question seem plausible and inevitable?" This question marks the first "how" question in the *Approach to Literature* series, asking students to account for how a particular effect—here, plausibility—is achieved.

The clearest development of this new line of questioning appears in four of the eight questions following Arnold's "Culture and Anarchy." These questions best illuminate the detailed analysis of both form and content to which this edition aspires. After asking students to compare the definition of culture and the key points Arnold makes to elements of another essay selection, the apparatus poses a series of questions aimed at uncovering how the essay is constructed and how its construction contributes to its work. First, students are asked to reread the essay, paying attention to "Arnold's method of presentation and argument. What has he gained by his special ordering of the ideas which he has used?" (167). This emphasis on the essay's structure is strengthened in the next two questions, which ask students to attend to Arnold's use of examples and metaphors/similes. Each question encourages students to justify how these elements assist or detract from the essay's persuasiveness. Finally, the last question turns explicitly to style: "Consider, for example, the difference in style between the concluding paragraphs of the essay, and, say, the section on Puritanism and the Nonconformists. What accounts for this difference?" (167). Although the phrasing of the question suggests a "haphazard" selection of two sections to compare, questions like these pave the way for ensuing editions of *Approach* to develop attention to more than the essay's content.

Third Edition, 1952

Although there are only slight changes between the revised second edition and the 1952 third edition, a few changes begun in the revised edition begin to come to fruition. The third edition elaborates the questions about style and advances a more substantive taxonomy differentiating kinds of essays. Brooks and Warren note differences between the "perceptible logic" typical of argumentative essays and the characteristics that mark personal essays in which "the organization and the tone are more complex—and in a sense, more important" (591). This edition also offers a new synopsis of what the authors perceive as key differences between these kinds of essays:

> [The personal essay] tends to emphasize attitudes and moods rather than a process of logical exposition; and consequently, it characteristically uses a great deal of concrete illustration, imagery, narrative, etc. In its extreme form, as a matter of fact, this type of the essay may seem to be little more than a presentation of the author's personal prejudices and whimsies. Often, writers of personal essays will prefer to approach their material by presenting some paradoxical situation or idea, or by an overinsistence on some aspect of an idea. (591)

This additional explanation moves beyond the organization and tone mentioned in the first part of the discussion to a more adept description of the form and structure of the personal essay, including its emphases, devices, approach, and movement. Additionally, the editors introduce a spectrum of essay-writing—from formal to informal and from more extreme forms of each to less extreme forms—alongside the spectrum of essay readers, who, the authors hope, are able to perceive the logic and complexities of these multiple essays.

Remembering how the editors previously characterized the personal essay as following the "apparent whim and impulse of the author himself or the apparently casual association of ideas" (the Montaigne question from the first edition, "Does this essay have any formal structure or is it merely haphazard? If it has a structure, what determines that structure?" is a good example) helps to pinpoint the development of stronger questions in the third edition. Specifically, in this edition Brooks and Warren pay greater attention to how the reader is figured in the essay, as well as the tone the essay establishes in relation to the reader.

Reader-oriented questions in this edition include the following:

- What is the tone of the essay? What do the allusions and quotations used by Lamb tell us of his attitude toward the reader? On what terms does he stand with the reader? What kind of reader does he envision?
- To whom is this essay addressed? The author writes: "We have forgotten, etc." Who is we? What is the tone of the essay?

Furthermore, the third edition offers more precise questions helping the student to engage style. Through modeling, the pedagogical apparatus asks students to articulate similar comparisons between essays. In some cases, the authors encourage students to account for and describe elements of tone, implied content, and specific textual devices—in order to home in on the style of the essay.

- Why does Lamb recur to China teacups at the end of his essay? Is he merely trying to justify the title? Or is some artistic function accomplished by this return? (592)
- Discuss the style of this essay, noting particularly the means by which the author establishes a particular tone. (579)
- How would you describe the style of this essay? The first paragraph, for example, has a number of echoes from the King James version of the Bible. (Can you point them out?) In what other ways is the style "literary"? Compare and contrast it with the style of Hemingway, of Bishop, and of Lamb in his informal essay, "Old China." (523)
- Is there any difference in style between Churchill writing as a historian and Churchill speaking as an orator? In this connection, consider very carefully the style of the last paragraph. (588)
- As a historian, Churchill is necessarily interested in giving facts—precise dates, places, even tables of statistics. Does he manage to make his facts "come alive"? Does he succeed in presenting the dramatic excitement as felt by himself and the British people? If so, how has he done this? Consider carefully the diction, the comparisons, and the rhythms of the relevant passages. (588)
- What is the function of the French quotations? Thurber sometimes translates the relevant passages. Would anything be lost if he used no quotations in French at all? (601)

Instructed by these precise directives to consider specific words and sentences, students are called upon to describe how textual elements work in concert to achieve a particular tone, style, and overall effect. Moreover, in the final question students are asked to pay attention to the intricate ways the text is constructed by considering how the text might change if it were missing one or more of its elements. This encouragement to engage style is developed still further in the next edition.

Fourth Edition, 1964

The fourth edition, the last to include essays, exemplifies many of the changes Brooks and Warren struggled to implement in their earlier discussions of the essay. Especially since the fifth edition omits nonfiction prose entirely, it seems that the genre of the essay posed challenges not usually present in Brooks and Warren's other textbooks: reading and interpreting literature not easily categorized as "imaginative" or "pure." Indicative of these challenges is that essays in the fourth edition now fall under the category of Discursive Prose. This is a substantial reorganization of the section on the essay: the rubric of "Discursive Prose" now combines four categories—the personal essay, the essay of idea and opinion, the critical essay, and biography. Surveying textbooks from 1956 to 1960, Richard M. Eastman observes that the genre of prose nonfiction "is virtually confined to the freshman course" and thus to the texts and anthologies marketed toward such a course (221). Clearly, this redesignation seeks to align forms of the essay more squarely with other modes of discourse—narration, persuasion, exposition, and description—on which another of their textbooks, *Modern Rhetoric,* relied throughout its editions.

The change of *Approach*'s overall heading to Discursive Prose also indicates larger theoretical changes within the text.[8] The fourth edition is more grounded in rhetorical purpose, a point emphasized at the beginning of each subsection through a discussion of the "occasion" to which writers respond (whether writing a personal essay, an essay of idea, a fictional story, etc.). This stronger focus on occasion usefully complicates the division between literary/belletristic writing and utilitarian writing which underlay earlier editions of the textbook. Moreover, rather than present form and style as merely aesthetic categories, this edition instead frames them as part of a rhetorical project, focusing on the connection of style and structure to "the writer's concern for precision and expressiveness in his exploration and discrimination of meanings" (432).

This shift toward a more rhetorical understanding of literature allows Brooks and Warren to expand their lexicon for and attention to the elements of style in writing, especially through developing richer questions for the apparatus. Nonetheless, their methods of reading poetry persist as a central way to attend to style, as demonstrated in the exercise example: "Study the characteristic sentence structure. Read sections aloud and catch the natural rhythm of the prose" (436). New to the pedagogical approach, however, is the opportunity for students to respond to readings by generating their own sets of questions. Instead of being directed by the editors, students are encouraged to develop questions that "would serve as a guide to a critical discussion of both content and method" as well as to make pertinent "comparisons with content or method of other essays" (491).

New questions also more fully interrogate sentence, paragraph, and holistic stylistics. One set focuses on "effective" parts of the text—"bits of description, turns of phrase, or bits of dialogue" that stand out to the student (517). The fourth edition also generally applies more pressure to essayistic structure and how essayistic prose differs from fictional prose. More questions emerge in the fourth edition that ask students to attend to specific stylistic and structural moments: "Consider the structure of the next to the last paragraph. By ordinary standards it is wandering and pointless. Do you find it effective here? If so, why?" (440)

The authors also finally return to some of their key essays, by Lamb and others, which have appeared throughout several editions. Although Brooks and Warren typically innovate most in the apparatus around new readings, this edition also presents a productive expansion of the questions for readings retained from edition to edition, which have seen only small modifications over several editions. The result is a more comprehensive and consistent method across the essays. This more even development of the apparatus also allows a new type of second-order question to surface: "What different kinds of styles does Whitman, according to this critic, employ? What examples of critical analysis do you find Jarrell using in distinguishing these styles?" (545). Here students are asked to not only locate and describe multiple styles used by a single author, but to also take into account the types of analysis used to make judgments about style.

In its greater attention to particular uses of structure and style in a wider array of the essay selections, Brooks and Warren's fourth edition thus illustrates the growth of seeds planted in earlier editions. Although a few of the questions still contain vestiges of earlier editions—such as a focus on discerning the "personality" of the author via the text—and although the rubric of clarity is often used to explain stylistic choices, the fourth edition of *An Approach to Literature* demonstrates the fruit of an evolving process whereby the editors grappled with essayistic style and how to help students to think about style outside the realms of fiction and poetry.[9] Reading across editions makes visible the strategies that Brooks and Warren used to adapt a literary approach to a genre that, for them, involved both literary and non-literary elements. The result was not only an enhanced theorization of how style functions in the genre of the essay, but also a more adroit effort to focus student attention on this important literary question.

Thus for Brooks and Warren, the essay—as a creature both literary and non-literary—was decidedly a critical problem, and a generative one. Most interesting is that their shifting pedagogical approach to essays over the course of this textbook's editions allows them eventually to accommodate in a "literary" way this not altogether literary genre. Struggling with the genre of the essay enabled Brooks and Warren to fine-tune their pedagogical methods—and indeed their understanding of essays and their style. The result was a more developed and consistent approach to the essay and essayistic style, as well as more fruitful questions for assisting students in reading and interpreting these challenging texts. With each new edition there was more to say, more to consider, and more attention to be paid to essays, their construction, and how their style mattered in rhetorical terms. Concomitantly, with each new edition of *Approach*, what students were asked to do and the types of readers they were asked to become shifted and developed. Students were encouraged to become more capable of pursuing their own inquiries and more competent at generating critical responses to complex textual questions. Imagined as careful readers who could make a case for what they noticed in texts, students were asked to become more focused and precise in both their responses to stylistic questions and in the way they noted connections and distinctions among genres.

Mark Jancovich notes that one reason Brooks and Warren's literature-based textbooks were so immensely influential is that they

> appeared at a time when there was no coherent practice for the teaching of literature *as literature*. Their strength was that they addressed this absence, and presented a series of pedagogical activities which could be used both inside and outside the classroom. More than any other New Critical activity, these text-books were responsible for redefining the object of literary study. They directed attention to the linguistic forms of the text, and defined the terms of reference within which literary studies largely continues to operate. (87)

Jancovich's point—that it was textbooks that largely developed and defined a practice of literary study (the study of "literature *as literature*") still largely in use today—rightly focuses our efforts to understand New Criticism through the enterprise that I would suggest mattered most to the New Criticism: helping students to read and study literature qua literature. Investigating the changes to this methodology as they were most present to students—that is to say, via textbooks and their complex, integrated, evolving pedagogical apparatuses—offers the richest site for rediscovering the analytical and interpretive practices Brooks and Warren actually advocated. Moreover, attending to these practical instantiations of New Criticism best reveals the pedagogical imperative at the heart of the New Critical project: how to teach teachers how to teach and students how to read texts as literature.

Made particularly evident through Brooks and Warren's struggle with the slippery genre of the essay is their strenuous commitment to empowering readers to consider form in rigorous ways. That they did so even when facing a genre whose literary style was less privileged and less well theorized than that of other genres demonstrates their marked dedication to this objective. Despite—perhaps because of—their anxious relationship to the elusive genre of the essay, over four editions of *An Approach to Literature* they continued to refine their pedagogical apparatus in service of this commitment, adapting their techniques for analyzing form used elsewhere to a genre usually not regarded as meriting such attention and formal analysis.

Through this examination of *An Approach to Literature*'s pedagogical trajectory, I aim to encourage more work of this kind—work that reveals specific acts of teaching—in order to illuminate more richly historical teaching practices in context, as well as their lasting influences on current pedagogy. The development of New Critical pedagogical practices, especially those showcased through Brooks and Warren's ongoing efforts to make interpretation of the essay and its style available for students, displays the difficult balance which must be struck between literary and rhetorical education, between the text and the reader. Noting even small changes across editions is important in discerning innovations in both literary and genre theory, as well as the ongoing process of adapting pedagogy to achieve the most effective classroom practices.

To enlist the concept of "style" differently, the style in which the New Critics taught has been so thoroughly absorbed into today's classroom practices that we tend to respond to it as we do a longstanding habit, as a "style to which we have become accustomed." Revisiting the particulars of how that pedagogical style entered North American classrooms to begin with, and how it developed productively over time, can help us respond to New Critical teaching methods not as mere customs used and abandoned without reflection, but rather as thoughtfully developed resources potentially adaptable for coming days.

Notes

1. For more on how textbooks instruct, interpellate, and discipline teachers in addition to students, see Hawhee, Libby Miles, and Reynolds.

2. Graff characterizes the context of the New Criticism as "part of the general revolt against empiricism which characterizes modern intellectual history—and which today animates those who believe themselves to be opponents of the New Criticism" (*Literature against Itself*, 137).

3. All of the primary scholars of New Criticism I've cited here agree that the New Critics did not, as usually charged, divorce the text entirely from historical contexts. Reviews at the time support this more nuanced understanding. See Jancovich, particularly Chapter 8, "Understanding Literature: Textbooks and the Distribution of the New Criticism."

4. The New Critics are not the only school of thought that Graff charges with falling into this trap. By Graff's account, many interpretive communities (up to 1979 when *Literature against Itself* was published) fell prey to the same binary oppositions, the result being that they "assigned ambitious cultural functions to literature while defining literature in a way that obstructed carrying out these functions" (147).

5. For an illuminating history of the collaboration on and release of these textbooks, see the introduction in Grimshaw. Apropos of the influence of *An Approach to Literature* specifically, sales of textbooks are notoriously difficult to gauge, but one number referenced in the correspondence between authors may act as a rough illustration: in under two years, a fourth edition of *An Approach to Literature* (1964) sold over 99,000 copies (Grimshaw, 264).

6. In his chapter on textbooks in *Fragments of Rationality*, Lester Faigley notes that studies focusing primarily on textbooks lack the ability to determine how these texts were used, appropriated, or challenged by teachers and students. Yet his assertion that "if textbooks are not a reliable source of data for how writing is actually taught, they do reflect teachers' and program directors' decisions about how writing should be represented to students" makes a useful distinction and, coupled with the context this chapter provides in terms of the reception of these texts, points to the ways that textbook study is important for understanding the representations of writing and reading, students and teachers (133).

7. Citations in this section reference the revised edition, published by F. S. Crofts, Inc.

8. As Kulisheck notes, textbooks such as *An Approach to Literature* furthered a "genre-approach in preference to the period or chronological approach," resulting in a curricular sea change as well: many liberal-arts colleges "completely revised . . . their curricular offerings . . . on an exclusively genre basis" (177).

9. For an alternate view on style—style as pleasure and not as clarity—see the work of Richard Lanham.

Bibliography

Brooker, Jewel Spears. "In Conclusion: Literature and Culture in the Last Essays of Cleanth Brooks." *South Atlantic Review* 60.4 (November 1995): 129–36.

Brooks, Cleanth. "Forty Years of 'Understanding Poetry.'" In *Confronting Crisis: Teachers in America,* ed. Ernestine P. Sewell and Billi M. Rogers, 166–76. Arlington: University of Texas at Arlington Press, 1979.

Brooks, Cleanth, John Thibault Pursur, and Robert Penn Warren. *An Approach to Literature.* Baton Rouge: Louisiana State University Press, 1936.

———. *An Approach to Literature,* rev. ed. New York: Appleton-Century-Croft, 1939.

———. *An Approach to Literature,* 3rd ed. New York: Appleton-Century-Croft, 1952.

———. *An Approach to Literature,* 4th ed. New York: Appleton-Century-Croft, 1964.

———. *An Approach to Literature,* 5th ed. Englewood Cliffs, NJ: Prentice-Hall, 1975.

Brooks, Cleanth, and Robert Penn Warren. *Understanding Poetry.* New York: Henry Holt, 1938.

Corbett, Edward P. J. "Teaching Style." In *The Territory of Language,* ed. Donald A. McQuade, 23–33. Carbondale: Southern Illinois University Press, 1986.

Eastman, Richard M. "On the Frequency of Certain Selections in Freshman Prose Anthologies." *College Composition and Communication* 11.4 (December 1960): 220–23.

Faigley, Lester. *Fragments of Rationality: Postmodernity and the Subject of Composition.* Pittsburgh: University of Pittsburgh Press, 1992.

Graff, Gerald. *Literature against Itself: Literary Ideas in Modern Society.* Chicago: University of Chicago Press, 1979.

———. *Professing Literature: An Institutional History.* Chicago: University of Chicago Press, 1987.

Grimshaw, James A., Jr., ed. *Cleanth Brooks and Robert Penn Warren: A Literary Correspondence.* Columbia: University of Missouri Press, 1998.

Hawhee, Debra. "Composition History and the Harbrace College Handbook." *College Composition and Communication* 50.3 (February 1999): 504–23.

Jancovich, Mark. *The Cultural Politics of the New Criticism.* Cambridge: Cambridge University Press, 1993.

Kulisheck, Clarence L. "The New Criticism and the New College Text." *The Journal of Higher Education* 25.4 (April 1954): 173–78, 227–28.

Lentricchia, Frank. *After the New Criticism.* Chicago: University of Chicago Press, 1980.

Miles, Josephine. "Review: *The Well Wrought Urn.*" *The Journal of Aesthetics and Art Criticism* 6.2 (December 1947): 185–86.

Miles, Libby. "Constructing Composition: Reproduction and WPA Agency in Textbook Production." *WPA: Writing Program Administration* 24.1–2 (Fall/Winter 2000): 27–51.

Reynolds, Nedra. "Dusting off Instructor's Manuals: The Teachers and Practices They Assume." *WPA: Writing Program Administration* 19 (1995): 7–23.

Stewart, Randall. "New Critic and Old Scholar." *College English* 15.2 (November 1953): 105–11.

Swardson, H. R. "The Heritage of the New Criticism." *College English* 41.4 (December 1979): 412–22.

Wagner, Geoffrey. "English Composition in the American University." *College Composition and Communication* 7.4 (1956): 225–28.

CHAPTER TEN

"A Kind of Dual Attentiveness"

Close Reading after the New Criticism

CECILY DEVEREUX

THE NEW CRITICISM is a school of thought now so old that it seems oddly anachronistic to discuss it in relation to contemporary reading practices. The dominant mode for literary analysis and the teaching of literature in North American post-secondary contexts from the 1930s until well into the 1970s, the New Criticism fell radically out of favor during the so-called theory wars of the last three decades of the twentieth century, when the discipline of English appeared to fracture along a line between "new," theoretically situated, historically contextualized critique and "old," putatively ahistorical analysis, which focused on language and form as it produces meaning in texts outside of—or without regard to—temporal and contextual referents. The New Criticism was justly accused of being myopic in its disposition to situate "universal" meanings not only without reference to cultural specificities, but also in the form and language of poetry largely written by white male writers; it thus acted as a primary factor in the formation of a canon whose aesthetic criteria excluded everyone else. As a result, while the New Criticism constituted a radical and invigorating school of thought in the early to mid-twentieth century (it was demonstrably new in relation to the late-nineteenth-century historicist approaches to reading it contested), by the last quarter of the century it had become a substantial impediment to development within a discipline no longer dominated—or, at any rate, less dominated—by white male academics.

Close reading, the New Criticism's primary gesture and most significant legacy, worked precisely against the kind of situated reading that characterizes theorized analysis. Because, that is, it is a practice of reading that attends to the ways in which a text produces values in relation to itself, as a more or less autonomous object that can be detached from its author and from the circumstances of its production, close reading did not lend itself well to late-twentieth-century investigations, for instance, of the conditions of authorship: the ways in which marginalized constituencies use language; the extent to which literature is imbricated in the reproduction of systems of power; and the social and political work of representation. Indeed it did not lend itself to any ideologically situated critique of literature undertaken in the necessary late-twentieth-century return to the foundations of an academy that, given the continued gaps between academic salaries along the lines of race and gender, proved an uneasy intellectual home for scholars "outside," as Spivak famously put it, "in the teaching machine."[1]

Within an academic discipline that itself foundationally and pervasively reproduced a system of social and political inequity, then, the New Criticism and its practice of close reading came to be understood as instruments for maintaining that system. In some late-twentieth-century debates about the destructive implications for English studies of race theory, feminist critique, postcolonialism, queer, class, cultural, and popular culture studies, close reading came to be represented by scholars outside the theory camp as the whipping boy of various leftist agendas. But the New Criticism and its practices were not simply and arbitrarily destroyed like the art of a deposed regime by bloodthirsty revolutionaries. Rather, as a school of thought that provided no strategies for assessing the social and political determinants in the production of language in specific contexts at specific times, the New Criticism really did function as what Audre Lorde would describe in 1979 as "the master's tools" (331).

Thus if exclusionary, male-dominated, and patriarchal scholarship characterized English studies during the first three quarters of the twentieth century and accordingly comprised what Lorde calls the "master's house," New Critical close reading could not be particularly useful to the work of dismantling that house—in the field of English, the university, and more widely. The New Criticism's role in an unequal workplace had to be assessed, and its effects on the discipline had to be addressed. As Jane Gallop suggests, "The time was ripe for . . . a course correction: ahistoricism had been persuasively linked to sexism, racism, and elitism; attacks on the canon had called into question the notion of timeless works; literary studies had been ahistorical for too long" (181).

By the end of the 1970s, close reading, under pressure from what were often represented as "special interest groups" (constituencies rendered "special" by virtue of their exclusion from the dominant category, most often through "differences" in gender, race, or sexuality), had largely vanished from classrooms and the analysis of literature. At any rate, it had ceased to function as the core of the discipline's training and critique—even to be acknowledged a valued practice. Close reading, as Terry Eagleton observes became "[l]ike thatching or clog dancing, . . . a dying art" (1), a vestige of the New Criticism that had, by then, as Frank Lentricchia puts it, met its "official" demise (xiii). No longer taught, no longer studied, no longer accorded any authority in the analysis of literature, the New Criticism was "dead"— as Lentricchia suggests, "an imposing and repressive father-figure" (xiii)— brought to its end through an act that might be understood, as Jonathan Arac has likewise intimated, as a kind of disciplinary "parricide" (347). The often vitriolic late-twentieth-century debates about whether theory or close reading was the better system for teaching and interpretation and about whether or not the New Criticism was really more historically engaged or less focused on the text as an autonomous artifact than it appeared to be gradually faded, displaced by other debates. With only a few exceptions—for instance, Lentricchia's volume, *After the New Criticism* (1980); Chaviva Hosek and Patricia Parker's 1985 collection, *Lyric Poetry: Beyond New Criticism* (1985); Mark Jancovich's study, *The Cultural Politics of the New Criticism* (1993)— hardly anyone mentioned the New Criticism in a direct and sustained way, indicated much concern with its demise, or mourned the loss of what Parker describes as its "program" (11–12).[2]

Now, however, as we enter the second decade of the twenty-first century, many academics have begun to reconsider the function of this school of thought as it pertains to critical practice and to pedagogy, with particular reference to close reading. Such reconsideration underpins recent analysis of the New Critical moment, such as that of Andrew DuBois and Frank Lentricchia in their 2003 edited volume, *Close Reading: The Reader;* Caroline Levine in a 2006 essay in *Victorian Studies* ("Strategic Formalism: Toward a New Method in Cultural Studies"); Stephen Schryer in a discussion in *PMLA* in 2007 ("Fantasies of the New Class: The New Criticism, Harvard Sociology, and the Idea of the University"); Andrew DuBois in a consideration of ethics, critics, and close reading in *University of Toronto Quarterly* in the same year; Garrick Davis, founder of the *Contemporary Poetry Review,* in an anthology of New Criticism titled *Praising It New: The Best of the New Criticism;* as well as many others, including, of course, the authors in this volume. Moreover, critics notably not associated with New

Critical practices, such as Gayatri Spivak ("Close Reading") and Jane Gallop ("The Historicization of Literary Studies and the Fate of Close Reading"), have called for a review of the work of close reading. Marjorie Levinson has weighed in with an extensive review of current writing on or within what she designates "the New Formalism," which aims, as she puts it, "to recover for teaching and scholarship in English some version of their traditional address to aesthetic form" (559).[3] Eric Savoy has made a case for what he calls "Queer Formalism." Perhaps most unexpectedly, in 2007 Terry Eagleton published *How to Read a Poem,* suggesting the importance for readers (of poetry, specifically) of attending to matters of form and language ("Tone, Mood and Pitch," "Syntax, Grammar and Punctuation," "Rhythm and Metre") historically associated with the domain of what I. A. Richards in 1929 called "Practical Criticism" rather than with ideologically situated analysis.

Given the emergence of the majority of these discussions of close reading from such contexts as feminism, poststructuralism, postcolonial critique, queer theory, and Marxism, it cannot be suggested that there are many academics who advocate a full-scale return to a school of thought whose time has come and gone, and in whose recession from classrooms and scholarly inquiry many still active in the profession were involved. Professional equity along the lines of race, gender, and sexuality has certainly not been fully achieved, and salary and promotion gaps between nonvisible-minority men and visible-minority women are still acutely evident across North American universities; and if New Critical practices can be understood to be implicated in creating these gaps, it is hard to make a case for taking them up again. Moreover, although in English studies, old exclusionary canons have been largely displaced as structuring principles for course syllabi and programs of research, dominance and marginality still obtain in many textbooks, anthologies, and areas of inquiry throughout the discipline. Thus the need to maintain pressure on the practices that demonstrably reproduced and reinforced the patriarchal academy continues to exist; and it is doubtful that any of the critics cited above, whatever their theoretical affiliations, could be accused of leading a retro-guard to restore a system whose unsituated formal analysis serves as index of the academy's inequities.

Nonetheless, these critics, along with many others, are making a collective and increasingly urgent call for some version of the old New Critical practice of attending to form and language, and, in particular, to return to teaching the "art" of close reading. Like Gallop, they argue that close reading was "the most valuable thing English ever had to offer" (183) and like Savoy, "invite the fainthearted formalists to overcome their embarrassment and institutional abjection" (80) and return to doing what they used to do. "Forward," as Eagleton puts it, "to antiquity!" (16).

If there is not, in fact, a rearguard plot to reaffirm patriarchy in the university (as some feminists have suggested there is in the various performances of "backlash" since the early 1980s[4]), then the rationale for the call to close reading is obscure. Why do so many scholars want close reading back? What has been lost with its eradication from scholarship and classrooms? What will be gained with its reinstatement? How is what happens in English studies now *less* than it was before—before theory, before new historicisms, before situated, archive-based critique? And, most importantly, what conditions in the discipline and the academy are indicated by the desire to return to close reading? The university, Bill Readings suggested a decade ago, is palpably "in ruins"; disciplines across the academy are charting decline[5]; apocalyptic reports of imminent disappearance, diminishing value, and disciplinary fragmentation proliferate, in English studies and elsewhere. The New Criticism "died" a long time ago; more recently the discipline has seen not only the "end of reading" (Eagleton, 1) but the "death" of theory itself—or, at any rate, as Jonathan Culler suggests, widespread reports of its death (Culler, 1). The disciplinary moment symptomized by the call for a return to close reading, then, is characterized by postness: "after the New Criticism" (Lentricchia, 1980), "after theory" (Eagleton, 2003), poststructuralist, -modern, -colonial, -feminist, and -human, what, as a 2003 Readers' Forum in *English Studies in Canada* (*ESC*) asked, is "left of English studies"?[6] What do we study? How do we teach it? And, crucially, how do we train others to do the work of the discipline?

The *ESC* Forum and many other such investigations, in tandem with the broad call for a return to close readings, suggest that the discipline of English, if not in ruins, is broadly aware of an identity crisis. Unlike the situation in the seventies and eighties, however, the current crisis is an effect less of political infighting or ongoing contests of margin versus center than of decentering itself, both as it involves repositioning what had been marginalized in relation to the dominant and as it signifies a gap at the core of disciplinary identity. Although the proliferation of disciplinary self-analysis in this first decade of the twenty-first century has yielded a substantial catalogue of concerns pertaining to the profession (what it is, what we do, why it matters), what is at the heart of this discussion across all its categories—what defines the gap—is what used to be called literature. Evident in discussions of the state of the discipline is an intuition that what has been lost is a coherent, collective, and, if always conditionally and provisionally, shared idea of the object of disciplinary study. The focus of English studies has become unclear, shifting over the past twenty-five years from literature through text across a range of discursive registers to a kind of studies that are sometimes Cultural Studies and sometimes just culturally situated, and not necessarily textual or language-based at all. Literature, it might be argued, is no longer the focus of English studies.

In fact, we, if there is any kind of first-person plural subject at all, do not teach what used to be called literature, but instead a range of cultural documents and practices that function not so much to demonstrate to students the lineaments and terms of "English" as a discernible disciplinary body but rather the extent to which what used to be called literature operates across disciplinary boundaries and is comprehensible not through the study of literature itself but through the lenses and positions of theoretical tools and systems that are mobilized in many disciplines. Accordingly, sociologists, historians, musicologists, anthropologists, philosophers, and English scholars might all "use" the same references to explore and articulate values in the material they study and teach. Although, as Terry Eagleton rightly observes, it is "one of the great myths or unexamined clichés of contemporary critical debate" that close reading was "destroyed" by "theory, with its soulless abstractions and vacuous generalities" (1), it is true, as Culler points out, that theory breaks down disciplinary boundaries. If we understand theory, as Culler defines it, "as work that succeeds in challenging and reorienting thinking in fields other than those in which it originates" (3), then it is, as he suggests, "inescapably interdisciplinary" (4) and minimizes distinctions between disciplines—at the level both of "approach" or methodology and of the object of inquiry. This effect is certainly evident in English, as scholars find themselves in a location that is still nominally identified as a discipline while becoming increasingly undifferentiated from other disciplines by methods and objects of analysis. While there is not necessarily any loss in this configuration—scholarship is unquestionably enriched by the movement of ideas across disciplinary boundaries—the effect for English studies, perhaps uniquely in the academy, has been a demonstrable diminishment in its engagement with its former object of inquiry, as well as of the disciplinary sense of what that object is. What has been lost is a shared sense of literature: what it is and why it matters.

In many ways, what there is to study in English is much more than was there before: the political critique of the literary that informed the theory-driven canon wars in the late twentieth century stretched the boundaries of "literature" to include writing by women and marginalized categories, non-English or colonial English and sometimes translated texts, nonliterary genres, print culture, and non-language-based symbolic systems and media.

It also gave rise to new canon of key theoretical, philosophical, historical, and scientific commentary that would constitute the groundwork of critique in English as in other disciplines. In other ways, however, interdisciplinary boundary-crossing has meant that this terrain is wide open and not the "property" of English studies. That is, if literature is not to be differentiated from any other kind of cultural production, the point of a discipline whose purpose is the study of literature becomes unclear. Anybody in English studies can read anything across any disciplinary terrain, and, indeed, can bring that reading to research and teaching as the knowledge in relation to which any text or process signifies; conversely, anybody equipped with the same theoretical toolbox can read literature and situate it in relation to the cultural context it reproduces, with and in relation to other documents and processes doing related work. English studies might thus be seen to have expanded to become, in one sense, everything, while in another, to have diminished into nothing.

Thus what is at stake in the current discussion of close reading is what close reading functioned to define and validate—both literature and the profession of literary studies. On the one hand, the question "What's left of English studies?" speaks to the problem of a discipline whose identity in the academy has been mystified; on the other hand, to the problem of literature itself as an identifiable, distinct, and meaningful element in of the field of cultural production; as a mode of discourse whose characteristics differentiate it from other kinds of discursive production and merit, if not problematic placement above other kinds of cultural production, at least attention to what it does and how it does it. The current conversation invites discipline-specific methodologies, practices of analysis that attend to the work itself and not only, as in some historicized or situated readings, its function as evidence or "symptom" of systems in which it is implicated. The call for a return to close reading is thus a call for English studies to define itself again with reference to what it is that English studies studies—just as it was for the New Critics, who undertook to "redefine the literary institution and its claim to professional status" (Jancovich, 144).

Gallop notes that it was the New Criticism and close reading that transformed studies in English from "a gentlemanly practice of amateur history" or what Searle describes as "the genteel cultivation of taste and sentiment" (528) into a profession (183): "We became a discipline, so the story goes, when we stopped being armchair historians and became instead painstaking close readers" (183). By this logic, without a definable, teachable methodology such as close reading, we are in danger of losing disciplinary identity. Indeed, Gallop suggests, we are in danger of becoming a "practice of amateur history" all over again: "While," she argues, "today's literary historians with their leftist leanings and insistence on understanding literature in a generally cultural and especially political context are hardly gentlemanly, still I fear they are—despite their archival work—amateurs. Certainly that is what our colleagues in history think" (183). In other words, according to Gallop, the archival and historical turn in English studies, while crucial to redefining the discipline and working toward forms of equality in the academy, has not only blurred the boundaries of the discipline but brought it back to much the condition in which the New Critics found it early in the early twentieth century when they developed a system of reading that would address the specificity and function of literature.

Although the New Critics were often accused of making the analysis of literature too "scientific," the effect of "practical criticism" was in many ways to affirm not the value of the discipline as an enterprise that is like science, but at a fundamental level the value of literature as cultural production. The New Critical canon registered the pervasively patriarchal structures—socially and of course also in the context of the university—from which close reading emerged; and New Critical analysis, obscuring the social and political circumstances in which authors and readers are imbricated, inevitably reproduced that patriarchal structure. But as Jancovich argues, the New Critics

> stressed that [literature or] the aesthetic was not inherently separate from human activity, but a form which should be fully integrated with all activities; that it should be established within a way of living that had acknowledged, and come to terms with, human nature. As a result, their literary criticism was not a form of scientism, but developed out of a reaction against positivist concepts of science. (144)

What Stephen Schryer describes as "the discipline's specialized techne" not only worked to "make criticism more scientific—that is, more predictable and rigorous" (665), but also "distinguish[ed] literary texts]," Searle suggests, "from other texts or other uses of language (particularly scientific language)" (528). The New Critical sense of literature, in other words, is that the ways in which humans negotiate language in texts whose function is artistic or aesthetic constitutes a vital area of scholarly inquiry, and, moreover, that the criticism of literary texts is a meaningful "form of activity itself" (Jancovich, 144), not so much because it elucidates cultural events or the circumstances conditioning an author's performance of identity but because it enables consideration of the text's own negotiation of language processes and attention to how constructions in form and language speak to and engage with contemporary moments.

The New Criticism thus both "redefined the profession of English" (Jancovich, 138) and reaffirmed the importance of literature as a human activity that merits systematic study. Its processes can be identified and named; its effects traced through analysis. Its negotiation of language to investigate complex and contradictory responses to environment, experience, and identity can be understood to be sufficiently complex to justify sustained, rigorous analysis. If, that is, the ways in which humans engage through language with the conditions that language both represents and constitutes is meaningful, then the systematic analysis of its meanings is also meaningful.

It is this kind of idealism that motivated the New Criticism and its work to develop a discipline dedicated to the study of literature. It is likewise this kind of idealism that motivates the current wave of critics calling for a return to close reading. The problem confronting these critics, however, is twofold. On the one hand is the question of the literary itself, and the problem of affirming the value of this form of human engagement in and with language without reconstructing old hierarchies separating "art" from other cultural work and "high" from "low" art. On the other is the problem of the New Criticism as an apparatus that simultaneously affirms through its practice of close reading the specificity of literature as a form of cultural production and reproduces a system within which the conditions of textual production and circulation are not considered as factors in the ways in which literature signifies. The problem, in other words, is how to reaffirm the literary without undermining the crucial late-twentieth-century expansion of the literary (and the aesthetic) beyond a male-dominated, Anglocentric, white canon of specific texts and particular genres and without undoing the expansion of the discipline as workplace and intellectual home for scholars whose marginality has only recently and tenuously been redressed. The problem is, in effect, how to dislodge the historicism that, in the view of scholars such as Gallop, has turned English studies away from the textual production of meaning to a consideration of its function, as Culler puts it, as "a symptom, whose causes are to be found in historical reality" (9)—and, importantly, how to do this without disarticulating analysis from history. The question is how to integrate close reading with social and political critique.

Jancovich maintains that the New Critics did undertake such an integrated practice, making "the critique of modern society the centre of their argument and approach" (144). By the same token, Eagleton argues that close reading has in fact always informed the practice of what he describes, in a kind of Arnoldian swerve, as "the twentieth century's towering literary scholars," for whom, he suggests, "there is a politics implicit in the painstaking investigation of the literary text" (8–9); and Culler holds that "formalism does not involve a denial of history, as is sometimes claimed" and that "it is precisely because language is historical through and through . . . that we must relate any linguistic event to the synchronic system from which it emerges" (9–10). But the fact remains that the New Criticism represents a problematic, exclusionary, and deeply biased notion of the literary and of the discipline, and that the New Criticism did not consider the historical as an integral factor the work of close reading—as contemporary critics suggest that any "new" practice of close reading must do.

In the current project of defining a disciplinary practice, Levinson describes a "new formalism" that takes up a "project of cultivating 'a historically informed formalist criticism'" (559). Caroline Levine, meanwhile, traces a movement toward what she calls "strategic formalism," a culturally situated method premised on the idea that "literary forms do not merely reflect social relationships but may help bring them into being" (625) and that demonstrates how "literary forms participate in a destabilizing relation to social formation, often colliding with social hierarchies rather than reflecting or foreshadowing them" (626). And Eagleton observes what he calls "a kind of dual attentiveness: to the grain and texture of literary works, and to those works' cultural contexts" (8). Such gestures, Levine suggests, do not disregard the cultural as a central location for the production of meaning, but emphasize it; they do not, Eagleton holds, diminish "the critic's social and political responsibilities" (16) but compellingly affirm them; they do not, Gallop suggests, return to what has often been seen in relation to New Critical practices (as it was for the philologically and historically oriented models of English studies prior to the New Criticism) as an authoritarian model of reading and teaching, but revitalize what she describes as "our most effective antiauthoritarian pedagogy" (185).

None of these critics proposes a reduction of the expanded literary field of the late twentieth century; what they all do propose, however, is a method, inspired by the methods of the New Criticism, that makes it possible to see cultural texts not necessarily as autonomous objects but nonetheless as works that generate their own meanings through the organization and particular use of language, not detached from social and political contexts or histories, but equally not detached from symbolic practice. What close reading thus seems to mean as it is represented by scholars calling for its return, is a not a de-emphasis of content per se (although, Gallop recommends teaching course materials with less reference to extradisciplinary and already established knowledge that must be given to students as context for understanding a text), but an emphasis of form as itself a symbolic practice and, as Fredric Jameson suggests, itself ideological. Caroline Levine draws attention to Jameson's "attention to the *ideology of form* as an effort to grasp the 'symbolic messages transmitted to us by the coexistence of various sign systems which are themselves traces or anticipations of modes of production'" (Jameson, qtd. in Levine, 625). Where the "dually attentive" practice of close reading that is tentatively identified as "new formalism" and "strategic formalism" differs from the older New Critical practice is precisely in its understanding of form as it produces values.

Formal practices have of course been productively charted over the discipline's history and formed the basis of New Critical analysis of rhetoric, narrative, genre, poetic meter and poetic form, structure, and figure. They represent what Eagleton describes as "the grain and texture of literary works." To consider them is thus to affirm "the literary"; to situate them in relation to "works' cultural contexts" is to affirm the extent to which literature—albeit an expansive and flexible category—is also distinct from cultural production generally. It is not that literature is more or less important than other kinds of writing and symbolic representation, but it does produce effects in language and sign systems in different ways. If disciplinary identity and distinctness matter, and if literature is the lost object of English studies and the thing sought in the impulse to return to close reading, then recognizing and engaging with those differences matters too.

There is always a danger in fundamentalism: this has been as evident in what Savoy describes as "the self-perpetuating circularity of raceclassgender" (80) or what Gallop suggests is the authority of historicism as it once was in New Critical practices of insisting on the autonomy and discrete form of the literary text. There is thus a clear danger in arguing for a critical practice necessary to the survival of the discipline. The point, however, is not necessarily to articulate an imperative with regard to the specifics of what we teach and study, nor to construct factions across the battlefield of the text and its interpretation (theorized close reading *versus* theory without close reading; literary *versus* nonliterary), but rather to continue to develop understanding of how what we teach and study shapes the discipline in which we work and the social structures we inhabit. The recent interest in returning to close reading in the context of ideologically situated criticism and in relation to the conditions of the academy might most compellingly indicate that the problems evident in the New Critical moment, while lessened, have not altogether disappeared. These systemic problems may well be similarly reproduced to some degree in a discipline organized around history and theory. If historicism and theory have not produced an academic ecosystem that has managed to move beyond the terms of the dominant and the marginal and is radically more equitable than that which characterized the New Critical moment, then there is still work to be done—the work of dually attentive close reading.

Notes

1. Spivak, *Outside in the Teaching Machine* (1993). With regard to continued inequity in the academic workplace, see, for instance, the data published by the Canadian Federation for the Humanities and Social Sciences (CFHSS) in 2006, which indicates that in Canadian universities in 2001 the salaries of nonvisible-minority women represent 68.9% and those of visible-minority women 55.4% of those of nonvisible-minority men. Statistics related to hiring and promotion in Canada in the first decade of the twentieth century are similar to widely published records in the US: in 2003 women, 59% of graduating students, comprise 31.7% of university teachers; First Nations, people with disabilities, and visible minorities represent, collectively, 22.5% of university teachers. Women occupy 29.9% of the highest ranking positions at American universities and 18.1% at Canadian universities (2003). See "Feminist and Equity Audits 2006" <www.fedcan.ca/english/pdf/issues/FEAAuditpostcardEng.pdf>.

2. Parker outlines the New Critical "program of treating the literary text as an isolated artifact or object, dismissing concern with author's intention and reader's response, and the tenet of the text's organic wholeness, its reconciliation of tension or diversity into unity" (11–12).

3. Levinson's essay provides an important overview of current criticism engaged with questions of form and formal analysis across a range of fields.

4. Susan Faludi, *Backlash: The Undeclared War against American Women* (New York: Crown, 1991).

5. See, for instance, Spivak on comparative literature in *Death of a Discipline* (2003).

6. Jo-Ann Wallace, ed., "Forum: What's Left of English Studies?" *English Studies in Canada* 29.1–2 (2003): 1–84.

Bibliography

Arac, Jonathan. "Afterword: Lyric Poetry and the Bounds of New Criticism." Hosek and Parker, 345–56.

Bauerlein, Mark. "What We Owe the New Critics." *The Chronicle of Higher Education,* 21 December 2007.

Culler, Jonathan. *The Literary in Theory.* Stanford: Stanford University Press, 2007.

DuBois, Andrew. "Ethics, Critics, Close Reading." *University of Toronto Quarterly* 76.3 (2007): 926–36.

Eagleton, Terry. *How to Read a Poem.* Oxford: Blackwell, 2007.

Gallop, Jane. "The Historicization of Literary Studies and the Fate of Close Reading." In *Profession 2007,* ed. R. G. Feal, 181–86. New York: MLA, 2007.

Green, Daniel. "Literature Itself: The New Criticism and Aesthetic Experience." *Philosophy and Literature* 27.1 (2003): 62–79.

Hosek, Chaviva, and Patricia Parker, eds. *Lyric Poetry beyond New Criticism.* Ithaca: Cornell University Press, 1985.

Jancovich, Mark. *The Cultural Politics of the New Criticism.* Cambridge: Cambridge University Press, 1993.

Lentricchia, Frank. *After the New Criticism.* Chicago: University of Chicago Press, 1980.

Levine, Caroline. "Strategic Formalism: Toward a New Method in Cultural Studies." *Victorian Studies* 48.4 (2006): 625–57.

Levinson, Marjorie. "What Is New Formalism?" *PMLA* 122.2 (2007): 558–69.

Lorde, Audre, "The Master's Tools Will Never Dismantle the Master's House" (1979). In *The Essential Feminist Reader,* ed. Estelle B. Freedman (New York: Modern Library, 2007), 331–35.

Parker, Patricia. "Introduction." In Hosek and Parker, 11–28.

Savoy, Eric. "Restraining Order." *English Studies in Canada* 29.1–2 (2003): 77–84.

Schryer, Stephen. "Fantasies of the New Class: The New Criticism, Harvard Sociology, and the Idea of the University." *PMLA* 122.3 (2007): 663–78.

Searle, Leroy F. "New Criticism." In *The Johns Hopkins Guide to Literary Theory and Criticism,* ed. Michael Groden and Martin Kreiswirth, 528–34. Baltimore: Johns Hopkins University Press, 1994.

Spivak, Gayatri Chakravorty. "Close Reading." *PMLA* 121.5 (2006): 1608–17.

———. *Outside in the Teaching Machine.* New York: Routledge, 1993.

Toward a New Close Reading

JOHN McINTYRE AND MIRANDA HICKMAN

A S WE ENTER a new millennium, our experiences of reading, once chiefly associated with the printed page, have undergone radical changes. Given the recent proliferation in our culture of digital text and hypertext, a dizzying array of new social media, storage devices, and e-readers, all of which present verbal text in new forms, we are increasingly prompted to take stock of our habitual reading practices and how they need to be adapted to new modes of transmission. We encounter verbal text on the web, in text messages, updates on Facebook, and blog posts. Accordingly, contemporary culture is proving fertile ground for the reconsideration of reading practices—and within literary studies, for a reevaluation of the approaches to reading associated with the New Criticism, suspicion of which for many years served as a kind of disciplinary shibboleth. In recent years, methods of close reading in particular have been increasingly invoked as they bear not only upon the category of "literature" but also on a much wider range of verbal text in various media, as well as on the semiotics of cultural texts more broadly.[1]

In "The Historicization of Literary Studies and the Fate of Close Reading," Jane Gallop laments what she perceives as a decline during the late 1980s and 1990s in literary studies of methods of close reading that have, in her view, provided the most valuable skills that the field offers. Even during the first days of "high theory" in the late 1970s and 1980s, when those committed to new currents in theory were refusing the "elitism" and "ahistoricism" of the New Criticism, approaches such as deconstruction in many respects carried on careful close readings whose maneuvers were very much indebted to the New Criticism. By the turn of the century, however, she notes, New Historicism and other historicizing approaches—at least as widely practiced—had contributed to a decline of close reading. And by this, Gallop means what most contemporary commentators who note the waning of close reading usually mean: the general assumption is that what close reading "reads" is, broadly speaking, aesthetic form. As Marjorie Levinson has recently noted, certainly the founders of New Historicism, themselves deeply invested in close reading, were not responsible for this trend; Thomas Laqueur likewise notes that the "new historicism, at least in its Berkeley version, engaged passionately with what are traditionally taken to be formalist questions" (50). But later New Historicist and related work was often read as displacing the emphasis on close reading for form with historical research. As Gallop observes, by 2000, archival work was regarded as paramount for jobseekers in the field, and many students were emerging from doctoral programs in literary studies without skills in close reading.

Gallop contends that if, in the name of removing from literary studies the dimensions of New Critical work with which we no longer want to be associated, we also jettison close reading, we lose an approach that has not only been crucial to the formation of the discipline of literary studies, but that is what we, distinctively, have to offer, both to our field and to neighboring disciplines. Insofar as it promotes active learning and empowers students to assert claims based on evidence they themselves can find, Gallop maintains that close reading provides our best defense against authoritarian, top-down forms of pedagogy. Like many others in the field today—Paglia, Graff, Eagleton, as well as those such as Heather Dubrow, Susan Wolfson, and Charles Altieri whom Levinson associates with the "New Formalism"—Gallop calls for a reinvigoration of close reading.

Such appeals have clearly constituted a major impetus for this volume. Likewise forming an important point of departure for the project and underscoring the importance of the historically reevaluative work undertaken by its essays is recent attention to a related phenomenon that Sharon Marcus and Stephen Best term "surface reading." In the introduction to "The Way We Read Now," their special issue of *Representations* published in fall 2009, Best and Marcus highlight this set of allied interpretive practices as playing a fundamental role in the "way we read now." Surface reading responds to an interpretive practice (which, following Fredric Jameson, they call "symptomatic reading") that has held significant sway over literary–critical practices since the 1970s, when New Criticism faded from the scene and the "metalanguages" of psychoanalysis and Marxism began to exert significant influence. This approach entails what Paul Ricoeur dubbed a hermeneutics of suspicion—i.e., proceeding with skepticism about what texts apparently present—and reads texts for latent content: manifest content is read as merely "symptomatic" of a deeper underlying logic, narrative, or ideology that waits to be uncovered by the discerning, "heroic" critic. As Best and Marcus have it, "when symptomatic readers focus on elements in the text, they construe them as symbolic of something latent or concealed" (3). According to Jameson, the "strong" critic has to "unmask" the text and "restore" to "the surface the history that the text represses."

By contrast, the essays gathered in "The Way We Read Now" feature recent critical approaches that depart from such symptomatic reading and turn, in some cases return, to varieties of "surface reading"—which involve attending to, interpreting, and evaluating what is evident in texts, rather than assuming that their most important dimensions are to be derived from distrusting what the textual surface suggests and exposing hidden depths. Among the contemporary varieties of surface reading they note, Best and Marcus highlight a practice of close reading that derives from the New Criticism, which focuses on revealing the "'linguistic density' and 'verbal complexity' of literary texts" (10). More generally, surface reading involves a "willed, sustained proximity to the text," directly reminiscent of the "aims of the New Criticism, which insisted that the key to a text's meaning lay within the text itself, particularly in its formal properties" (10).[2]

Animating the project of *Rereading the New Criticism* is an argument that Best and Marcus do not address but that their comments imply: that today's reinvigorated forms of close and surface reading can valuably be informed by—in fact, need the support of—historically based reevaluations of the New Criticism of the kind this volume offers. Most obviously, such reevaluation can bring forward specific classic readings from the New Critics and their predecessors that can guide contemporary close readings. While latter-day critics would no doubt not always wish to emulate the letter of these readings (we may not want to read for irony, ambiguity, and paradox), their spirit of close critical attention can nonetheless inspire today's work, and their readings can shape contemporary commentary both through what they model and how they go awry. As Connor Byrne's article notes, such approaches are especially useful when confronting literary texts that present forms of readerly "difficulty," which the New Critics, championing the difficulty of both modernist writers (such as Eliot) and their predecessors (such as Donne), prided themselves on being able to meet with specific critical techniques.[3]

What the New Critics sought to discover in a text through close reading

were those aspects of it beyond its thematics—what comprised its "form"—
which in their view constituted the dimensions of it that made it distinctively
"literary," and thus in need of specifically literary analytical and interpretive practice. In these days of anxious reassessment of what literary studies
itself studies, this indicates another issue that reengagement with the history
of the New Criticism can illuminate. Much recent interest in the New Criticism stems from its signature theoretical concern: how to read a literary text
qua literary text, rather than as historical document, registration of a moral
or philosophical position, set of themes, or witness to the cultural currents
of an era. What dimensions—what "differentia" or "residuary tissue" (as
Ransom put it in "Criticism, Inc." [349])—remain when one turns aside from
what the text provides at the level of content? And what difference do these
dimensions make to the text's content? One of the prime New Critical con-
tentions was that, if read closely for this "residuum" (Brooks, ii), "poetry
gives us knowledge" of a kind not otherwise available, not accessible through
other modes of discourse.[4] Recent work from Charles Altieri, whom Marjorie Levinson associates with the New Formalism, engages these New Critical
efforts to theorize such "literary knowledge," reads them as having fallen
short and considers how to follow this lead of the New Critics into deeper
knowledge of the value of "dispositions"—states of mind, body, and feeling—that poetry, if closely read with attention to what it does distinctively
qua poetry, can uniquely help us to achieve. "For me," Altieri notes, "all the
ladders start with the New Criticism" (259).

But all this should not imply that renewing engagement with New Critical close reading and its theoretical underpinnings pertains only to literary
studies. The relevance of close reading to other disciplines constitutes another
compelling issue toward which this volume gestures. As Best and Marcus
note, since the 1980s, literary critics have felt "licensed to study objects other
than literary ones, using paradigms drawn from anthropology, history, and
political theory"; and by the same token, other such fields have "themselves
borrowed from literary criticism an emphasis on close reading and interpretation" (1). In this new era, approaches to reading and interpretive techniques
honed in the domain of literary studies have come into increasing use in
neighboring disciplines.

In another special issue of *Representations,* appearing in Fall 2008 and
entitled "On Form," members of the journal's editorial board present essays
that variously insist upon the rich potential inherent in reading for form
across the disciplines. Encapsulating the issue's mission, Thomas Laqueur
recalls that the interdisciplinary journal was in fact originally established out
of interest in how texts in different fields often employ similar forms: the
founders shared a concern with "genre and plot that seemed to structure

events in the world as well as on the page and on canvas; in the figures of metaphor, synecdoche, and metonymy that informed novels, political theory, and legislation alike . . . in historical isomorphism, that is, an 'identity' or 'similarity' . . . of form between seemingly different contemporaneous or temporally distant domains" (51).

It is in this spirit that the contributors to this special issue of *Representations* bring self-consciously formalist interpretive strategies to their objects of study—whether the British film documentary *Seven Up,* passages from Flaubert and Melville, the Florentine Codex, military history, the evolution of the modern crematorium, a specific edition of Rousseau's *Social Contract,* or the ephemera of notes and meeting agendas associated with *Representations* itself. Considering the "intellectual and emotional responses" that prompt many commentators today to return to formalist readings, Samuel Otter suggests that their keywords "often signal . . . a sense that there has been a loss of recalcitrance, idiosyncrasy, and surprise in textual analysis." A prevailing feeling animating the return to form is that "Critics move too quickly through text to context or from ideology to text, without conceding the 'slowness of perception' that the Russian formalist Victor Shklovsky described as characteristically produced by verbal art" (117). Otter's invocation of a giant figure from an earlier stage of formalist interpretation reminds us that the New Critics were certainly not the only voices advocating for varieties of "close reading"during the first half of the twentieth century[5]: Otter highlights the importance of a careful engagement with that earlier history with an eye to enriching contemporary critical practices. Marjorie Levinson likewise notes in "What Is New Formalism?" that when reassessing formalisms of the past, we should not focus exclusively on the New Criticism, though it is still the New Criticism that is most closely associated in contemporary North American contexts with early to mid-twentieth-century formalist analysis: we need also to "introduce students to a wider array of formalisms: Russian formalism; Aristotelian and Chicago school formalism; the culturally philological formalism of Erich Auerbach and Leo Spitzer; the singular projects of William Empson, F. R. Leavis, I. A. Richards, Northrop Frye, Kenneth Burke, Wayne Booth" (563).

Such historical work can not only inform new varieties of close reading, but can also foster close critical reading of the very critical strategies involved in different forms of close reading. Bradley Clissold's reading of William Empson comes to mind here, with its suggestion that the tools of formal analysis can yield valuable and provocative results when brought to bear not only on Empson's poetry but also on his literary criticism, as well as the relations obtaining between the two. And in rereading the New Criticism itself closely, we need to consider the ethical implications of bringing into play again its techniques, theoretical concerns, and assumptions. As Cecily Devereux's essay emphasizes, among the reasons for the New Criticism's fall from dominance was its inter-imbrication with understandings of literary canon, academic culture, and aesthetic and literary values that today's academics can no longer countenance. She stresses the importance of remembering, in other words, the ethical blind spots of the New Criticism, especially in its institutional varieties, that involved it in the perpetuation of a patriarchal, Eurocentric, elitist academy many have labored over the past four decades to overturn. This, coupled with the emphasis of the New Critics themselves on ethics—as Robert Archambeau points out—can sensitize us anew to the ethical valences of acts of close reading.

Archambeau suggests that New Critical work itself, with its indebtedness to the "Romantic tradition of aesthetics-as-ethics launched by Schiller and Coleridge"—which advocated balanced, disinterested subjectivity, developed through engagement with aesthetics, as a precondition to citizenship—indicates an important form of ethical thought for our time. In this vein, another insightful recent meditation on the ethics associated with New Critical thought is Jane Gallop's "The Ethics of Reading" (2000). Reflecting upon her pedagogical experiences, Gallop argues for the widespread applicability of close reading to the study of texts, whether literary or otherwise. Gallop goes so far as to locate the *sine qua non* of literary studies not in the objects that it addresses—always a problematic paradigm—but rather in the specific interpretive approaches it takes to those objects. For Gallop, what makes her courses specifically "English" courses "are not the books we read, but the way we read the books we read"—that is, "close reading" (7). Starting from this cue, Gallop argues for a return to careful close reading as the best way of attending to what texts actually communicate, rather than to what we assume they say because of our own projections. In Gallop's view, close reading provides a crucial way of contending with, and learning from, the "otherness" of texts: paying close attention to the claims by which they transport us beyond what we already think.

In both their acts of historical reevaluation and the interpretive methods they enact, the essays in this volume demonstrate the cogency of this claim. For Gallop and for us, the value of close reading extends even beyond what it has to offer to interpretive rigor, pedagogical strategies, and the process of defining and legitimizing the discipline of literary studies: the value of close reading resides also in how it can help us to attend to, and engage with, the voices which fill the world around us. "Close reading," Gallop points out, "can thus be a crucial part of our education. . . . Close reading can equip us to learn, to be open to learning, to keep on learning" (11). Notwithstanding her reservations about the relationship of close reading to the exclusionary canon that New Criticism fostered, Gallop's remarks here notably emphasize the "openness" of close reading, in marked contrast to the now longstanding (and as we hope to have shown, misguided) claims for its prohibitively "closed" nature. Instead of a practice of close reading which would seek to keep the world out, a carefully articulated and historically engaged close reading "is not just a way of reading but a way of listening. It can help us not just to read what is on the page, but to hear what a person really said. Close reading can train us to hear other people" (12).

As close reading enjoys a renaissance not just within English departments but throughout the academy; as we find ourselves, accordingly, focusing once again upon "reading for form," it is for something more than just a simple lesson in literary history that we return to the work of critics such as Richards, Empson, Ransom, Tate, Brooks, and Warren. We can return profitably to them better to appreciate the complex relationship that has always obtained among strategies of close reading, disciplinary practices, and ethical principles.

Notes

1. In "The Strategy of Digital Modernism," which investigates "DAKOTA"—a digital text by Young-Hae Chang's Heavy Industries putatively developed out of a "close reading" of Ezra Pound's Cantos I and II—Jessica Pressman observes that there has been much discussion in recent work on digital literature about the applicability of traditional literary methods of "close reading" to digital text and the distinctive, "media-specific" reading experiences it generates. She suggests that

> Digital literature demands a close reading practice that incorporates not only the external cultural and historical influences affecting the text (for example the politics, historical perspective, or embodiedness of the reader and/or author), but also the media-specific aspects (for example the specificities of Flash as an authoring tool and the significance of the work's distribution online rather than on CD-Rom). YHCHI's statement that *Dakota* is "based on a close reading" demands that we read *Dakota* in relation to *The Cantos* and at the same time reflexively reassess our own close reading practices. YHCHI's claim thus poses a challenge to investigate the relationship between the texts in question and presents an opportunity to consider the efficacy of applying the print-based standard of literary criticism, close reading, to electronic literature.

2. In our view, it is somewhat of a misnomer to call such New Critical reading "surface reading," since, though it does not approach texts with "suspicion," it often does

move from the more to the less evident, the apparent to the hidden—if not always in the spirit of "unmasking," at least to uncover what is not initially apparent.

3. In *Cultural Capital* (1993), John Guillory notes that "difficulty itself was positively valued in New Critical practice. . . . [I]t was a form of cultural capital" (168).

4. See the introduction to Brooks and Warren for the concept of "literary knowledge" (xiii); see also Tate.

5. As much commentary has pointed out, the New Critics shared many fundamental assumptions with the Russian formalists—about, for example, the importance of focusing on the literary text qua literary text, and about the autonomy of literature; but as Donald Childs notes, the New Critics would not become familiar with Russian Formalist work until the late 1940s (120).

Bibliography

Altieri, Charles. "Taking Lyrics Literally: Teaching Poetry in a Prose Culture." *New Literary History* 32.2 (2001): 258–81.

Best, Stephen, and Sharon Marcus. "Surface Reading: An Introduction." *Representations* 108 (Fall 2009): 1–21.

Brooks, Cleanth. *The Well Wrought Urn: Studies in the Structure of Poetry.* 1947. London: Dennis Dobson, Ltd., 1949.

———, and Robert Penn Warren, eds. *Understanding Poetry.* 1938. 3rd ed. New York: Holt, Rinehart and Winston, 1966.

Childs, Donald. "New Criticism." In *Encyclopedia of Contemporary Literary Theory,* ed. Irene Makaryk, 120–24. Toronto: University of Toronto Press, 1993.

Cohen, Margaret. "Narratology in the Archive of Literature." *Representations* 108 (Fall 2009): 51–75.

Gallop, Jane. "The Ethics of Close Reading: Close Encounters." *Journal of Curriculum Theorizing* 16.3 (Fall 2000): 7–17.

———. "The Historicization of Literary Studies and the Fate of Close Reading." In *Profession 2007,* ed. R. G. Feal, 181–86. New York: MLA, 2007.

Guillory, John. *Cultural Capital: The Problem of Literary Canon Formation.* Chicago: University of Chicago Press, 1993.

Laqueur, Thomas. "Form in Ashes." *Representations* 104 (Fall 2008): 50–72.

Levinson, Marjorie. "What Is New Formalism?" *PMLA* 122.2 (March 2007): 558–69.

Loesberg, Jonathan. "Cultural Studies, Victorian Studies, and Formalism." *Victorian Literature and Culture* 27.2 (Sept. 1999): 537–44.

Otter, Samuel. "An Aesthetics in All Things." *Representations* 104 (Fall 2008): 116–25.

Pressman, Jessica. "The Strategy of Digital Modernism." *Modern Fiction Studies* 54.2 (Summer 2008): 302–26.

Price, Leah. "From *The History of a Book* to a 'History of the Book.'" *Representations* 108 (Fall 2009): 120–38.

Ransom, John Crowe. *The World's Body.* 1938. Baton Rouge: Louisiana State University Press, 1968.

Tate, Allen. "Literature as Knowledge." 1941. *Essays of Four Decades.* Chicago: The Swallow Press, 1968.

SUGGESTED READINGS

Primary (in chronological order)

FORERUNNERS OF THE NEW CRITICISM

Eliot, T. S. *The Sacred Wood* (1920)
———. *Homage to John Dryden* (1924)
Richards, I. A. *Principles of Literary Criticism* (1924)
Riding, Laura and Robert Graves. *A Survey of Modernist Poetry* (1927)
Richards, I. A. *Practical Criticism* (1929)
Empson, William. *Seven Types of Ambiguity* (1930)
Leavis, F. R. *New Bearings in English Poetry* (1932)
———. *How to Teach Reading: A Primer for Ezra Pound* (1932)

NEW CRITICS AND RELATED CONTEMPORARIES

Twelve Southerners, *I'll Take My Stand* (1930)
Burke, Kenneth. *Counter-Statement* (1931)
Blackmur, R. P. *The Double Agent: Essays in Craft and Elucidation* (1935)
Ransom, John Crowe. *The World's Body* (1938)
Brooks, Cleanth, and Robert Penn Warren, eds. *Understanding Poetry* (1938)
Brooks, Cleanth. *Modern Poetry and the Tradition* (1939)
Ransom, John Crowe. *The New Criticism* (1941)
Wellek, René, and Austin Warren. *Theory of Literature* (1942)
Wimsatt, W. K., and Monroe Beardsley. "The Intentional Fallacy" (1946)
Brooks, Cleanth. *The Well Wrought Urn: Studies in the Structure of Poetry* (1947)

Wimsatt, W. K., and Monroe Beardsley. "The Affective Fallacy" (1949)

Tate, Allen. *Essays of Four Decades* (1969)

Secondary

Atherton, Carol. *Defining Literary Criticism: Scholarship, Authority, and the Possession of Literary Knowledge, 1880–2002*. Basingstoke: Palgrave Macmillan, 2005.

Baldick, Chris. "The Modernist Revolution: 1918–1945." Chapter 3 of *Criticism and Literary Theory, 1890 to the Present*. London: Longman, 1996.

———. *The Social Mission of English Criticism, 1848–1932*. New York: Oxford University Press, 1987.

Eagleton, Terry. *How to Read a Poem*. Malden, MA: Blackwell, 2007.

Elton, William. *A Glossary of the New Criticism*. Chicago: The Modern Poetry Association, 1948.

Fekete, John. *The Critical Twilight: Explorations in the Ideology of Anglo-American Literary Theory from Eliot to McLuhan*. London: Routledge, 1977.

Graff, Gerald. "What Was New Criticism?" Chapter 5 of *Literature against Itself: Literary Ideas in Modern Society*. Chicago: University of Chicago Press, 1979.

———. *Professing Literature: An Institutional History*. Chicago: University of Chicago Press, 1987.

Guillory, John. "Ideology and Canonical Form: The New Critical Canon." Chapter 3 of *Cultural Capital: The Problem of Literary Canon Formation*. Chicago: University of Chicago Press, 1993.

Jancovich, Mark. *The Cultural Politics of the New Criticism*. Cambridge: Cambridge University Press, 1993.

Leitch, Vincent B. *American Literary Criticism from the Thirties to the Eighties*. New York: Columbia University Press, 1984.

Levinson, Marjorie. "What Is New Formalism?" *PMLA* 122.2 (March 2007): 558–69.

MacDonald, Rónán. *The Death of the Critic*. London: Continuum, 2007.

Schryer, Steven. "Fantasies of the New Class: The New Criticism, Harvard University, and the Idea of the University." *PMLA* 122.3 (2007): 663–78.

Spurlin, William J., and Michael Fischer, eds. *The New Criticism and Contemporary Literary Theory*. New York: Garland Publishers, 1995.

CONTRIBUTORS

ROBERT ARCHAMBEAU is professor of English at Lake Forest College. His books include *Word Play Place* (1998), *Home and Variations* (2004), and *Laureates and Heretics* (2010). He is the editor of *Letters of Blood and Other English Works by Göran Printz-Påhlson* (2011), and co-editor of *The &NOW Awards: The Best Innovative Writing* (2009). His essays and poems have appeared in many books and journals, including *Poetry, The Chicago Review,* and *The Cambridge Literary Review.* Formerly the editor of the literary journal *Samizdat,* he has received grants and awards from the Academy of American Poets, the Illinois Arts Council, and the Swedish Academy.

CONNOR BYRNE received his doctorate from Dalhousie University in 2010. His teaching and research interests include Anglo-American modernism, urbanism, and everyday life studies. He is currently at work on a project concerning modernism's ordinariness.

BRADLEY D. CLISSOLD is associate professor of twentieth-century British literature, film studies, and popular culture at Memorial University. He has published on James Joyce, Virginia Woolf, *Candid Camera, The Big Lebowski,* and bowling. Currently he is at work on two collections of essays entitled *Are You Being Served? Servants and Service in Popular Culture* and *i_hate_shakespeare.com: Shakespearean Authority in the Age of New Media,* and a monograph entitled *Exchanging Postcards: The Correspondence of Vernacular Modernism.*

CECILY DEVEREUX is associate professor in the Department of English and Film Studies at the University of Alberta. She has published on English-Canadian women's writing, imperialism and gender, First-Wave feminism, eugenics, and white slavery. Current research focuses on the travels and performances of women working in dance in North America, 1869–1909.

ADAM HAMMOND received his doctorate from the University of Toronto in 2011. His dissertation, *1934: Generic Hybridity and the Search for a Democratic Aesthetic*, investigates the theorization of hybrid artistic genres in response to the political crises of Stalinism and fascism in the mid-1930s. His current research on Wyndham Lewis, Erich Auerbach, W. H. Auden, Marshall McLuhan, and Edward W. Said focuses on the legacy of late-modernist internationalism in post-WWII debates about multiculturalism. His work has appeared in *Style*, *The Walrus*, and *The Dalhousie Review*.

MIRANDA HICKMAN is associate professor of English at McGill University. Her most recent book is *One Must Not Go Altogether with the Tide: The Letters of Ezra Pound and Stanley Nott* (2011). Other work includes *The Geometry of Modernism* (2006) and articles on H. D., Ezra Pound, and the legacy of Raymond Chandler in *Twentieth Century Literature, Paideuma,* and *Studies in the Novel*. Recent essays have appeared in *The Cambridge Companion to H. D.* (2011), *The Cambridge Companion to Modernist Women Poets* (2010), *Ezra Pound in Context* (2010), and *James Joyce: Visions and Revisions* (2009). Her current research focuses on women in early-twentieth-century criticism and the construction of critical authority.

TARA LOCKHART is assistant professor of English at San Francisco State University. Her published work considers essayists such as Edward Said and Gloria Anzaldúa, the literary and pedagogical possibilities of the essay genre, hybridity in writing, and style.

ALEXANDER MACLEOD is associate professor in the Department of English and the coordinator of the Atlantic Canada Studies program at Saint Mary's University. His research examines the relationship between literary regionalism, cultural geography, and spatial theory and has been published in many leading Canadian journals, including *Canadian Literature, Studies in Canadian Literature, Essays on Canadian Writing,* and *Canadian Notes and Queries*.

JOHN D. McINTYRE is associate professor of twentieth-century literature and culture at the University of Prince Edward Island. He has published articles on Conrad, Joyce, Robertson Davies and Harold Pinter. He is currently working on a project examining the representation of islands in modernist literature and culture.

ALASTAIR MORRISON is a Nicolson Fellow and doctoral student in the Department of English and Comparative Literature at Columbia University. His dissertation, entitled *Instrumental Christianity*, examines the relationship between poetic form, sacramental religion, and discourses of social welfare in late nineteenth and twentieth-century literature. His work on Mordecai Richler has appeared in *Canadian Literature*.

AARON SHAHEEN is UC Foundation Associate Professor of English at the University of Tennessee at Chattanooga, where he specializes in American literature of the late nineteenth and early twentieth centuries. He has published articles in *The Southern Literary Journal, American Literary Realism, ATQ,* and *The Henry James Review*. His monograph *Androgynous Democracy: Modern American Literature and the Dual-Sexed Body Politic* (2010) examines the ways in which American modernists used scientific, religious, and racial notions of androgyny to formulate models of national cohesion.

JAMES MATTHEW WILSON is assistant professor in the Department of Humanities and Augustinian Traditions at Villanova University. He is the author of many articles on the intersection of theology, philosophy, and literature, particularly in Irish and American modernism. A poet and a critic of modern and contemporary poetry, he is the author of a chapbook of poems, *Four Verse Letters* (2010) and the forthcoming monograph, *Timothy Steele: A Critical Introduction* (2012).

INDEX